INUYASHA

VOL. 10
Action Edition

Story and Art by
RUMIKO TAKAHASHI

English Adaptation by Gerard Jones

Translation/Mari Morimoto
Touch-Up Art & Lettering/Wayne Truman
Cover and Interior Graphics & Design/Yuki Ameda
Editor (1st Edition)/Julie Davis
Editor (Action Edition)/Julie Davis
Assistant Editor/Michelle Pangilinan

Managing Editor/Annette Roman
Editor in Chief/Alvin Lu
Director of Production/Noboru Watanabe
Sr. Dir. of Licensing and Acquisitions/Rika Inouye
VP of Sales & Marketing/Liza Coppola
Sr. VP of Editorial/Hyoe Narita
Publisher/Seiji Horibuchi

INUYASHA is rated "T+" for Older Teens. It may contain violence, language, alcohol or tobacco use, or suggestive situations.

Printed in Canada.

Published by VIZ, LLC
P.O. Box 77010
San Francisco, CA 94107

1st Edition published 2001

Action Edition
10 9 8 7 6 5 4 3 2
First printing, March 2004
Second printing, October 2004

INUYASHA

VOL. 10   Action Edition

STORY AND ART BY
RUMIKO TAKAHASHI

CONTENTS

Long ago, in the "Warring States" era of Japan's Muromachi period (Sengoku-jidai, approximately 1467-1568 CE), a legendary doglike half-demon called "Inu-Yasha" attempted to steal the Shikon Jewel, or "Jewel of Four Souls," from a village, but was stopped by the enchanted arrow of the village priestess, Kikyo. Inu-Yasha fell into a deep sleep, pinned to a tree by Kikyo's arrow, while the mortally wounded Kikyo took the Shikon Jewel with her into the fires of her funeral pyre. Years passed.

Fast forward to the present day. Kagome, a Japanese high school girl, is pulled into a well one day by a mysterious centipede monster and finds herself transported into the past, only to come face to face with the trapped Inu-Yasha. She frees him, and Inu-Yasha easily defeats the centipede monster.

The residents of the village, now fifty years older, readily accept Kagome as the reincarnation of their deceased priestess Kikyo, a claim supported by the fact that the Shikon Jewel emerges from a cut on Kagome's body. Unfortunately, the jewel's rediscovery means that the village is soon under attack by a variety of demons in search of this treasure. Then, the jewel is accidentally shattered into many shards, each of which may have the fearsome power of the entire jewel.

Although Inu-Yasha says he hates Kagome because of her resemblance to Kikyo, the woman who "killed" him, he is forced to team up with her when Kaede, the village leader, binds him to Kagome with a powerful spell. Now the two grudging companions must fight to reclaim and reassemble the shattered shards of the Shikon Jewel before they fall into the wrong hands.

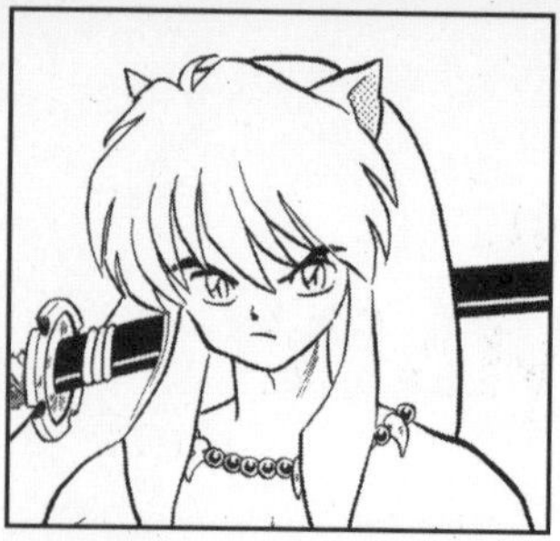

KAGOME
A modern-day Japanese schoolgirl, Kagome is also the reincarnation of Kikyo, the priestess who imprisoned Inu-Yasha for fifty years with her enchanted arrow. Kagome has the power to see the Shikon Jewel shards wherever they may be hidden.

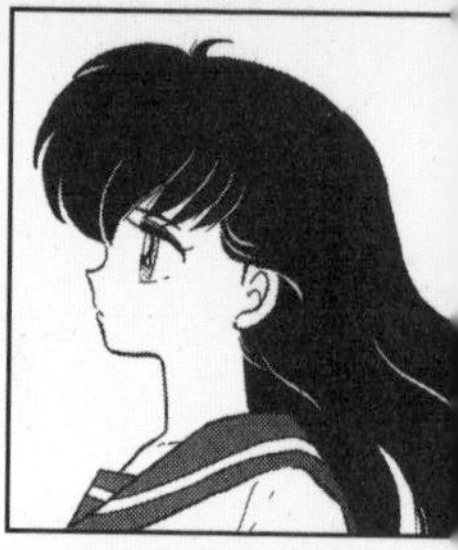

INU-YASHA
A half-human, half-demon hybrid, Inu-Yasha assists Kagome in her search for the shards of the Jewel. The charmed necklace he wears allows Kagome to restrain him with a single word.

KIKYO
A powerful priestess who died protecting the Shikon Jewel, and has been resurrected by magic. She and Inu-Yasha once shared a special bond.

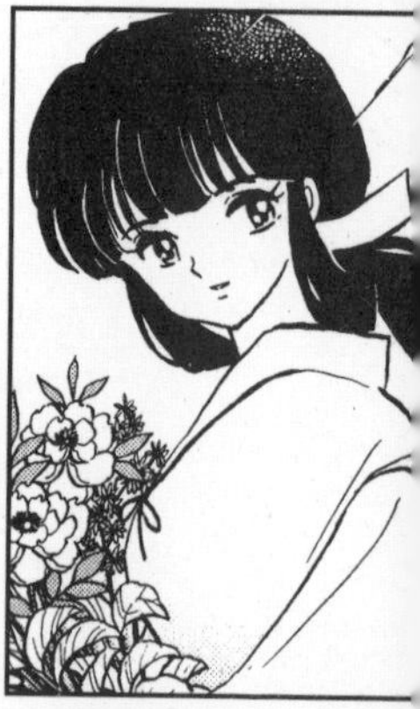

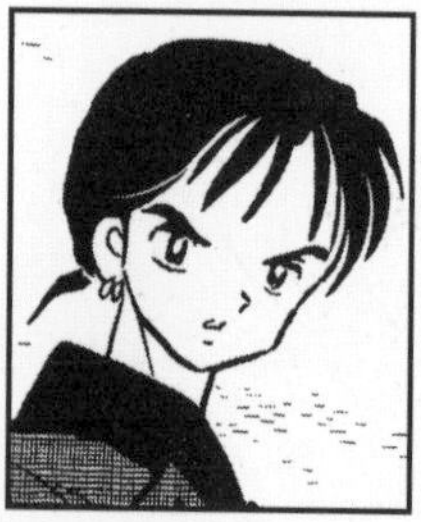

MIROKU
An easygoing Buddhist priest with questionable morals, Miroku is the carrier of a curse passed down from his grandfather. He is searching for the demon Naraku, who first inflicted the curse.

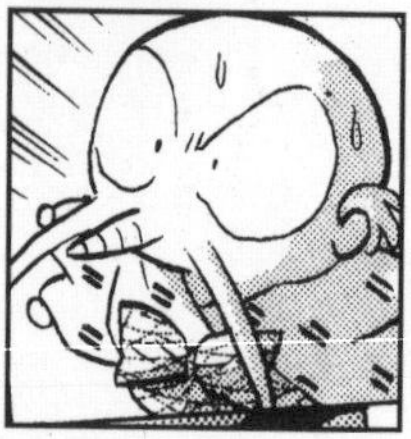

MYOGA
A flea demon and Inu-Yasha's servant. His bloodsucking seems to have the ability to weaken certain spells.

KAEDE
The little sister of the deceased priestess Kikyo, now an old woman and head of their village. It's her spell that binds Inu-Yasha to Kagome by means of a string of prayer beads and Kagome's spoken word—"Sit!"

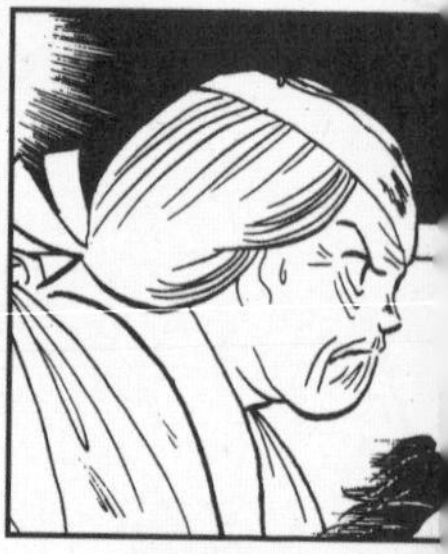

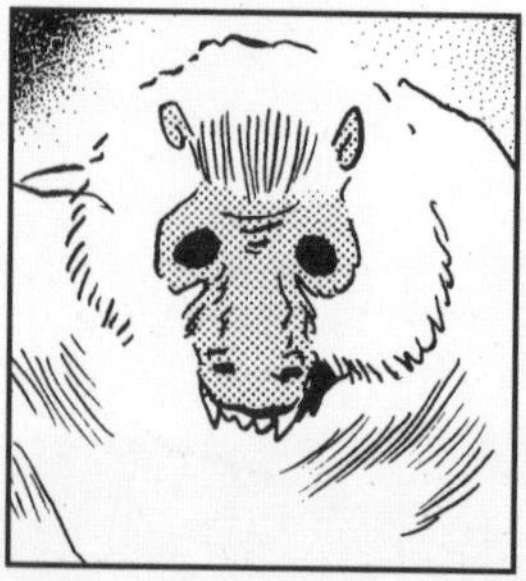

NARAKU
This enigmatic demon is responsible for both Miroku's curse and for turning Kikyo and Inu-Yasha against one another.

SHIPPO
An orphaned young fox-demon who enjoys goading Inu-Yasha and playing tricks with his shape-changing abilities.

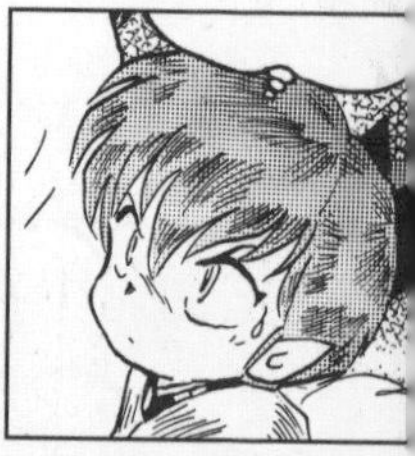

SCROLL ONE

THE MUMMY

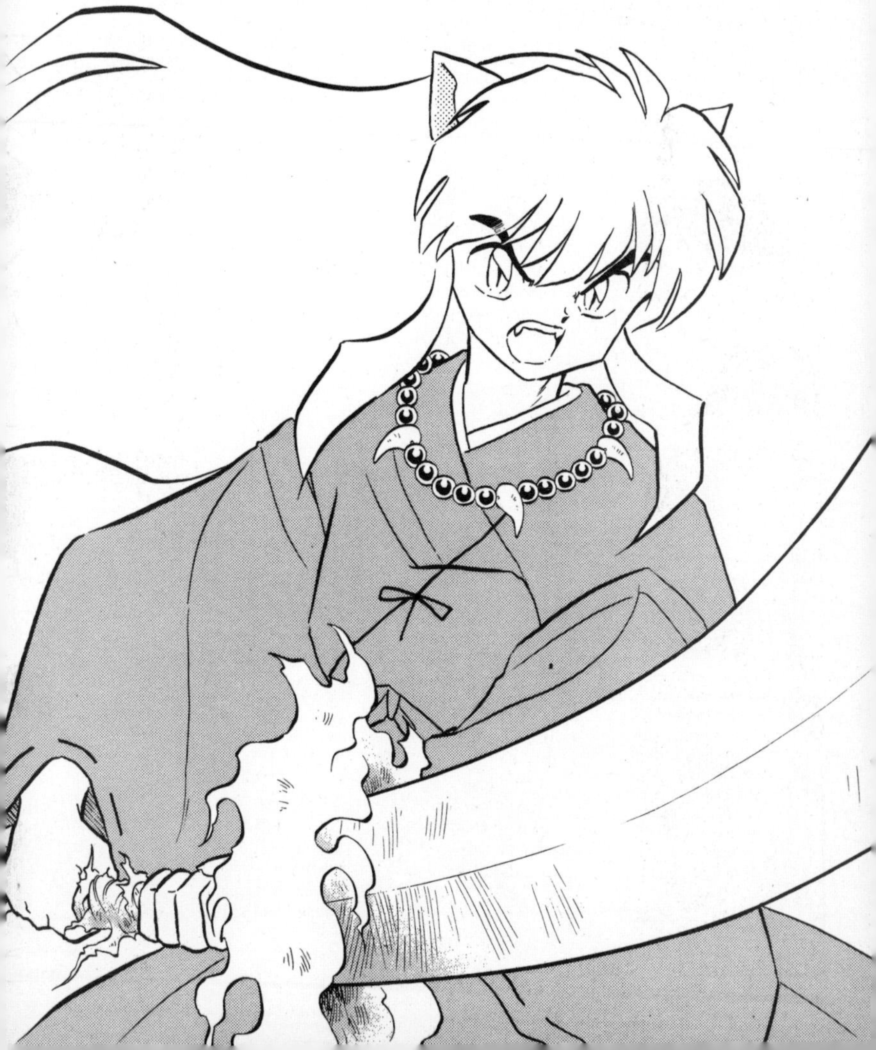

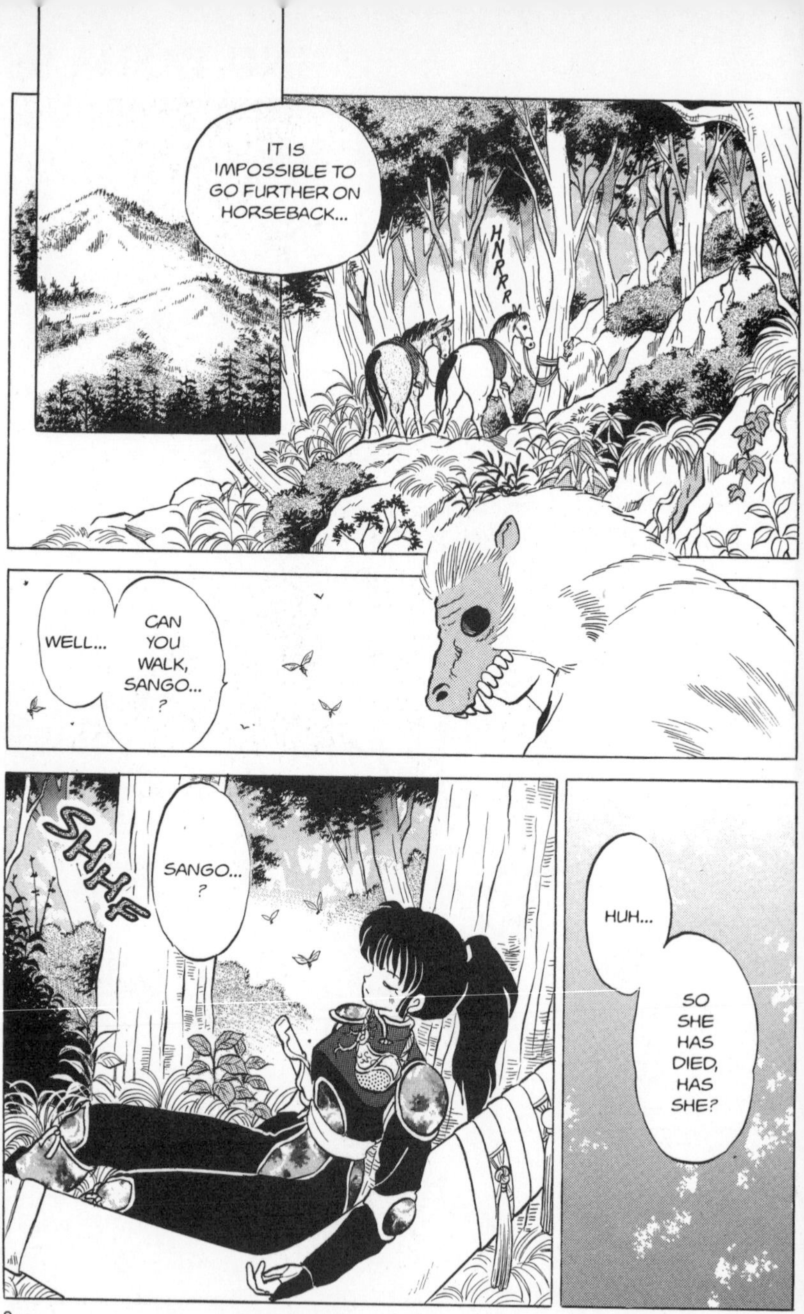
IT IS IMPOSSIBLE TO GO FURTHER ON HORSEBACK...
HNRRR
WELL...
CAN YOU WALK, SANGO...?
SHHF
SANGO...?
HUH...
SO SHE HAS DIED, HAS SHE?

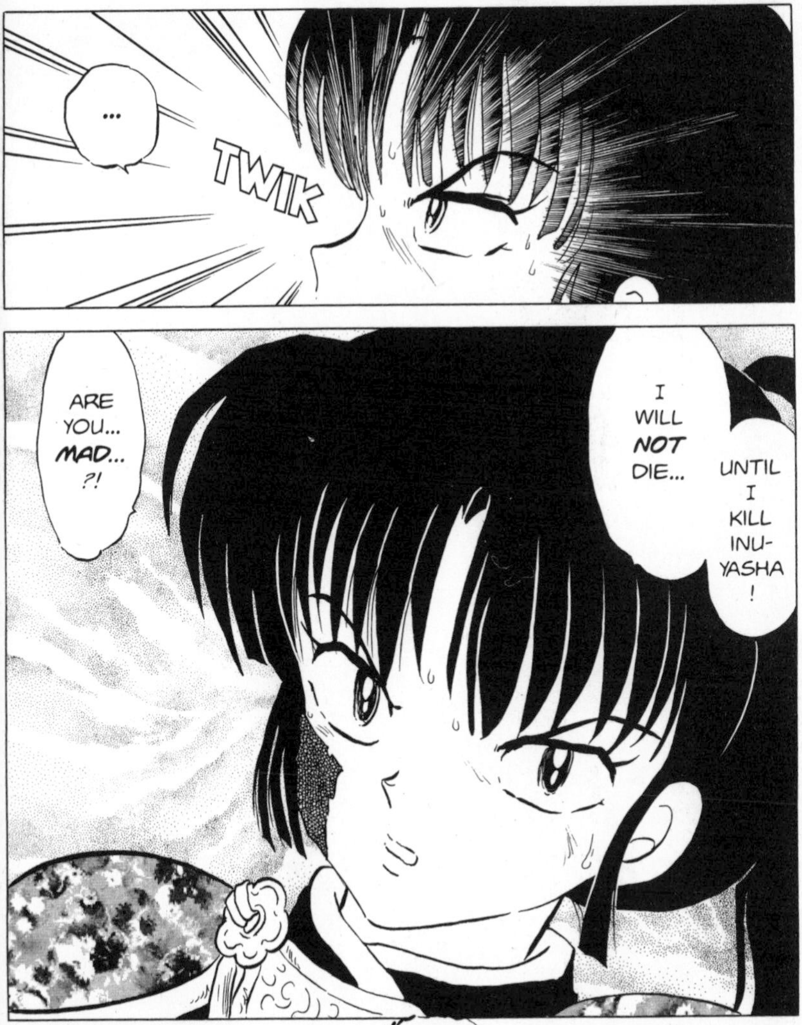
...
TWIK
ARE YOU... **MAD...** ?!
I WILL **NOT** DIE...
UNTIL I KILL INU-YASHA!
HEH...
THAT'S ALL WELL AND GOOD...

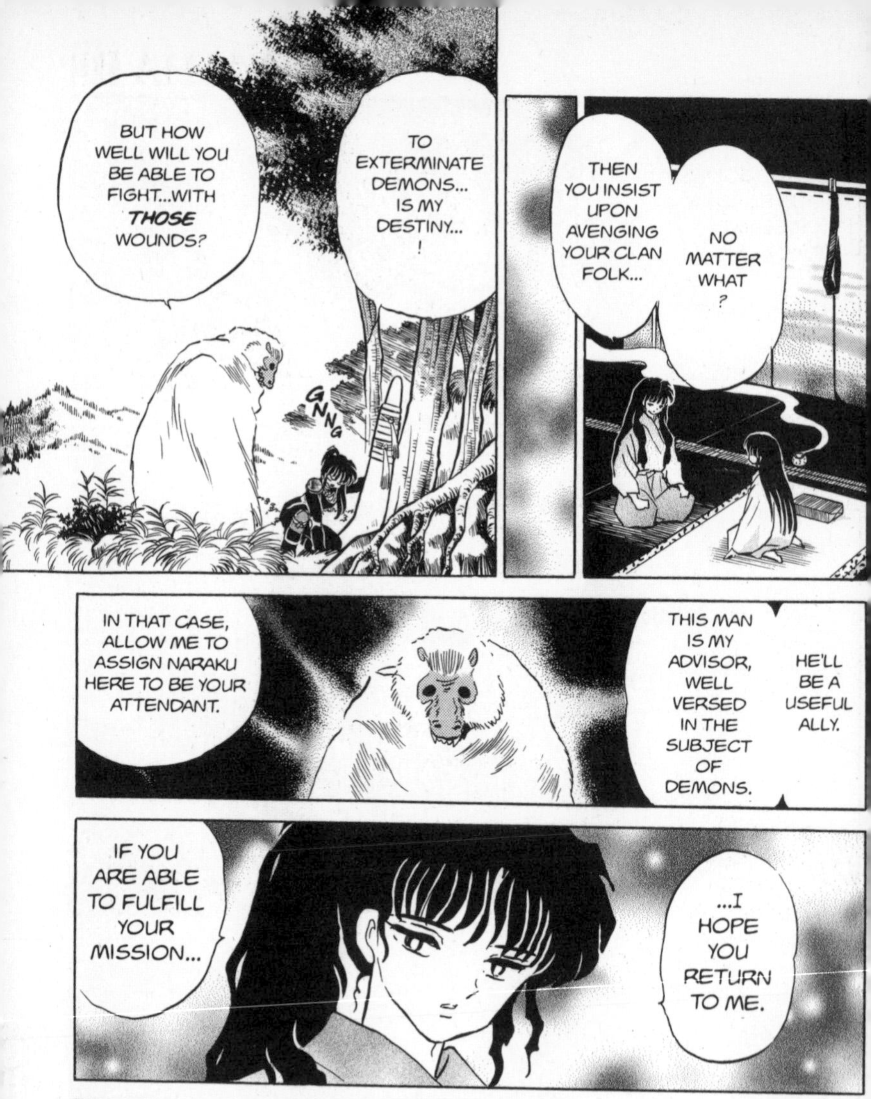
BUT HOW WELL WILL YOU BE ABLE TO FIGHT...WITH *THOSE* WOUNDS?
TO EXTERMINATE DEMONS... IS MY DESTINY... !
GNNG
THEN YOU INSIST UPON AVENGING YOUR CLAN FOLK...
NO MATTER WHAT ?
IN THAT CASE, ALLOW ME TO ASSIGN NARAKU HERE TO BE YOUR ATTENDANT.
THIS MAN IS MY ADVISOR, WELL VERSED IN THE SUBJECT OF DEMONS.
HE'LL BE A USEFUL ALLY.
IF YOU ARE ABLE TO FULFILL YOUR MISSION...
...I HOPE YOU RETURN TO ME.
I'LL NEVER RETURN...
SHHF
...I DON'T HAVE MUCH LONGER...

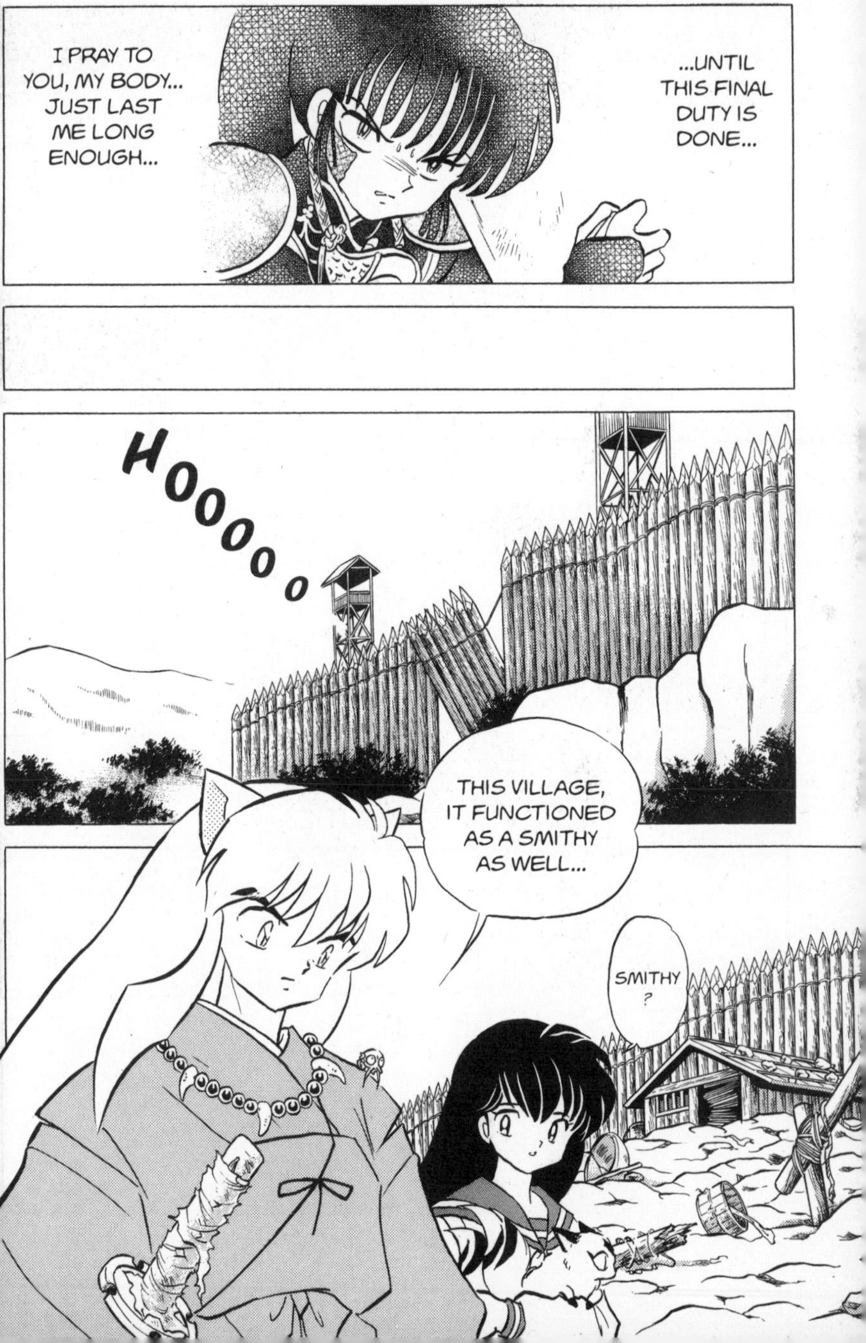
I PRAY TO YOU, MY BODY... JUST LAST ME LONG ENOUGH...
...UNTIL THIS FINAL DUTY IS DONE...
HOOOOOO
THIS VILLAGE, IT FUNCTIONED AS A SMITHY AS WELL...
SMITHY ?

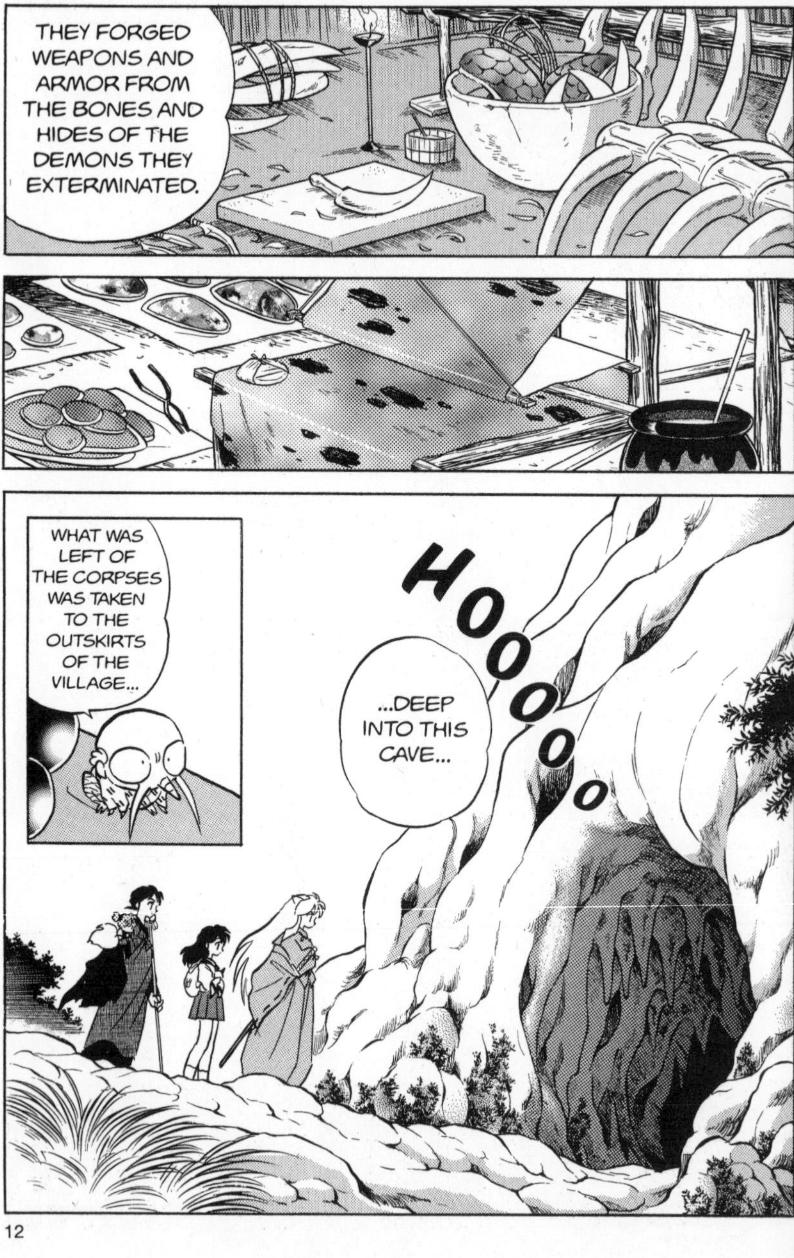
THEY FORGED WEAPONS AND ARMOR FROM THE BONES AND HIDES OF THE DEMONS THEY EXTERMINATED.
WHAT WAS LEFT OF THE CORPSES WAS TAKEN TO THE OUTSKIRTS OF THE VILLAGE...
HOOOOOO
...DEEP INTO THIS CAVE...

THIS...
IS WHERE
THE SHIKON
JEWEL WAS
BORN...
?

THIS
PLACE...

IT MAKES
ME
NAUSEOUS...

...I
CAN'T
GO IN
THERE...

HEY!
WAIT
UP!

NO!
YOU
HURRY
UP!

KRNCH
KRNCH
KRNCH

WERE YOU
PLANNING
TO LEAVE
ME
BEHIND?!

LADY
KAGOME,
IF YOU ARE
AFRAID...
FEEL
FREE TO
LEAN ON
ME...

KNCH KNCH

HEY!
I KNOW
WHAT
YOU'RE
AFTER!

!

GLINT...

13

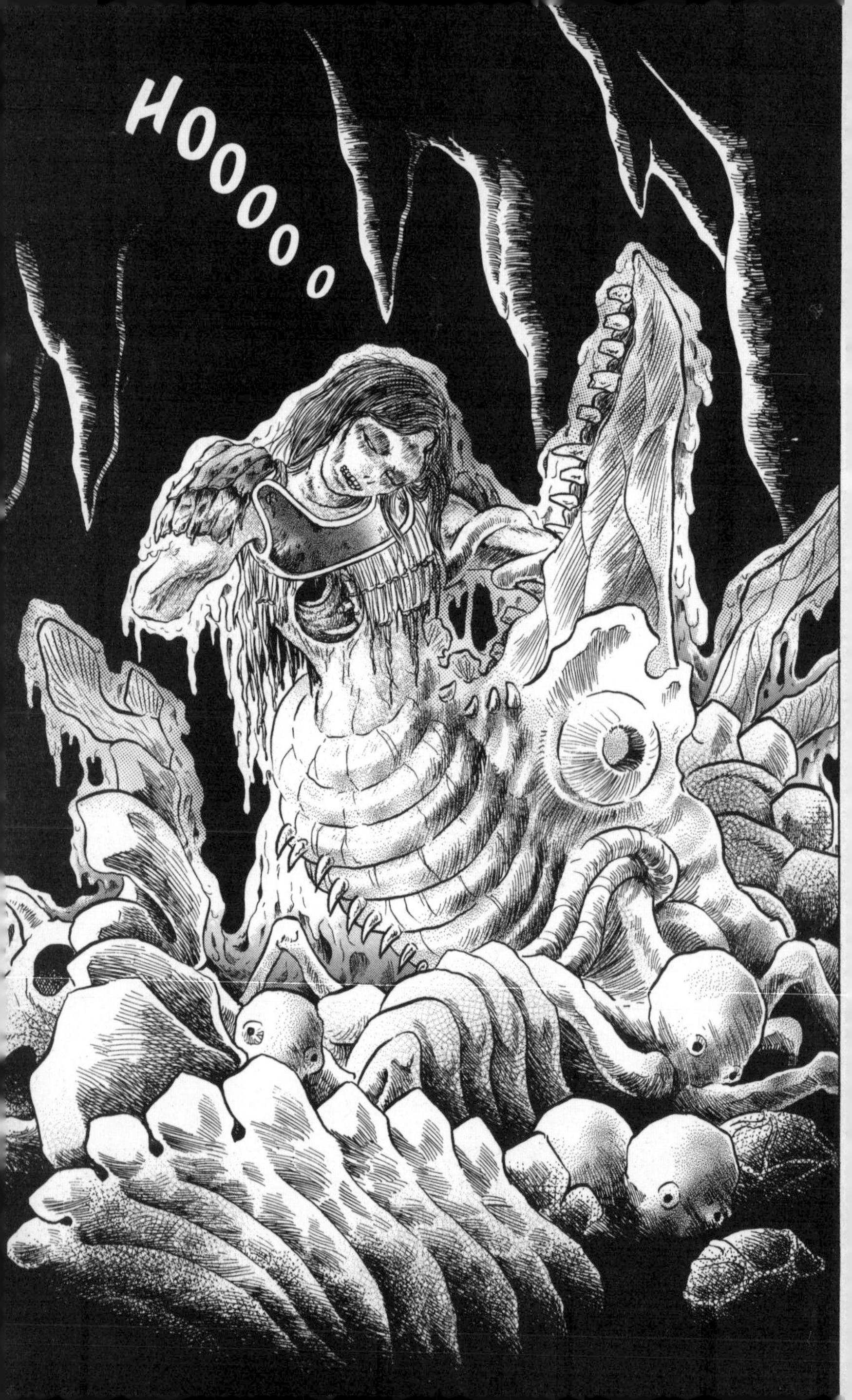
HOOOOOO

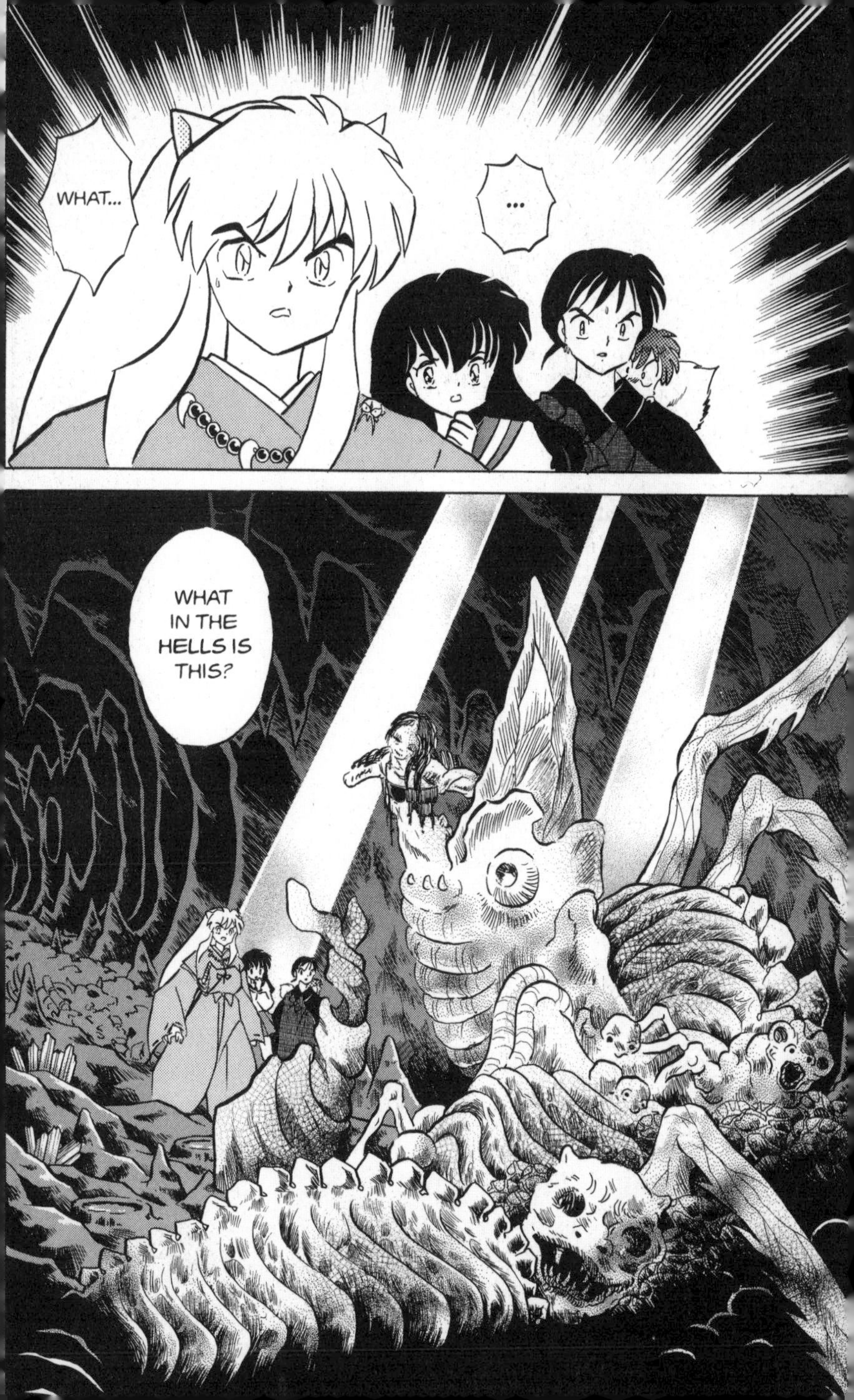
WHAT...
...
WHAT IN THE HELLS IS THIS?

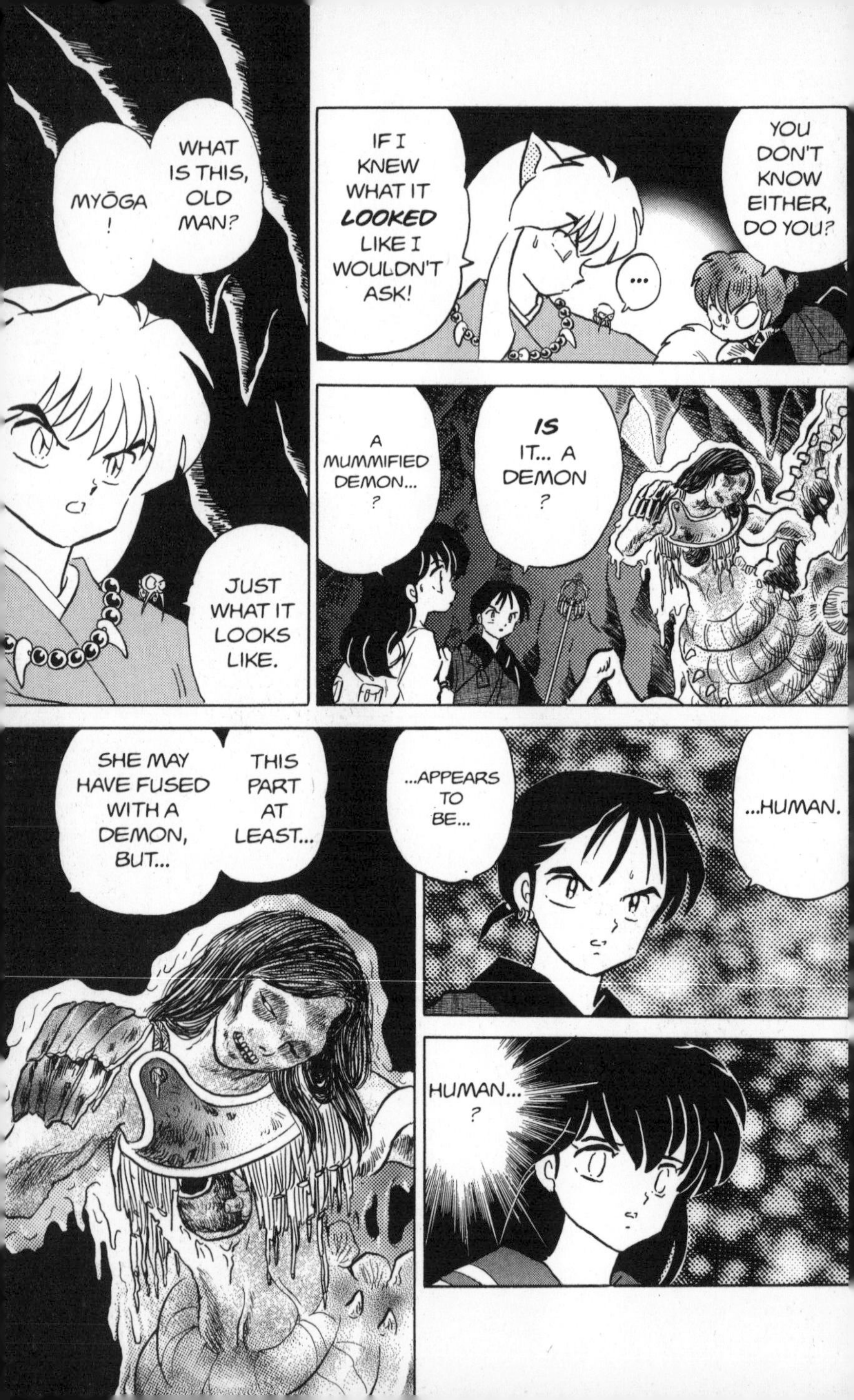
MYŌGA!
WHAT IS THIS, OLD MAN?
JUST WHAT IT LOOKS LIKE.
IF I KNEW WHAT IT **LOOKED** LIKE I WOULDN'T ASK!
...
YOU DON'T KNOW EITHER, DO YOU?
A MUMMIFIED DEMON...?
IS IT... A DEMON?
SHE MAY HAVE FUSED WITH A DEMON, BUT...
THIS PART AT LEAST...
...APPEARS TO BE...
...HUMAN.
HUMAN...?

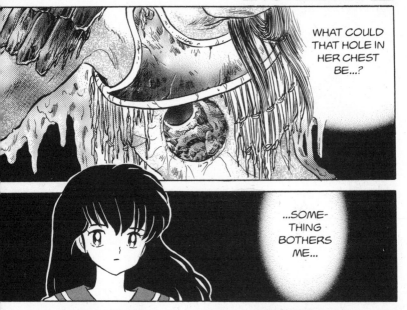

WHAT COULD THAT HOLE IN HER CHEST BE...?

...SOMETHING BOTHERS ME...

IN THE END, IT SEEMS...

WE WILL NEED TO ASK A VILLAGER AFTER ALL.

CRUMPLE

ARE YOU IN PAIN, SANGO...?

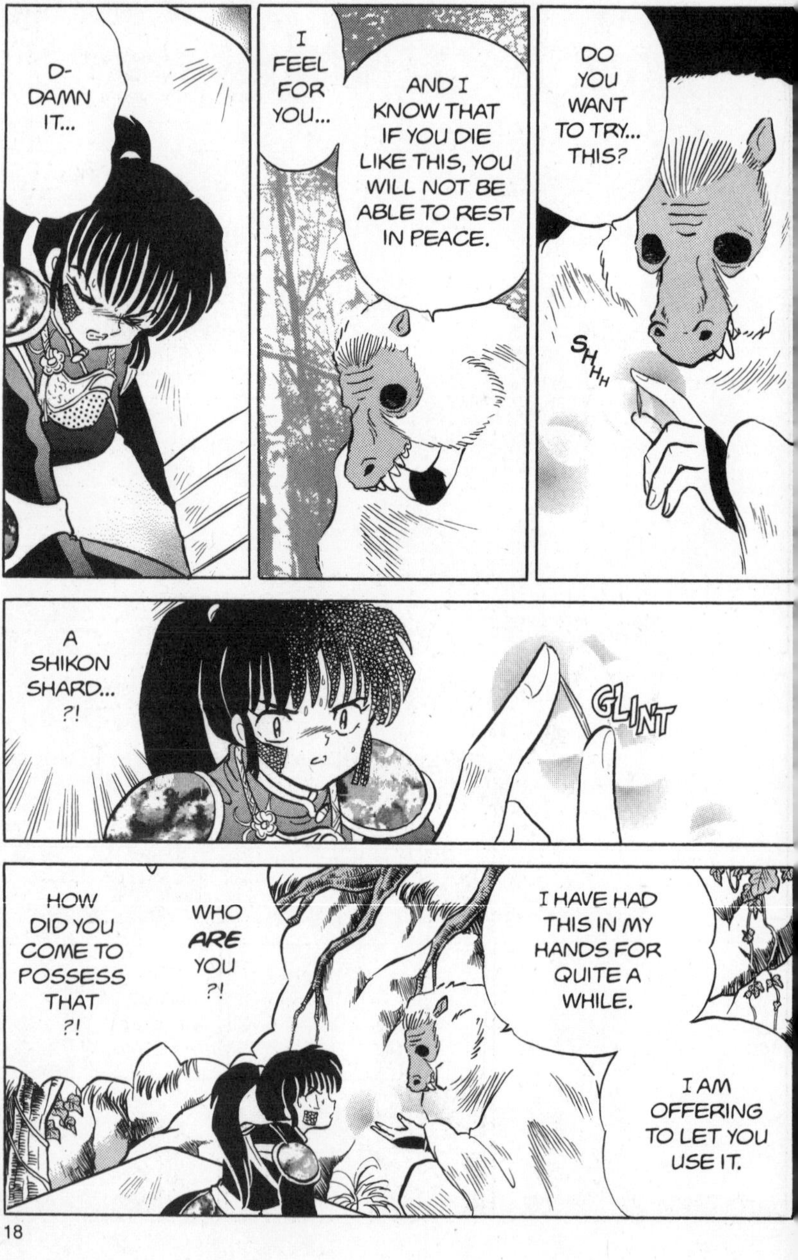
D-DAMN IT...
I FEEL FOR YOU...
AND I KNOW THAT IF YOU DIE LIKE THIS, YOU WILL NOT BE ABLE TO REST IN PEACE.
DO YOU WANT TO TRY... THIS?
SHHH
A SHIKON SHARD...?!
GLINT
HOW DID YOU COME TO POSSESS THAT?!
WHO ARE YOU?!
I HAVE HAD THIS IN MY HANDS FOR QUITE A WHILE.
I AM OFFERING TO LET YOU USE IT.

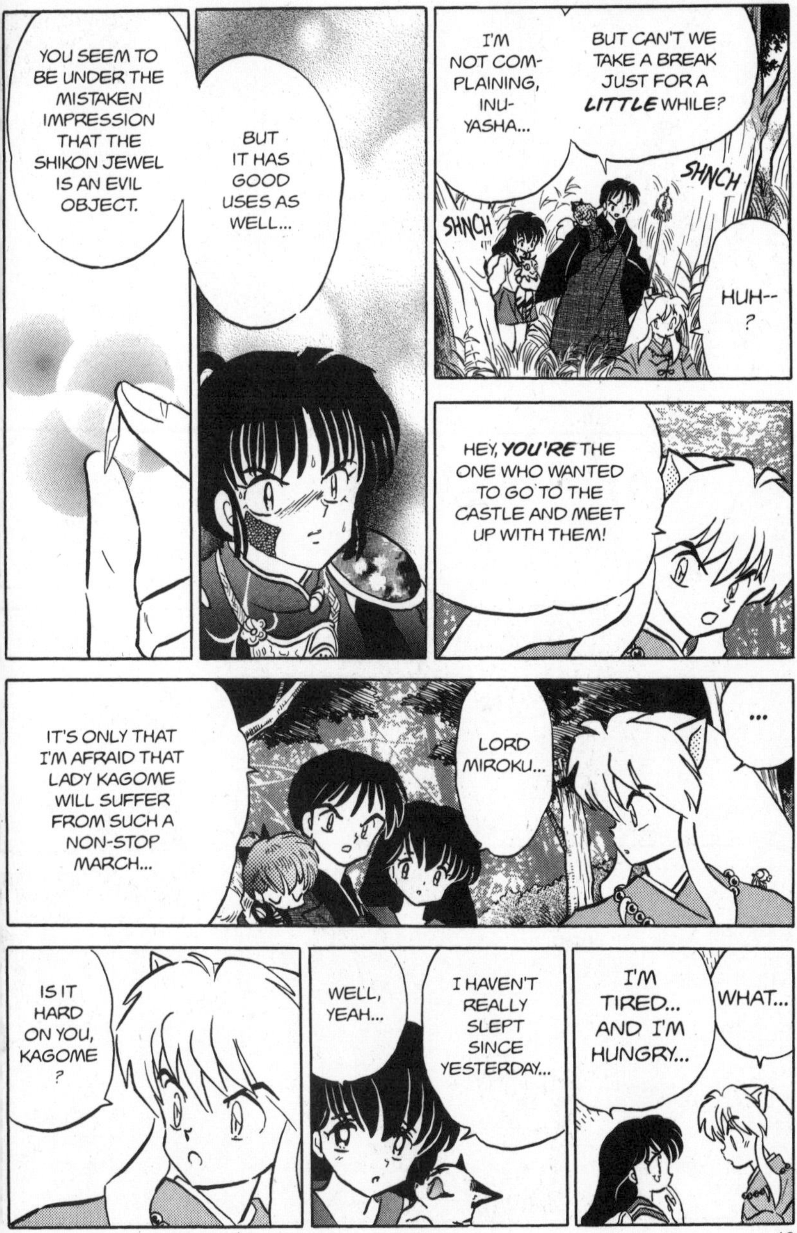
YOU SEEM TO BE UNDER THE MISTAKEN IMPRESSION THAT THE SHIKON JEWEL IS AN EVIL OBJECT.
BUT IT HAS GOOD USES AS WELL...
I'M NOT COMPLAINING, INU-YASHA...
BUT CAN'T WE TAKE A BREAK JUST FOR A *LITTLE* WHILE?
SHNCH
SHNCH
HUH--?
HEY, *YOU'RE* THE ONE WHO WANTED TO GO TO THE CASTLE AND MEET UP WITH THEM!
IT'S ONLY THAT I'M AFRAID THAT LADY KAGOME WILL SUFFER FROM SUCH A NON-STOP MARCH...
LORD MIROKU...
...
IS IT HARD ON YOU, KAGOME?
WELL, YEAH...
I HAVEN'T REALLY SLEPT SINCE YESTERDAY...
I'M TIRED... AND I'M HUNGRY...
WHAT...

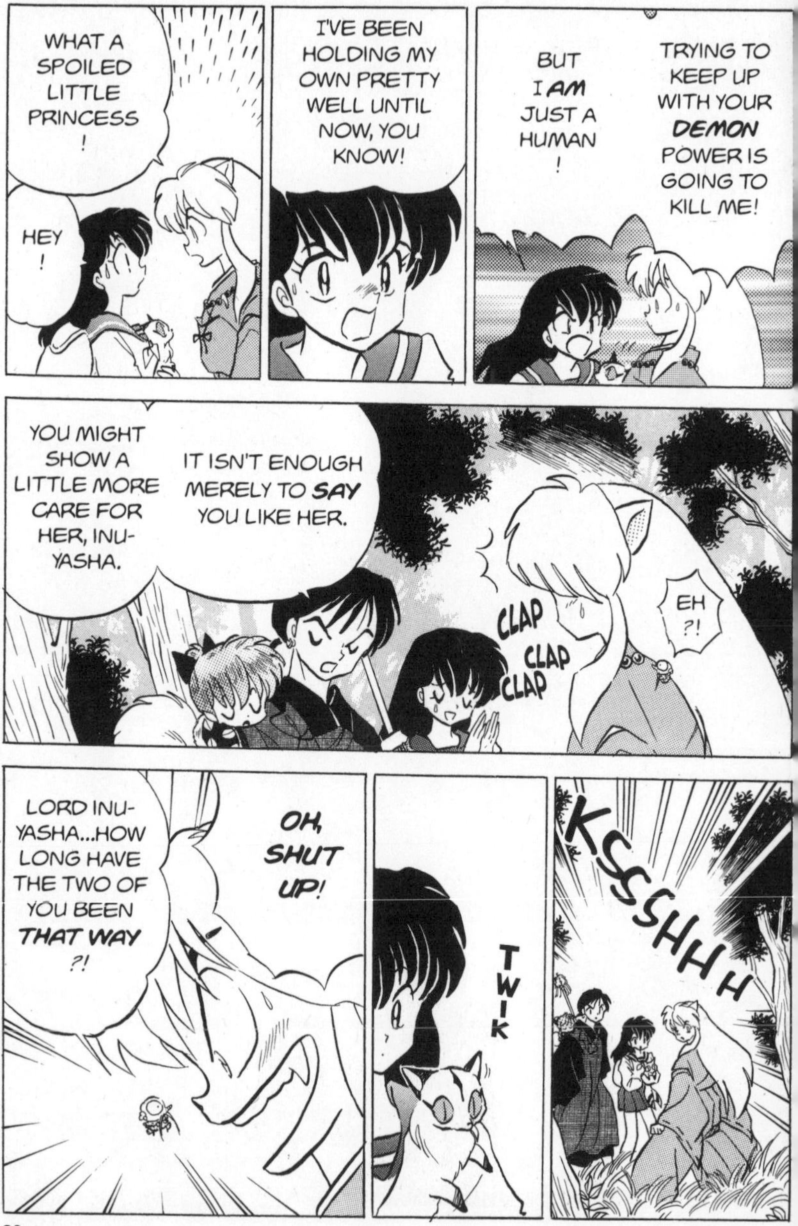
WHAT A SPOILED LITTLE PRINCESS!
HEY!
I'VE BEEN HOLDING MY OWN PRETTY WELL UNTIL NOW, YOU KNOW!
BUT I **AM** JUST A HUMAN!
TRYING TO KEEP UP WITH YOUR **DEMON** POWER IS GOING TO KILL ME!
YOU MIGHT SHOW A LITTLE MORE CARE FOR HER, INU-YASHA.
IT ISN'T ENOUGH MERELY TO **SAY** YOU LIKE HER.
CLAP
CLAP
CLAP
EH?!
LORD INU-YASHA...HOW LONG HAVE THE TWO OF YOU BEEN **THAT WAY**?!
OH, SHUT UP!
TWIK
KSSSHHHH

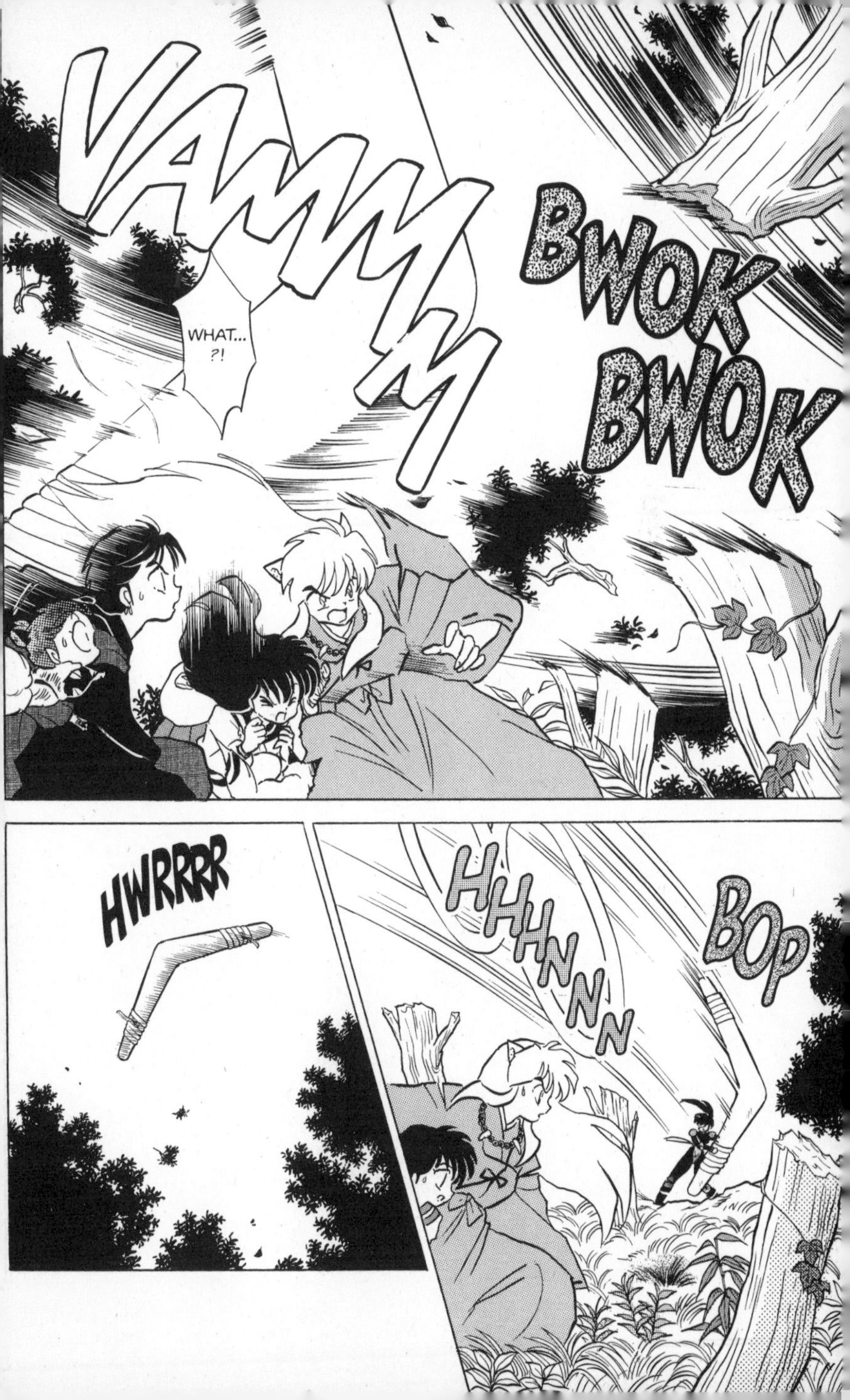
VAMMMM
WHAT... ?!
BWOK BWOK
HWRRRR
HHHNNNN
BOP

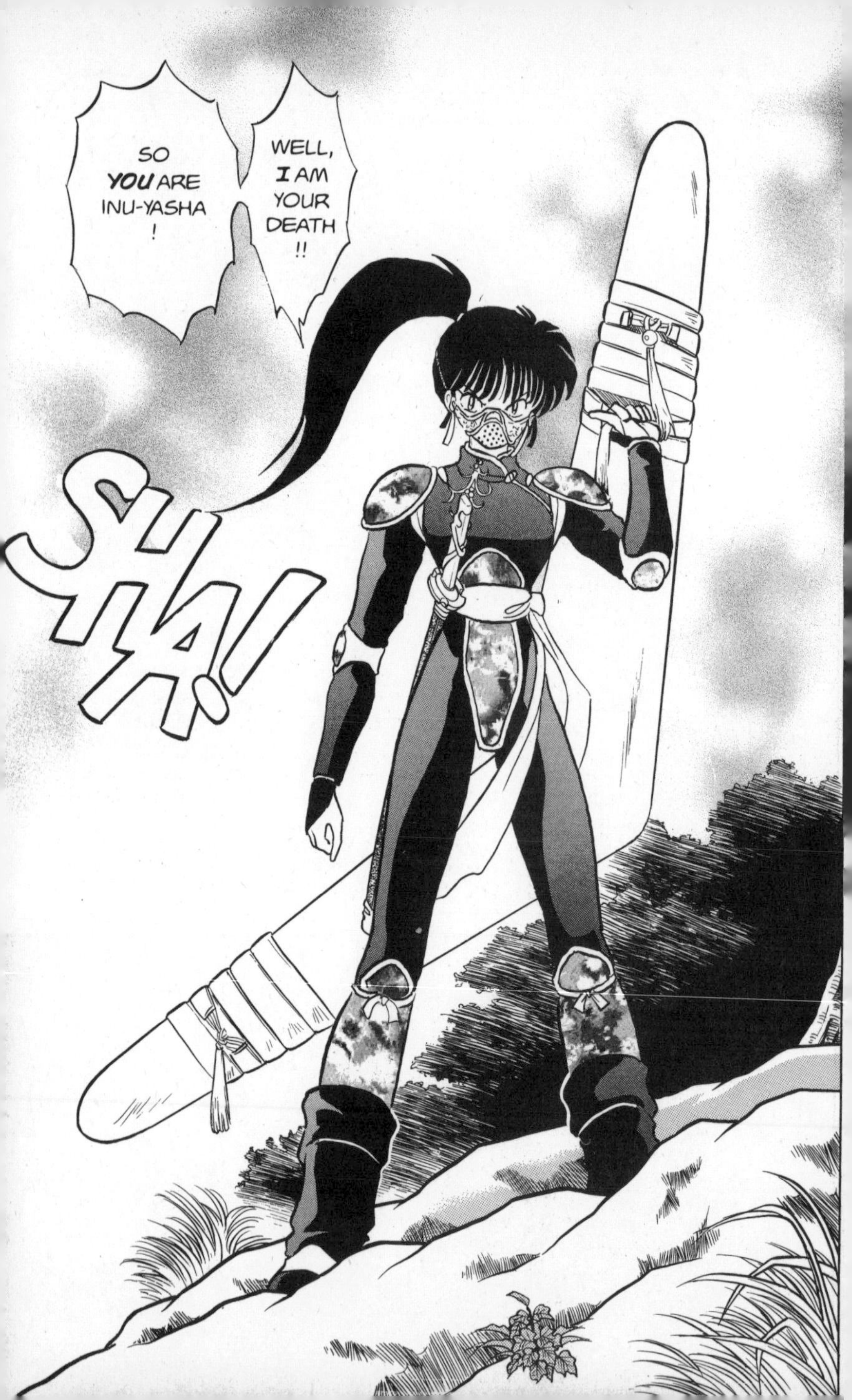
SO *YOU* ARE INU-YASHA !
WELL, *I* AM YOUR DEATH !!
SHA!

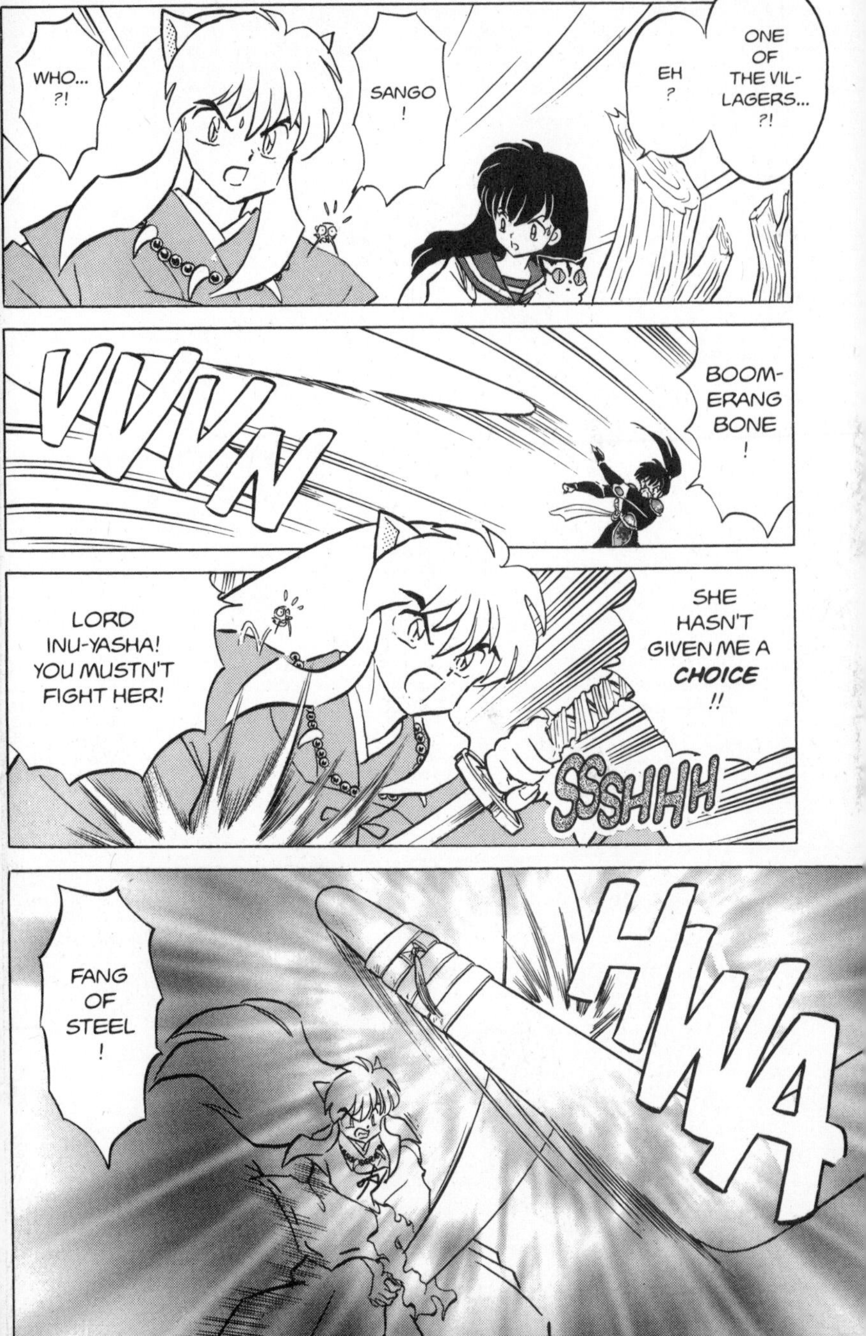
WHO... ?!
SANGO !
EH ?
ONE OF THE VIL- LAGERS... ?!
VVVN
BOOM- ERANG BONE !
LORD INU-YASHA! YOU MUSTN'T FIGHT HER!
SHE HASN'T GIVEN ME A **CHOICE** !!
SSSHHH
FANG OF STEEL !
HWA

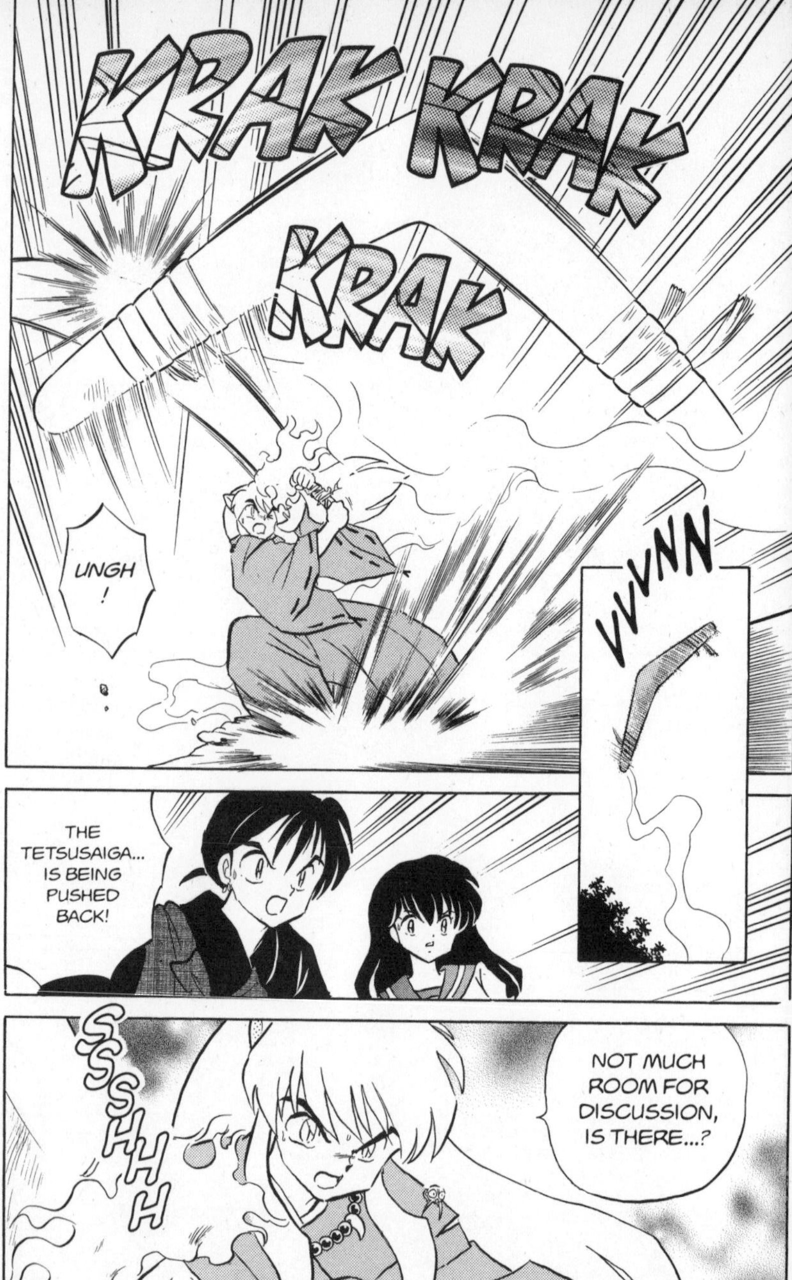
KRAK KRAK
KRAK
UNGH!
VVVNN
THE TETSUSAIGA... IS BEING PUSHED BACK!
SSHHHH
NOT MUCH ROOM FOR DISCUSSION, IS THERE...?

SCROLL TWO

VENGEANCE

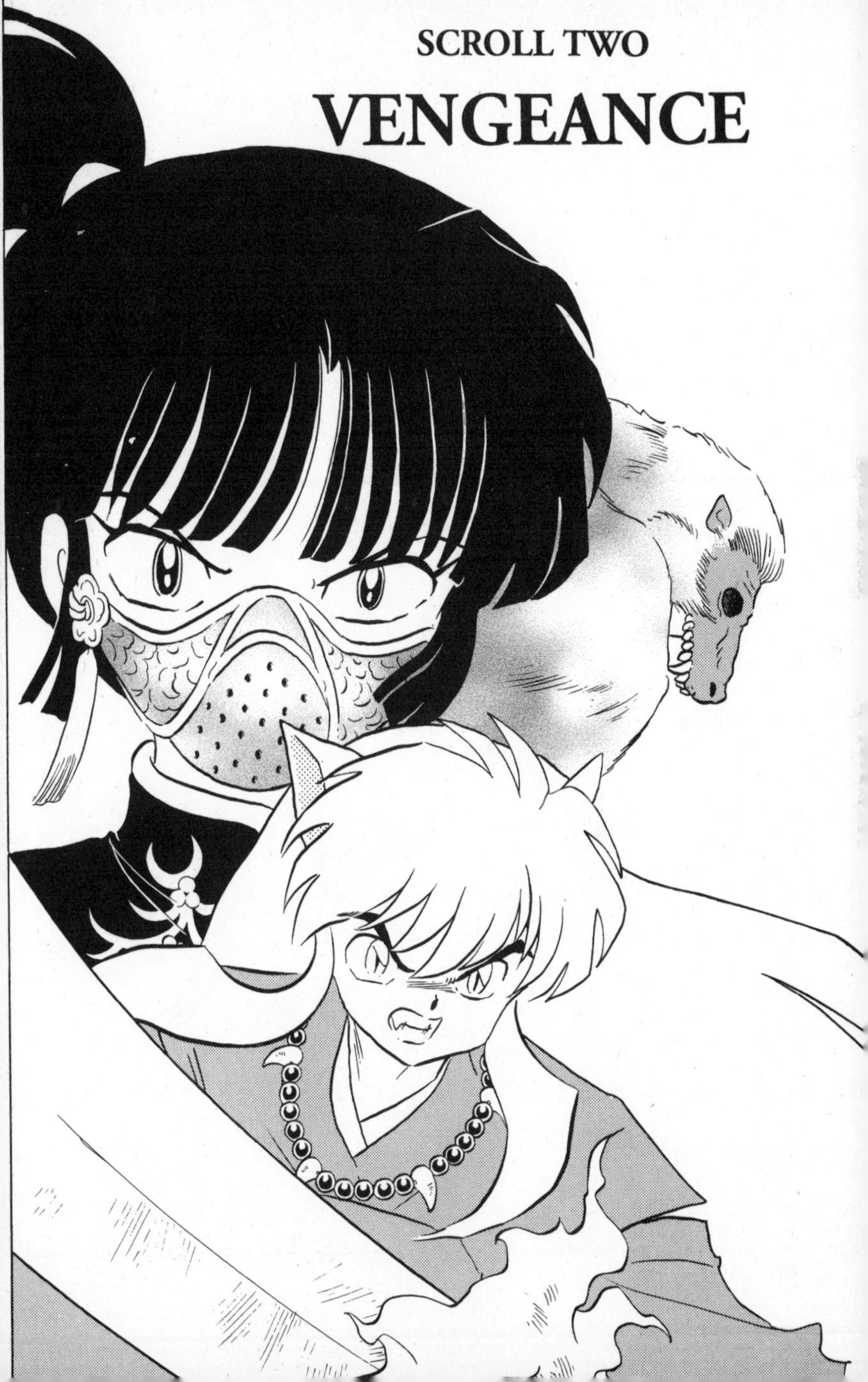

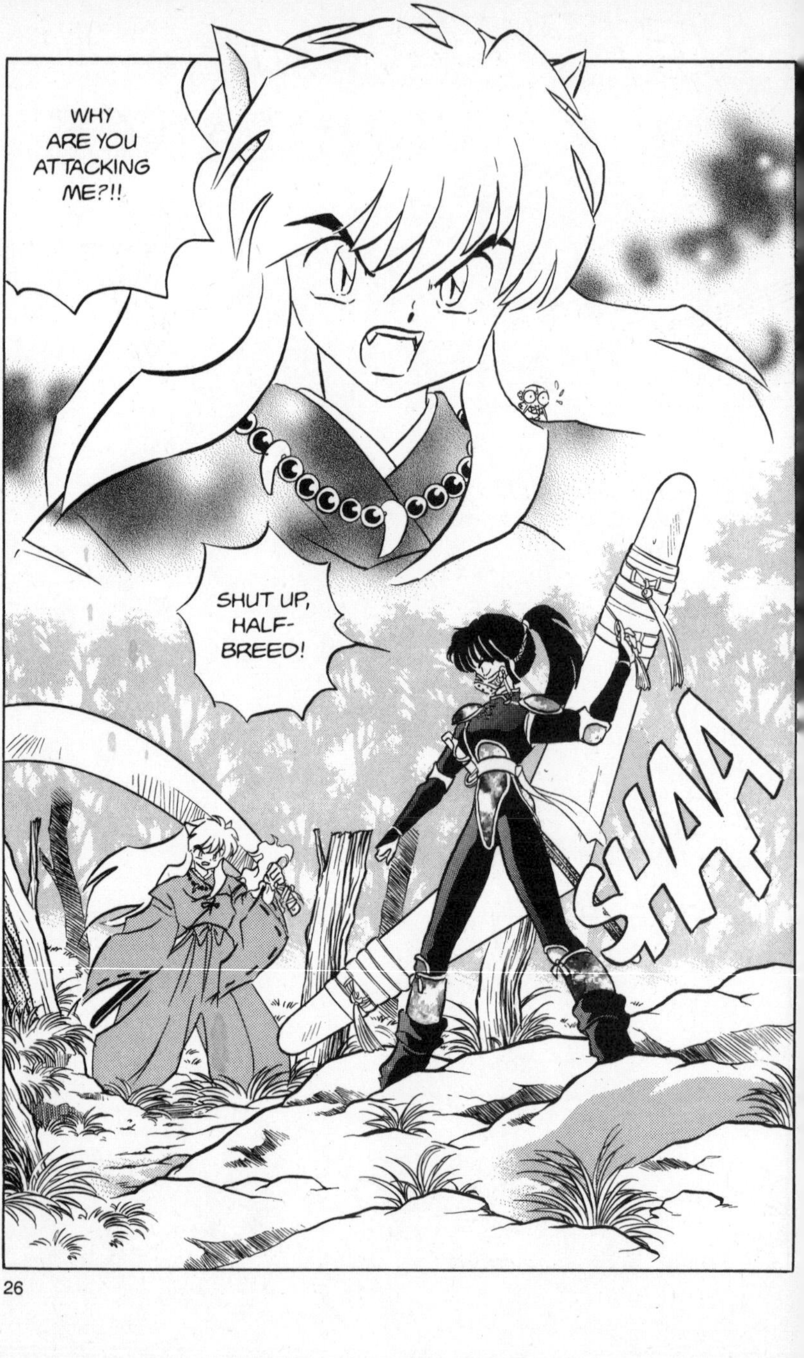
WHY ARE YOU ATTACKING ME?!!
SHUT UP, HALF-BREED!
SHAA

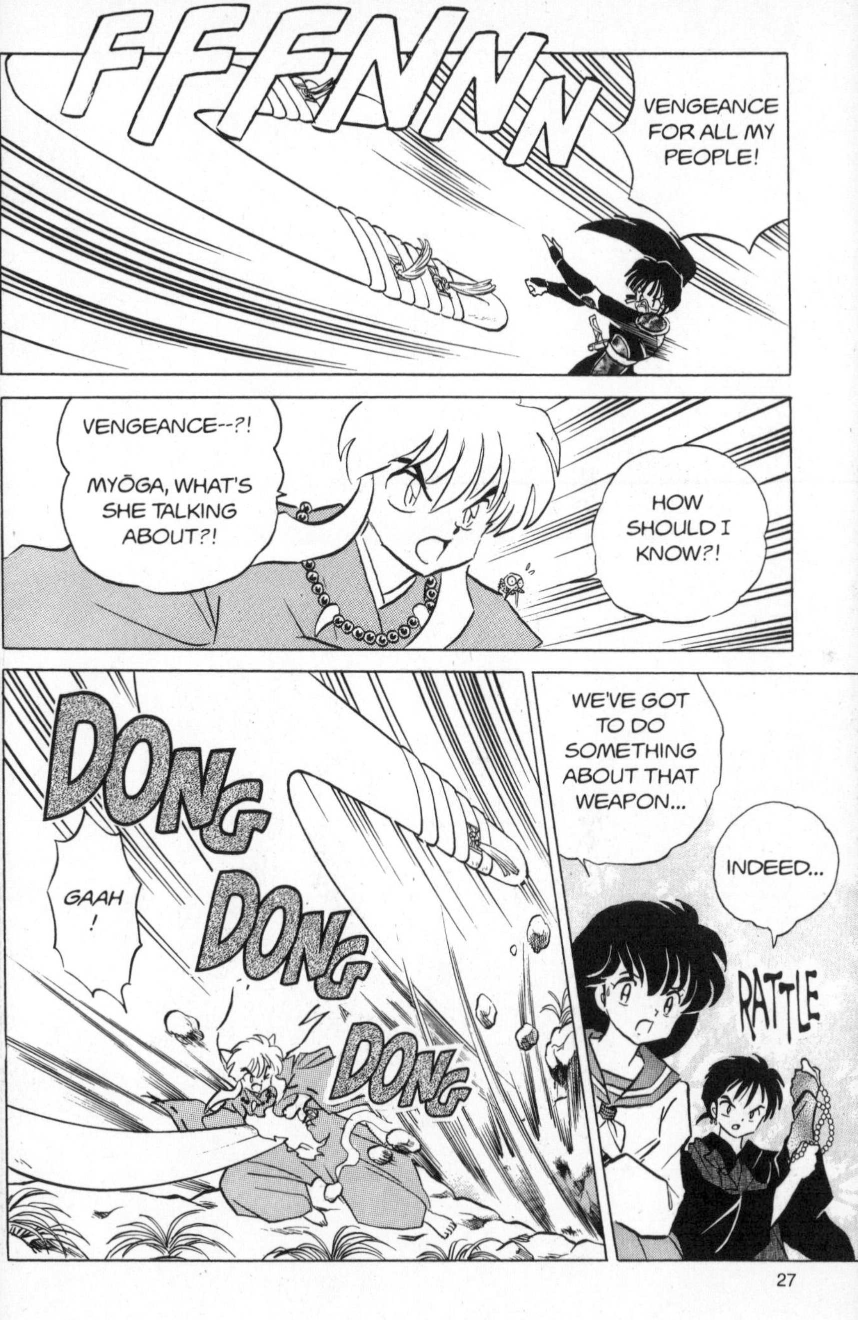
FFFNNN
VENGEANCE FOR ALL MY PEOPLE!
VENGEANCE--?!
MYŌGA, WHAT'S SHE TALKING ABOUT?!
HOW SHOULD I KNOW?!
DONG
GAAH!
DONG
DONG
WE'VE GOT TO DO SOMETHING ABOUT THAT WEAPON...
INDEED...
RATTLE

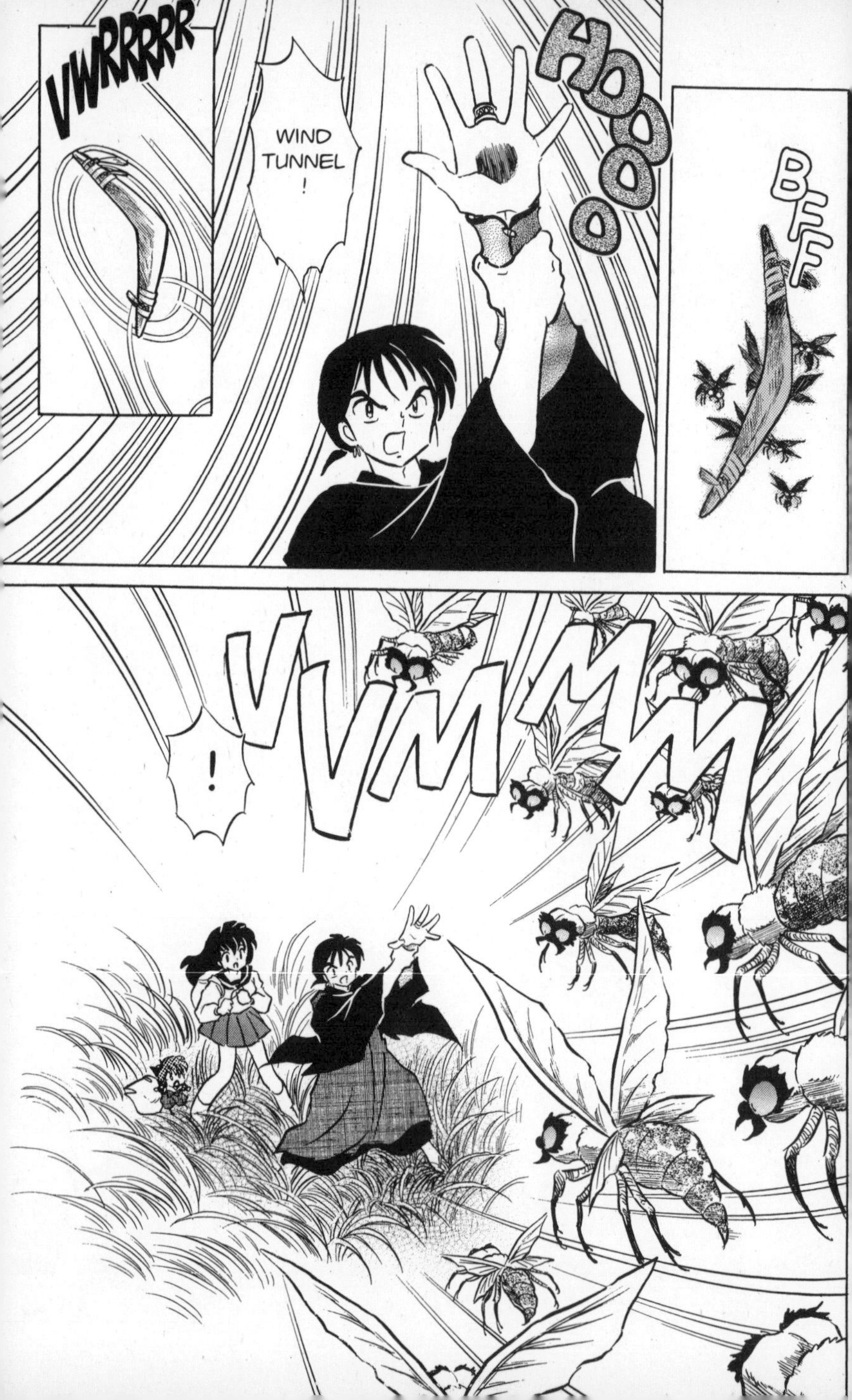
VWRRRRR
WIND TUNNEL !
HOOOOO
BFF
!
VVMMMM

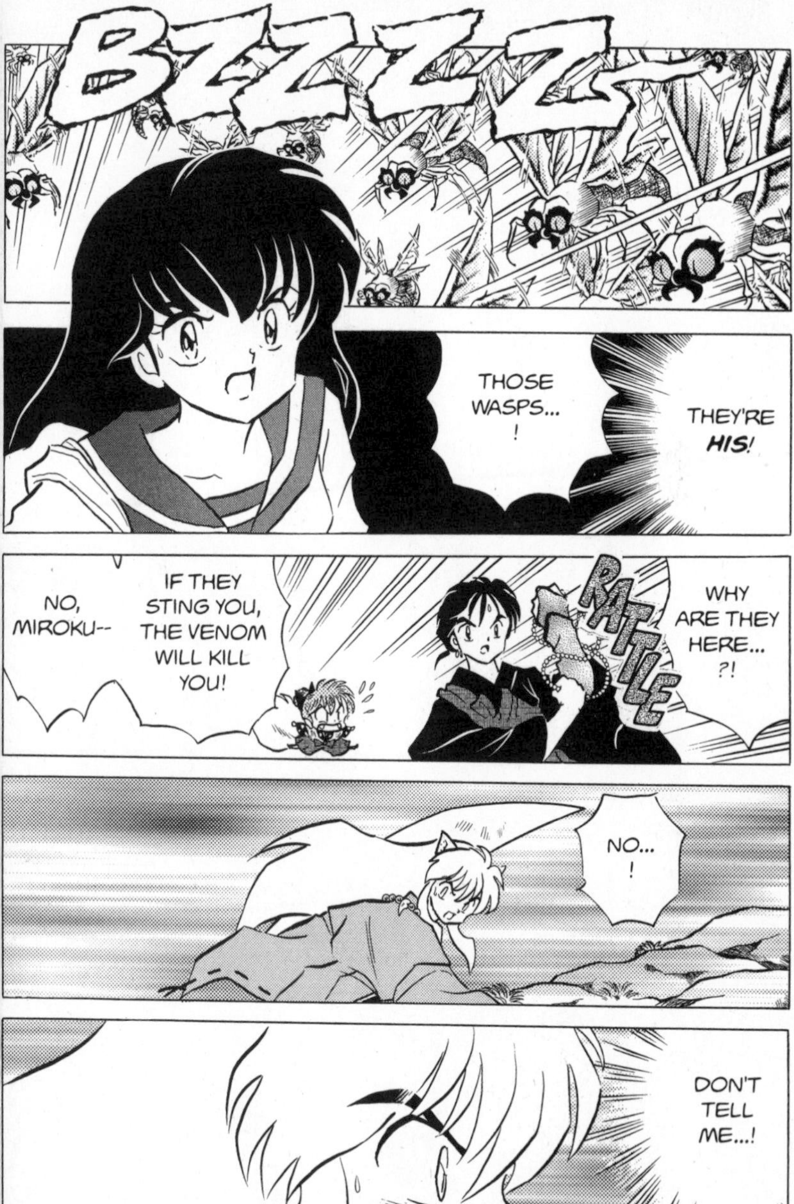
BZZZZ
THOSE WASPS... !
THEY'RE **HIS**!
NO, MIROKU--
IF THEY STING YOU, THE VENOM WILL KILL YOU!
RATTLE
WHY ARE THEY HERE... ?!
NO... !
DON'T TELL ME...!

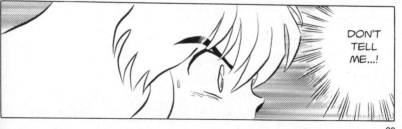

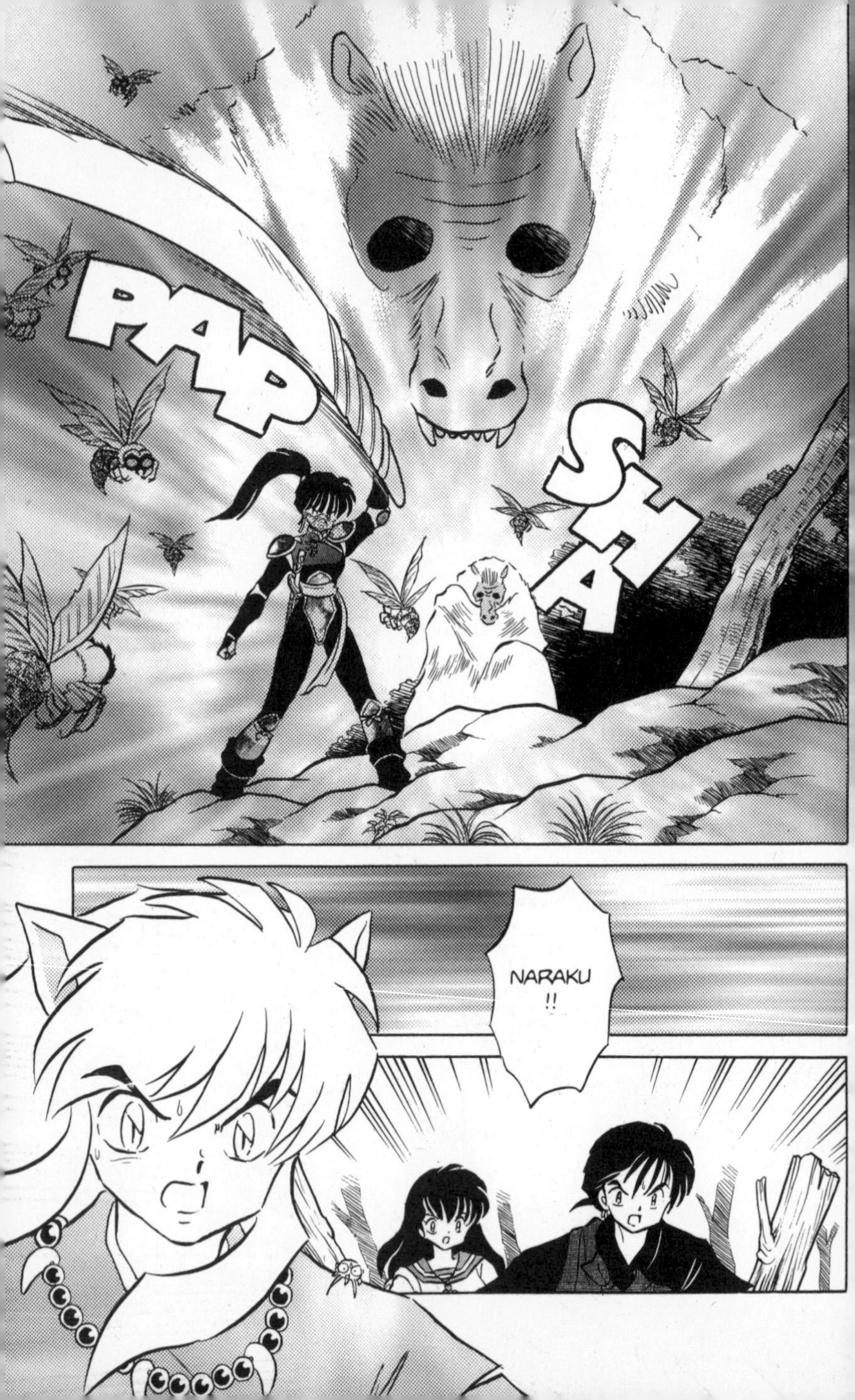
PAP
SHA
NARAKU !!

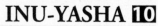

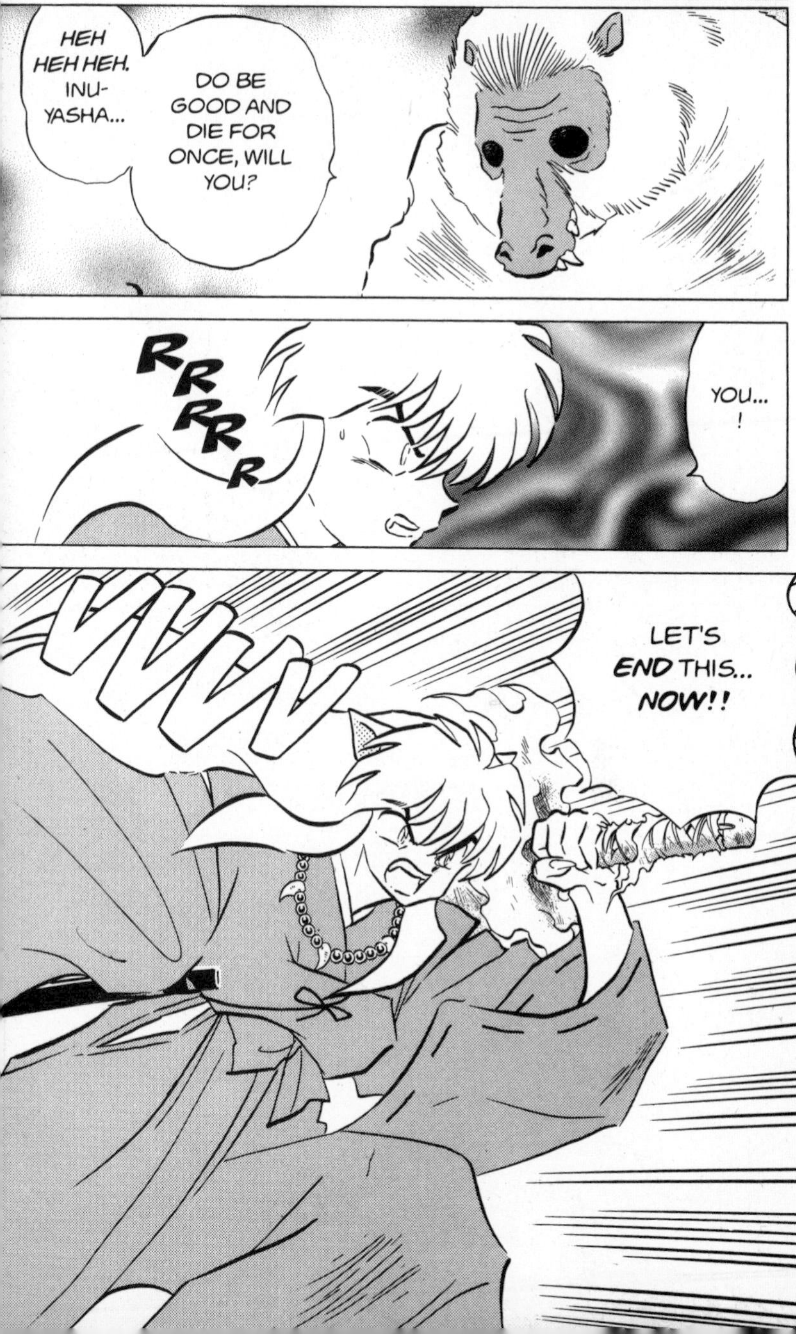
HEH HEH HEH. INU-YASHA...
DO BE GOOD AND DIE FOR ONCE, WILL YOU?
RRRRR
YOU... !
VVVV
LET'S **END** THIS... **NOW!!**

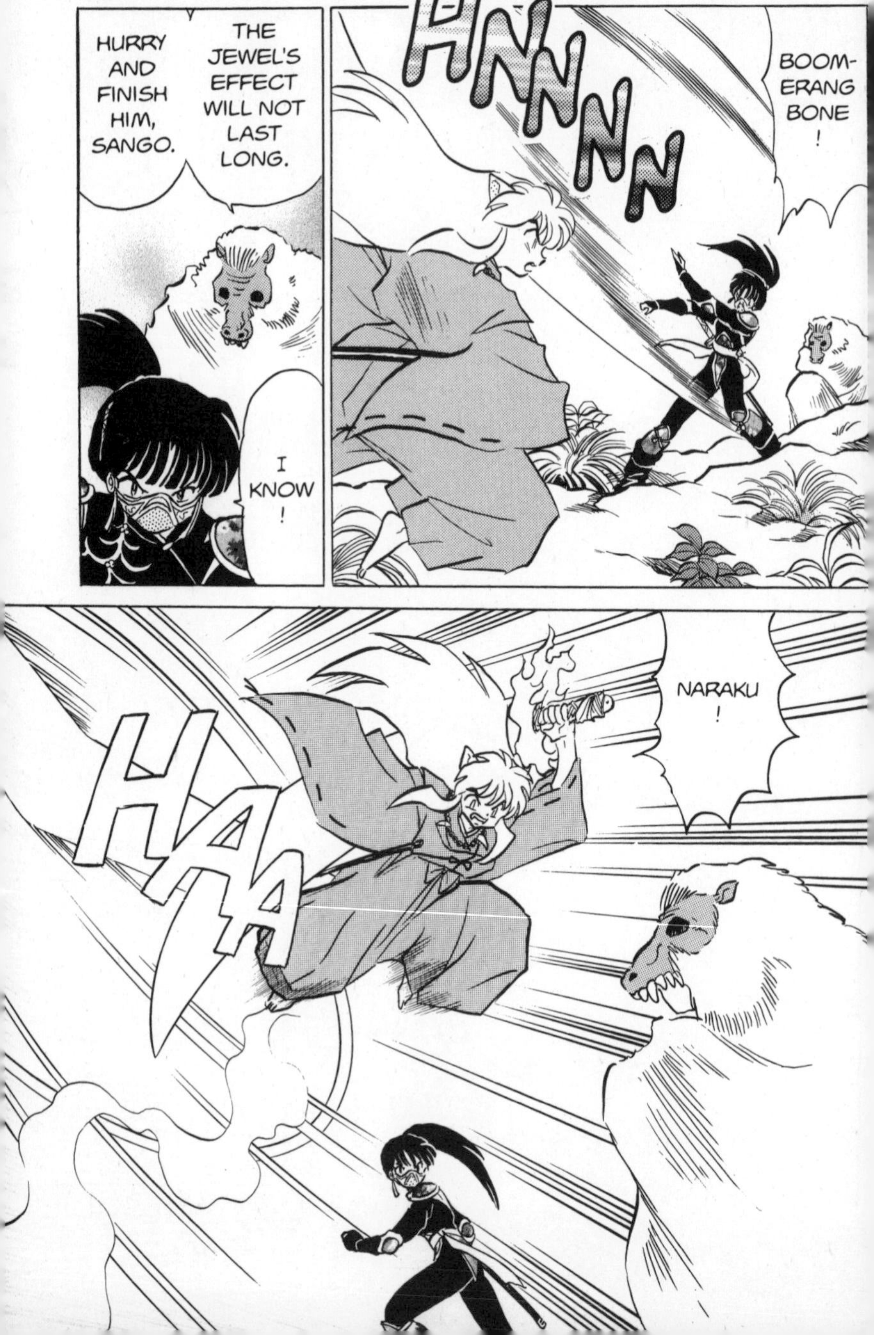
HURRY AND FINISH HIM, SANGO.
THE JEWEL'S EFFECT WILL NOT LAST LONG.
I KNOW!
HNNNNN
BOOMERANG BONE!
HAA
NARAKU!

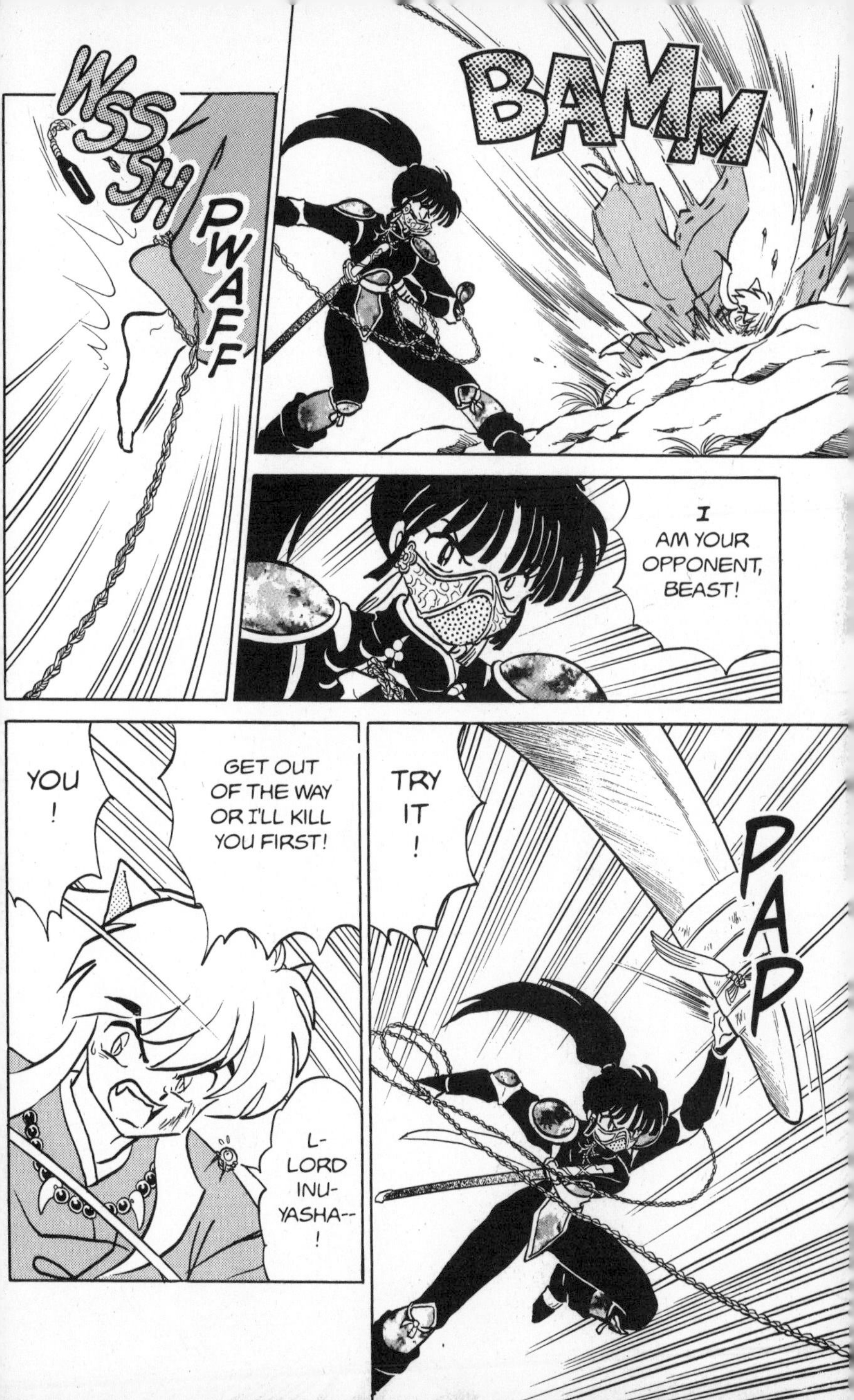
WSSSH
PWAFF
BAMM
I AM YOUR OPPONENT, BEAST!
YOU!
GET OUT OF THE WAY OR I'LL KILL YOU FIRST!
L-LORD INU-YASHA--!
TRY IT!
PAP

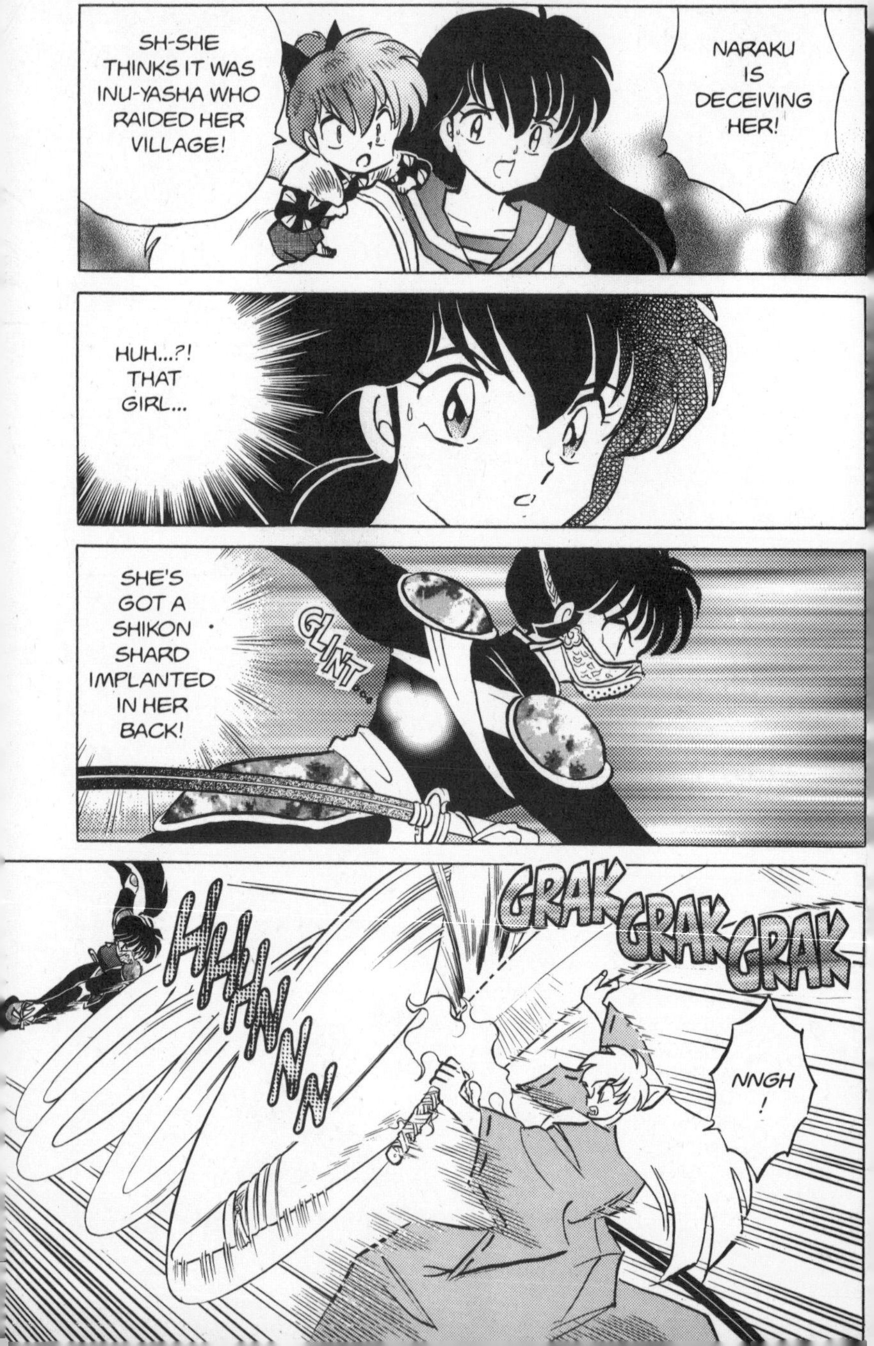
SH-SHE THINKS IT WAS INU-YASHA WHO RAIDED HER VILLAGE!
NARAKU IS DECEIVING HER!
HUH...?! THAT GIRL...
SHE'S GOT A SHIKON SHARD IMPLANTED IN HER BACK!
GLINT
HHHNNNN
GRAK GRAK GRAK
NNGH!

WHNNNN

FWAA

BEFORE HER WEAPON RETURNS TO HER...!

POISON POWDER!

HSSSSH

DOM

WHOA!

POISON GAS?!

HAK HAK

HMF.

I SEE DEMONS WITH DOG EARS HAVE SENSITIVE NOSES TOO.

GUHH!

I CAN'T GET CLOSE TO HER!

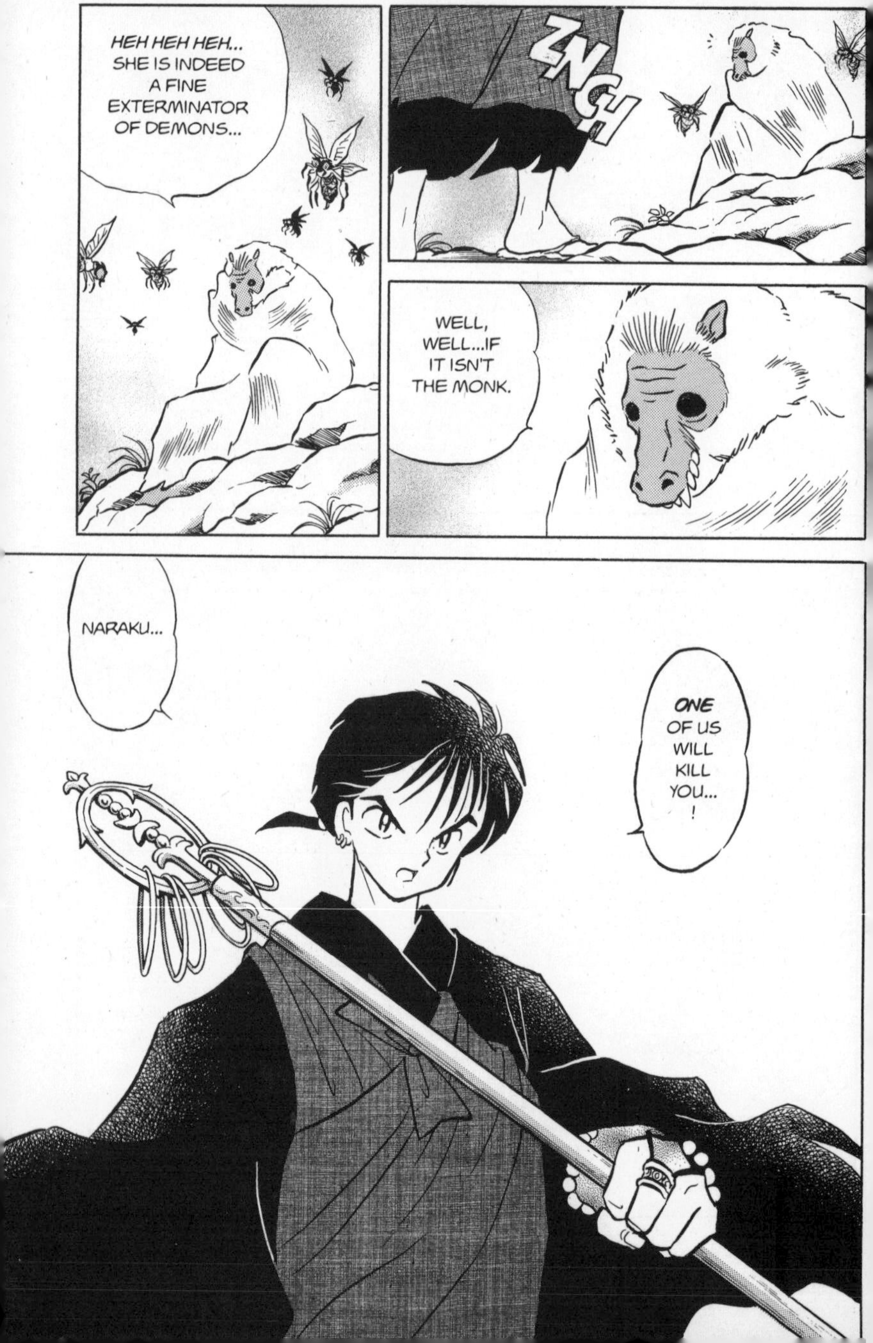
HEH HEH HEH... SHE IS INDEED A FINE EXTERMINATOR OF DEMONS...
ZNCH
WELL, WELL...IF IT ISN'T THE MONK.
NARAKU...
ONE OF US WILL KILL YOU...!

I CAN'T ALLOW THAT.

YOU SEE...

VERY SOON, ALL THE SHIKON SHARDS...

...WILL BE MINE!

I DON'T KNOW WHAT YOU'RE PLOTTING, BUT...

HSSST

FWA

IT ENDS NOW !!

SSSHHH

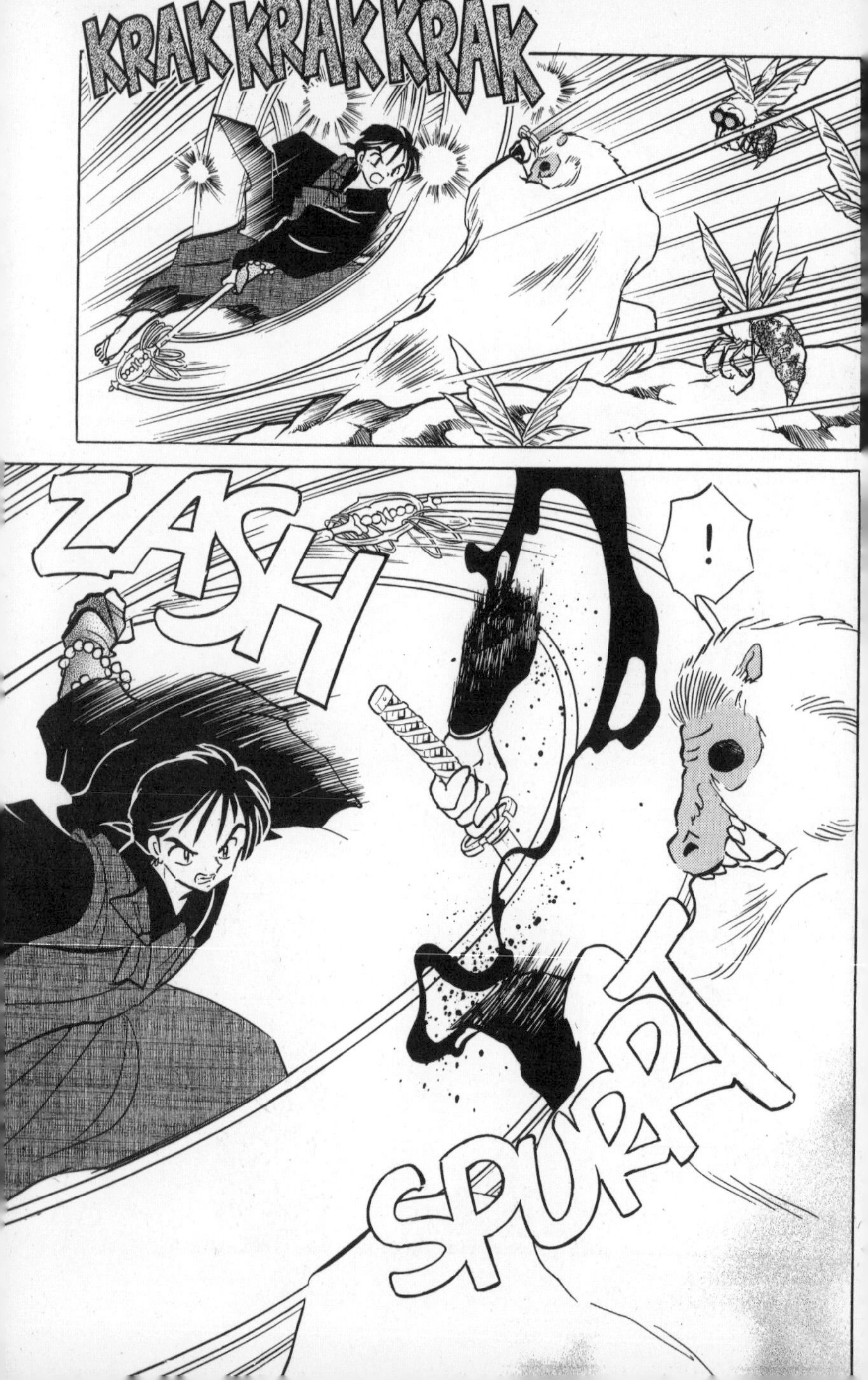
KRAK KRAK KRAK
ZASH
!
SPURT

HE
DID
IT!

PREPARE
TO DIE!

FEH.

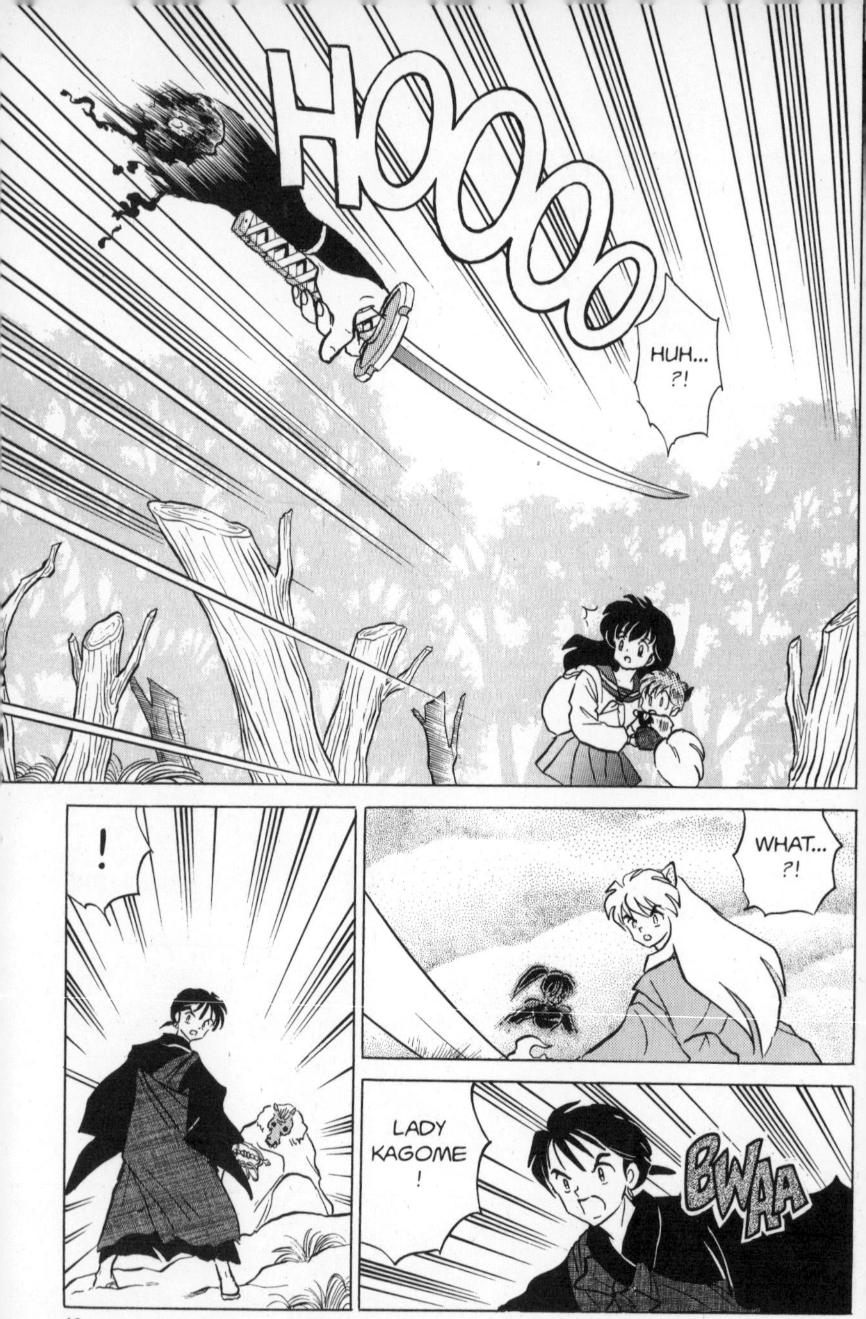
HOOOOO
HUH... ?!
!
WHAT... ?!
LADY KAGOME!
BWAA

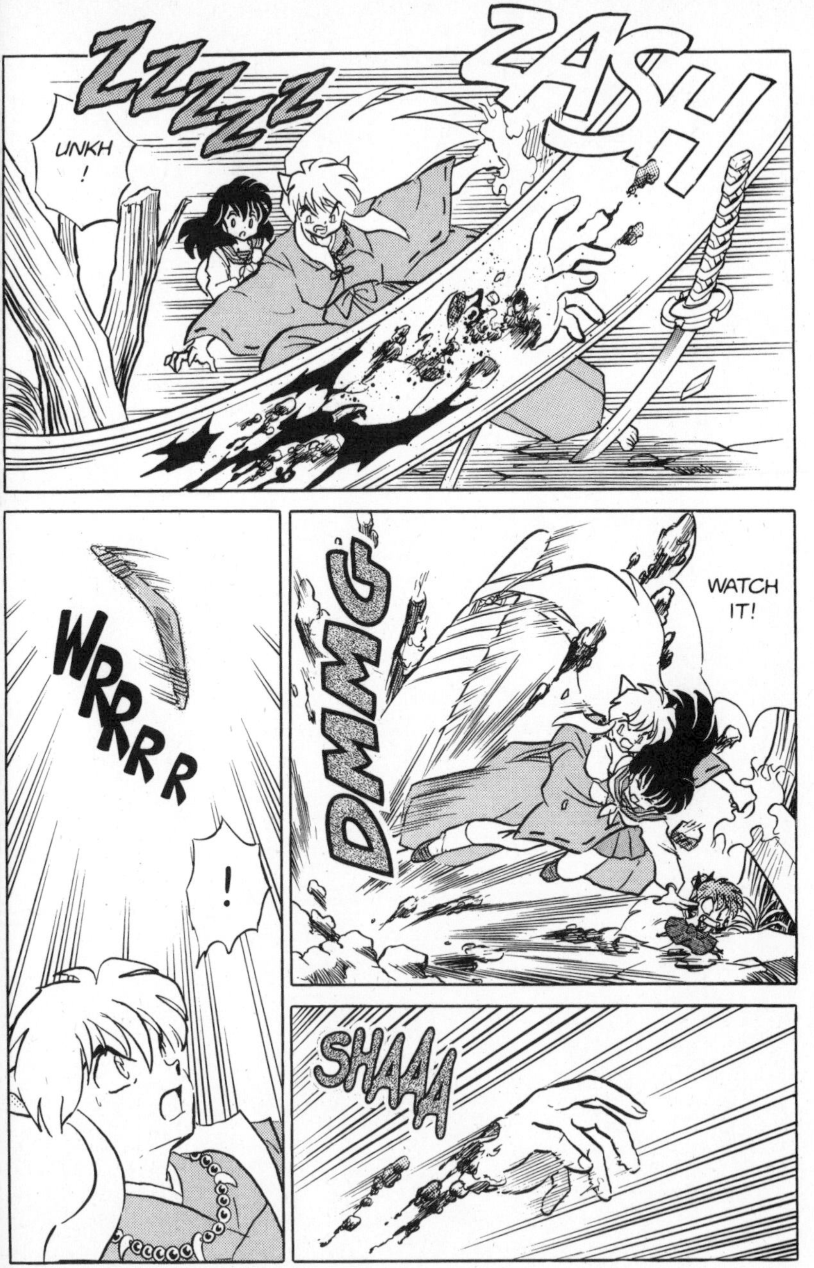
ZZZZZZ
UNKH!
ZASH
WRRRRR
!
DMMG
WATCH IT!
SHAAA

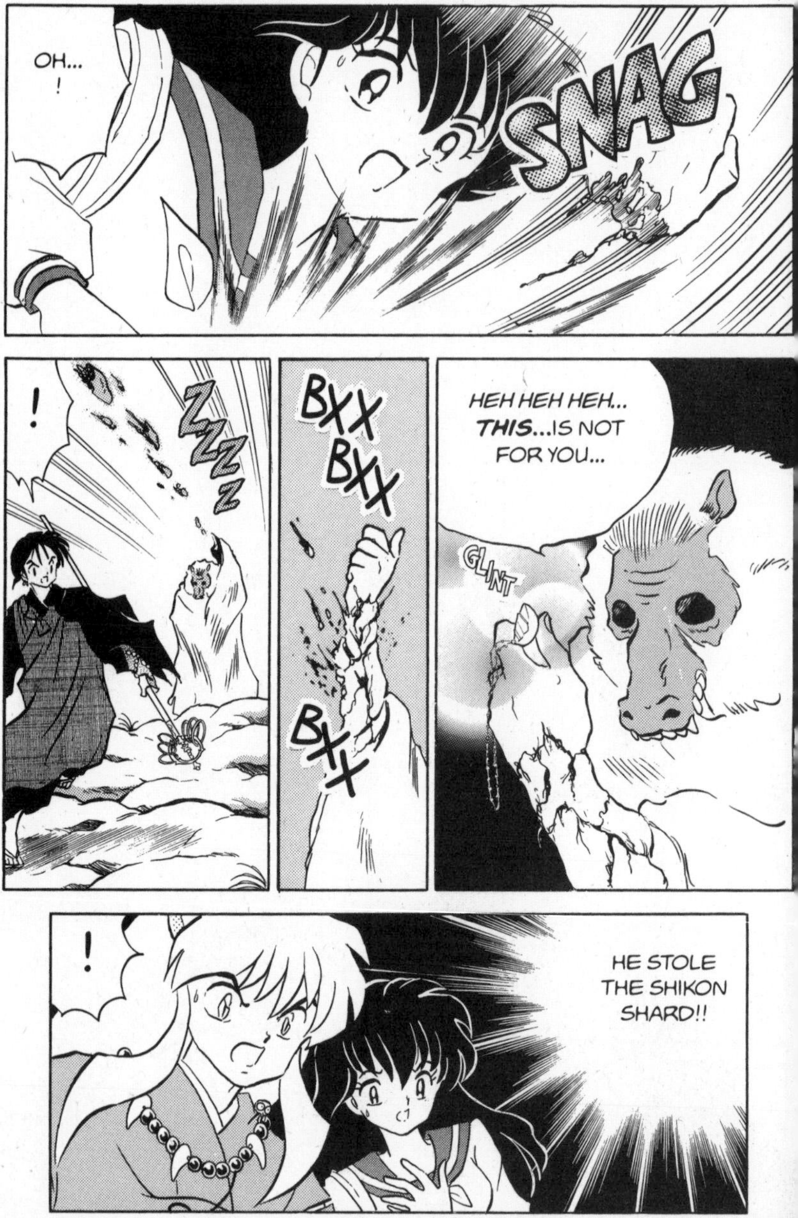

OH... !
SNAG
!
ZZZZ
BXX
BXX
BXX
GLINT
HEH HEH HEH... THIS...IS NOT FOR YOU...
!
HE STOLE THE SHIKON SHARD!!

SCROLL THREE

SUSPICIONS

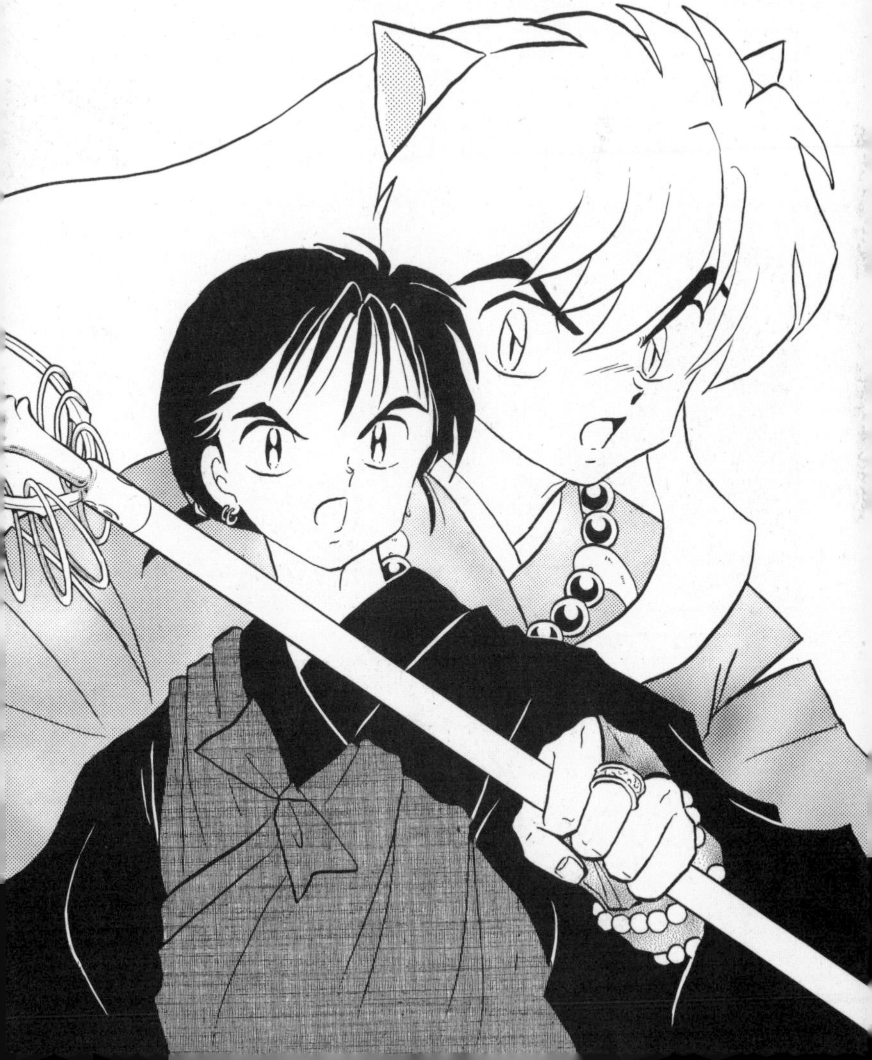

NOW THAT I POSSESS THE SHIKON SHARD, THERE IS NO LONGER ANY NEED FOR ME TO WAIT....

ROOOOOARR

NARAKU... STOP!

FARE-WELL, INU-YASHA!

I WON'T LET YOU GET AWAY!

VSH

44

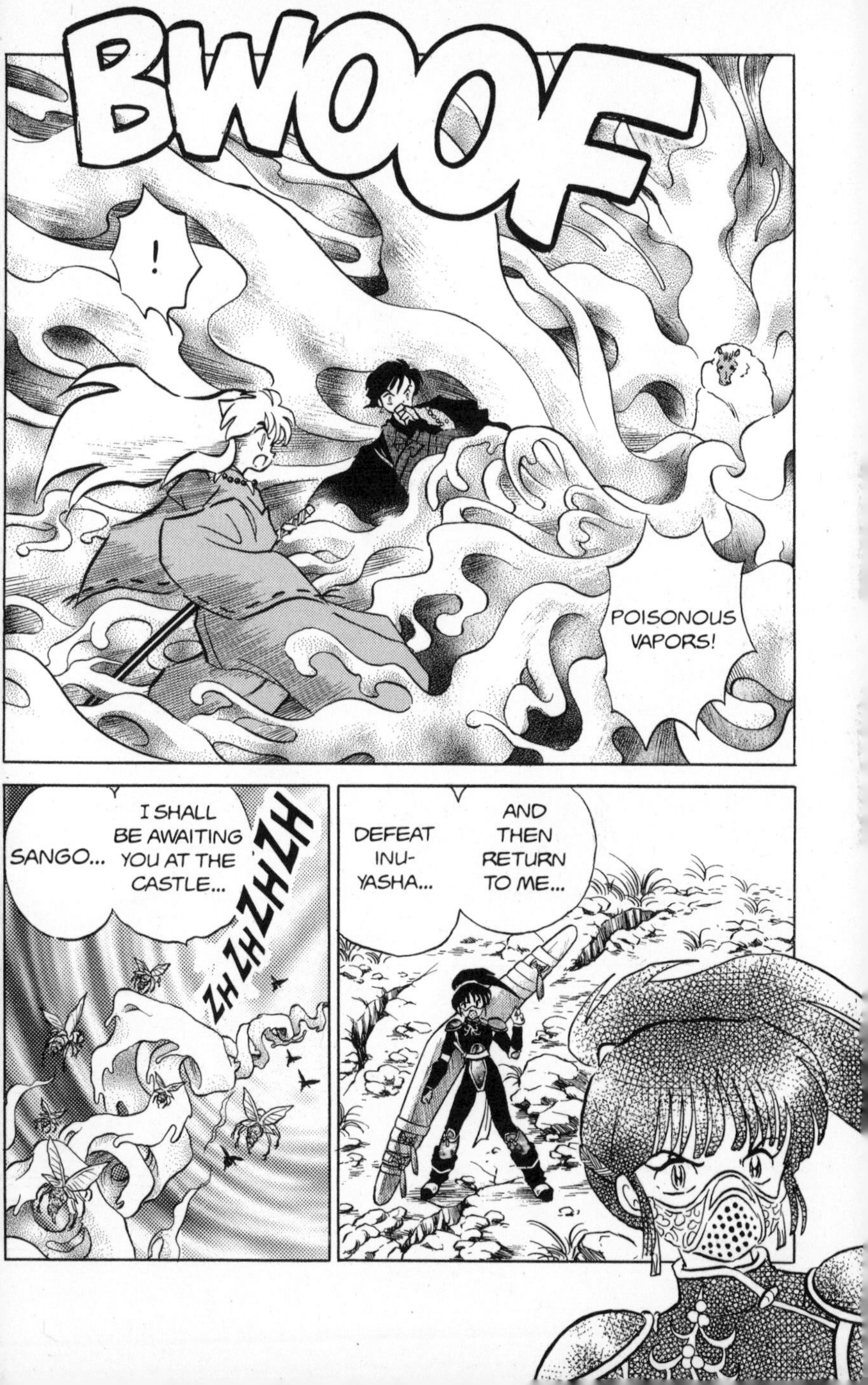
BWOOF
!
POISONOUS VAPORS!
SANGO...
I SHALL BE AWAITING YOU AT THE CASTLE...
ZH ZH ZHZHZH
DEFEAT INU-YASHA...
AND THEN RETURN TO ME...

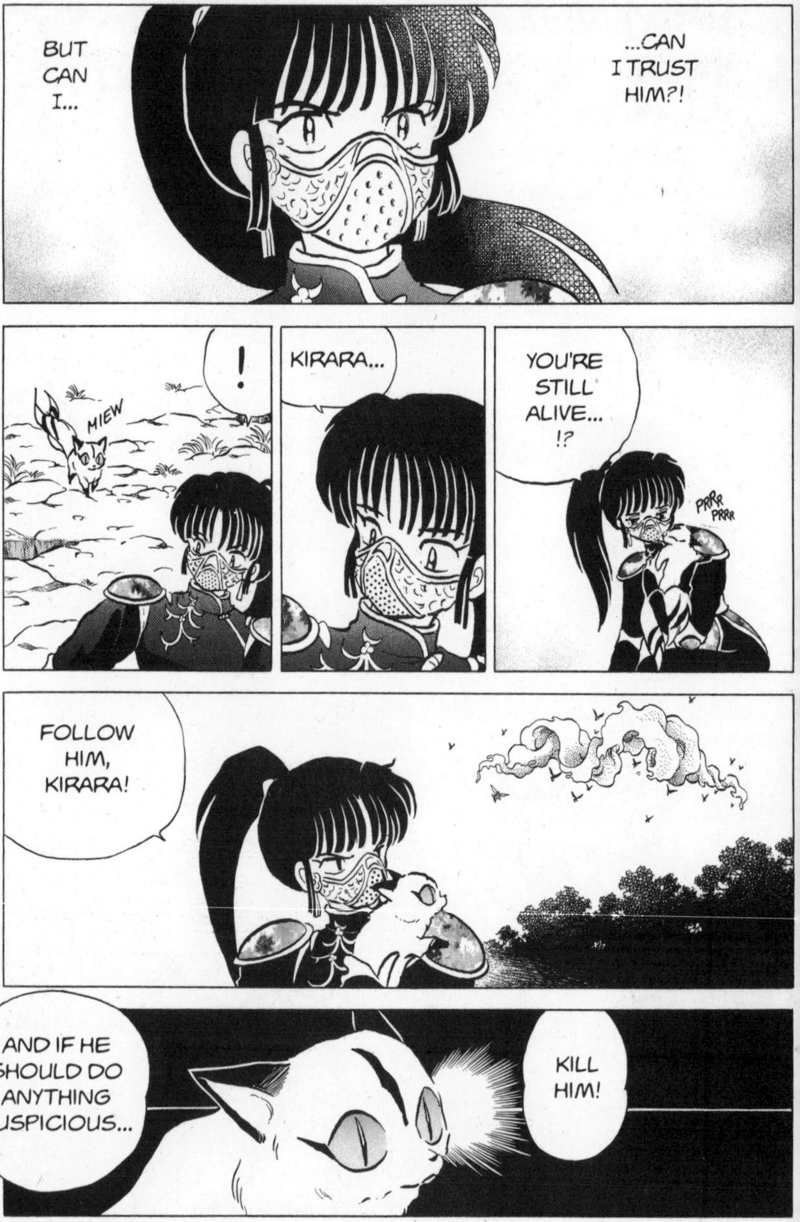
BUT CAN I...
...CAN I TRUST HIM?!
MIEW
!
KIRARA...
YOU'RE STILL ALIVE... !?
PRRR PRRR
FOLLOW HIM, KIRARA!
AND IF HE SHOULD DO ANYTHING SUSPICIOUS...
KILL HIM!

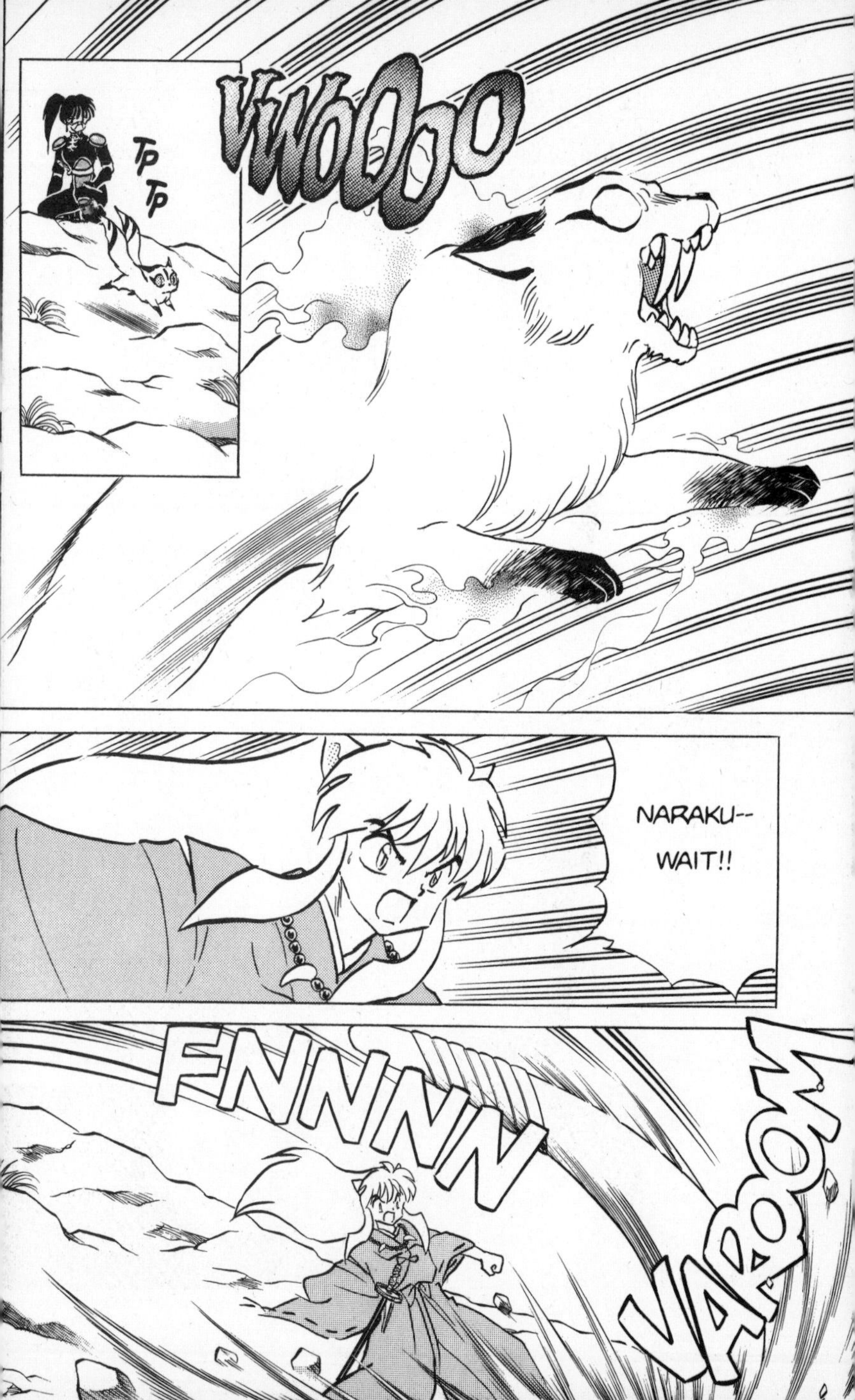
TP TP
VWOOOOO
NARAKU-- WAIT!!
FNNNNN
VAROOM

VNNNN

PAPG

NKH
!

PREPARE FOR EXTERMINATION-- HERE AND NOW!

CAN'T YOU GIVE IT *UP!?*

FWAA

I'VE GOT TO TAKE HIM DOWN QUICKLY....

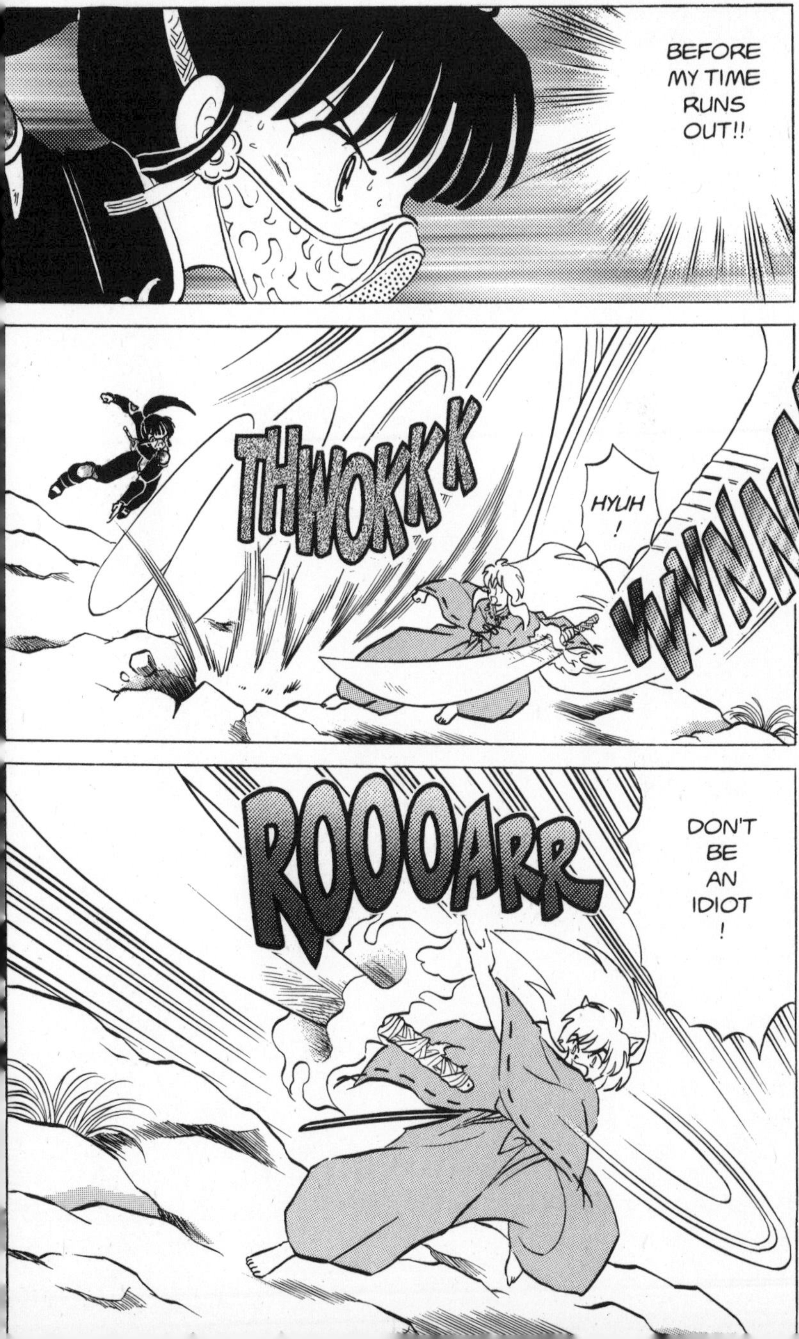
BEFORE MY TIME RUNS OUT!!
THWOKKK
HYUH!
WVNNNN
ROOOARR
DON'T BE AN IDIOT!

POISON DUST!

KWAAAA

!

PNNNG

MY FILTER MASK... CURSE IT...!

BWIP

!

GNG

FSH

WHY IN ALL THE HELLS... ...IS HE RESCUING ME?!

YOU FOOL!!

YOU STILL DON'T GET IT, DO YOU!? NARAKU'S DUPING YOU!!

SHOVE

AND MEANWHILE....

...YOU'RE BLEEDING TO DEATH!

WH... AT...?

!

BLUP

DRRRRIP

I DIDN'T REALIZE IT WAS SO BAD....

WHY HAVEN'T I FELT...THE PAIN...?

INU-YASHA, ARE YOU ALL RIGHT?!

I AM, YEAH.

SSHHHD

WAAH! SHE'S DEAD!

NO... SHE'S JUST FAINTED!

INU-YASHA, THIS GIRL...

SHE'S GOT A SHIKON SHARD IMPLANTED IN HER BACK...

...

THAT EXPLAINS IT...

FROM THE BLOOD SCENT ON HER I COULD TELL THAT SHE WAS SEVERELY INJURED FROM THE BEGINNING... BUT...

THAT BASTARD NARAKU STUCK THE SHARD INTO HER...

...TO KEEP HER FIGHTING UNTIL SHE DIED.

NNNH...

I CAN'T LOSE SIGHT OF HIM!

ZZHHH

KRII

BLAST IT!!

HYUUUU

RRROAR

CLATTER

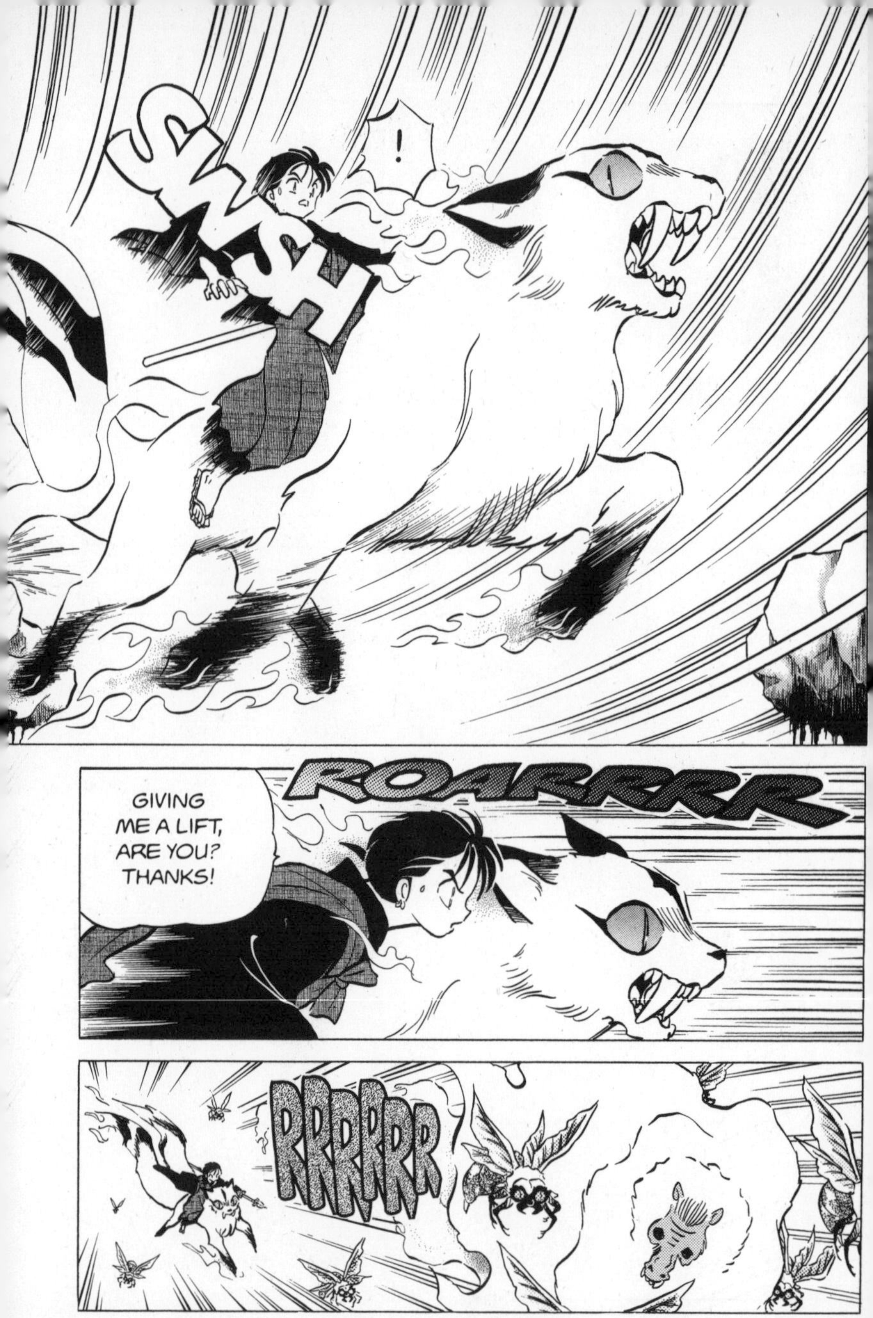
SWISH
!
ROARRRR
GIVING ME A LIFT, ARE YOU? THANKS!
RRRRRR

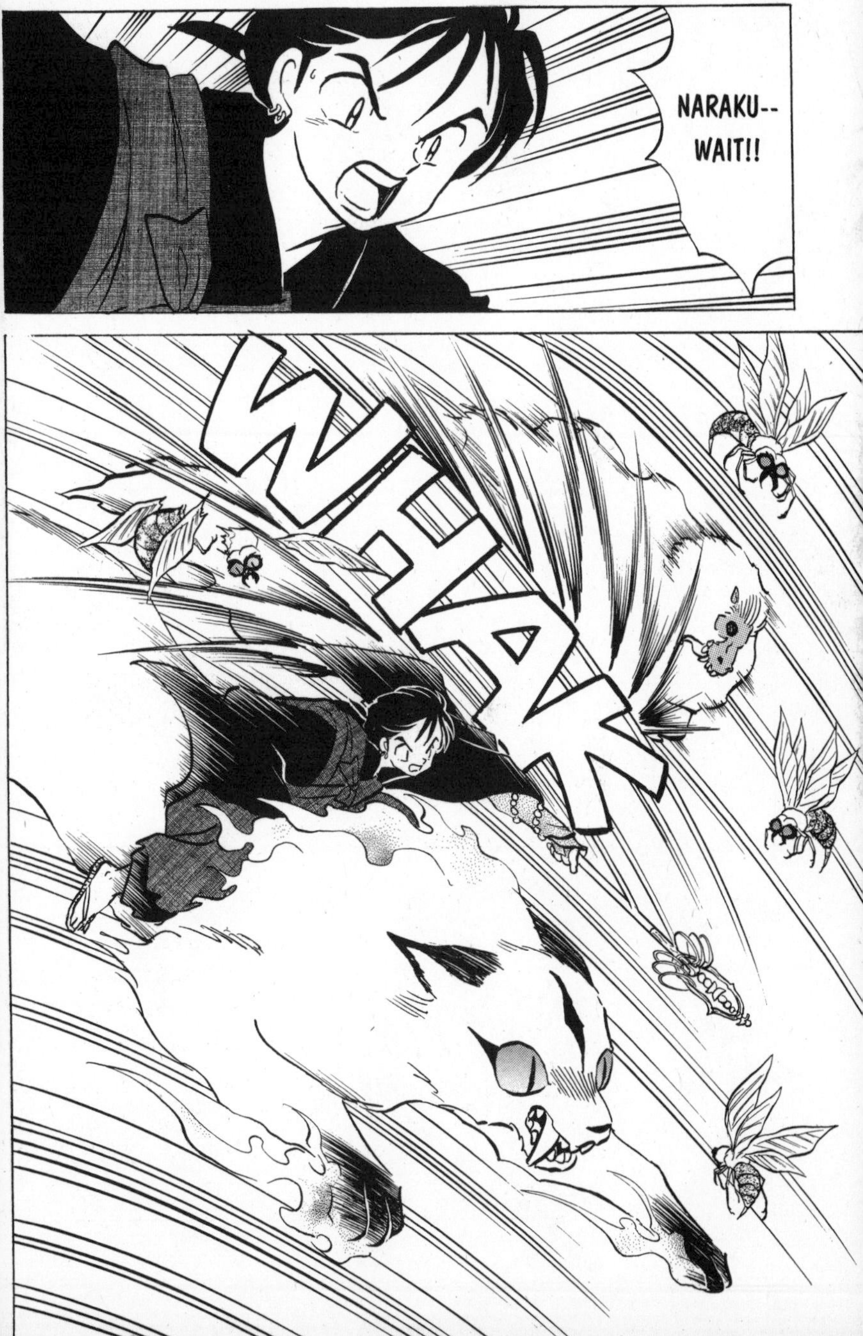
NARAKU-- WAIT!!
WHAK

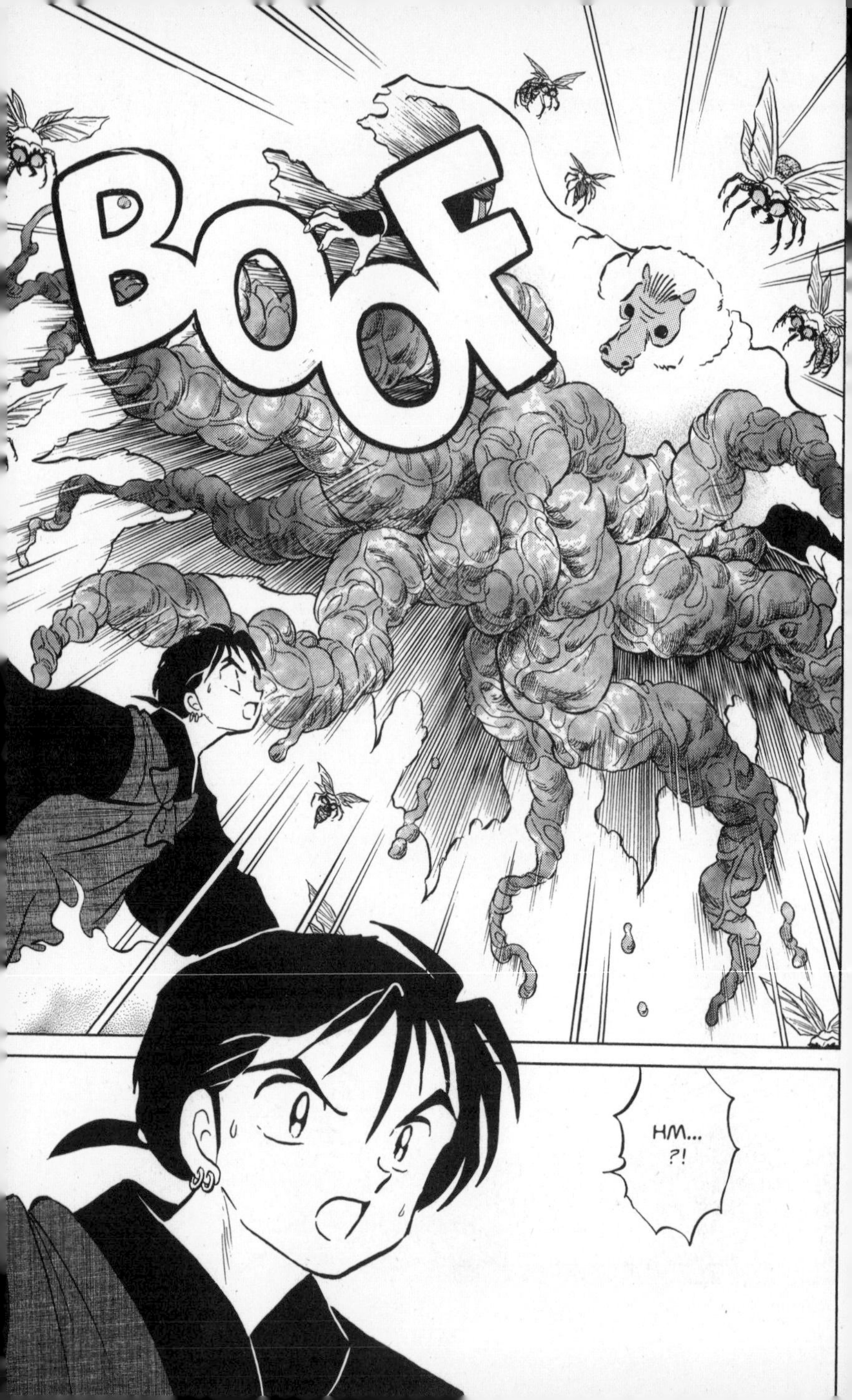
BOOF
HM...
?!

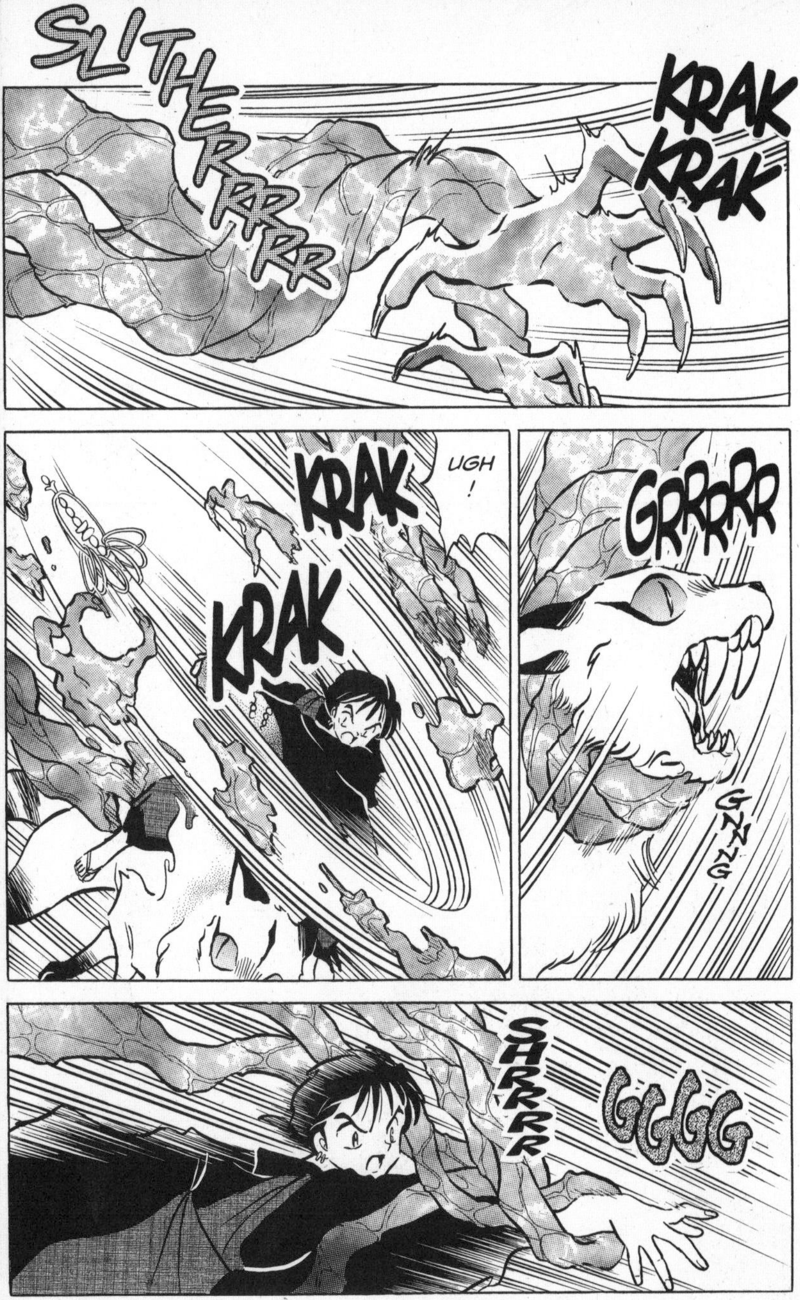
KRAK
KRAK
SLITHERRRRRR
GRRRRR
GNNG
UGH!
KRAK
KRAK
SHRRRR
GGGG

SCROLL FOUR

STRATEGIES

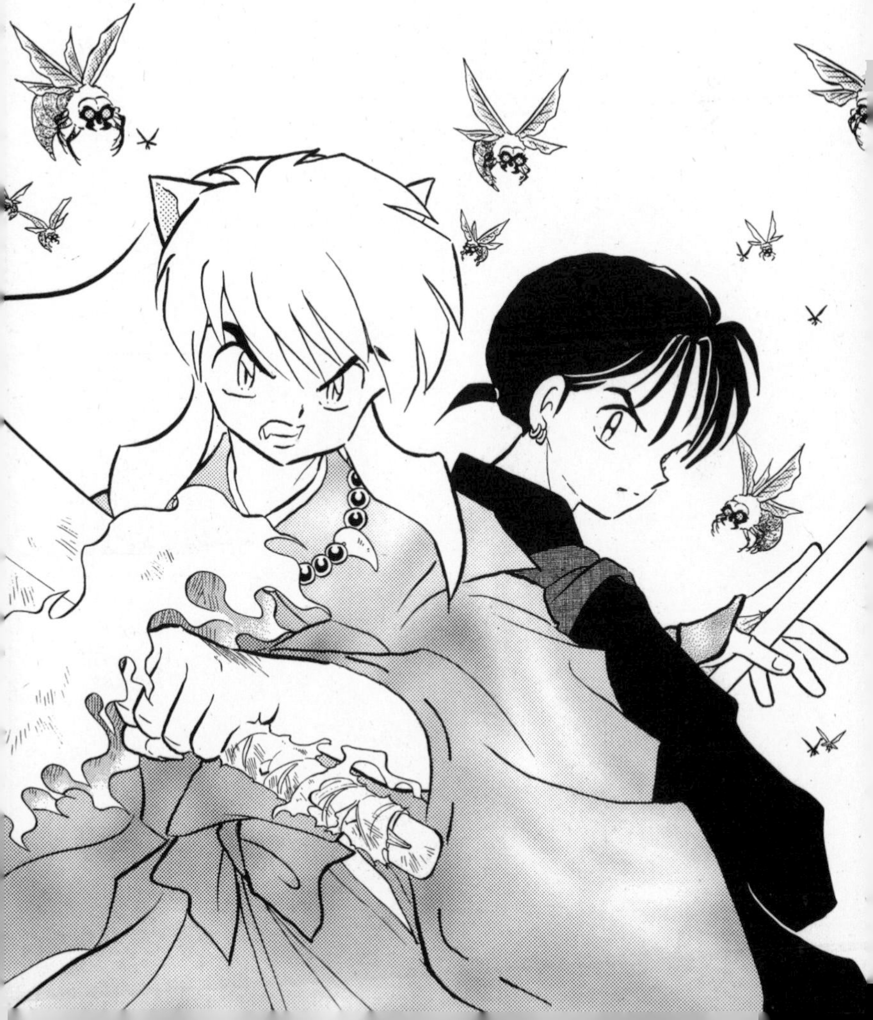

YOU BACK AMONG THE LIVING?

YOU...!

LET ME DOWN!

WHAT ARE YOU PLANNING TO DO WITH ME!?

WHAT--!

WE'RE CHASING AFTER NARAKU--

BECAUSE HE TOOK MY SHIKON SHARD...

poip

LISTEN... IT'S *SANGO*, RIGHT?

IF YOU KEEP SWALLOWING NARAKU'S LIES, I'M GOING TO DROP YOU RIGHT HERE!

WHA...!

SHEESH...

AND YOU WONDER WHY NO ONE TRUSTS YOU....

PAY NO ATTENTION TO HIM. HE MAY LOOK FIERCE....

BUT HE'S BASICALLY A BIG CUDDLY PUPPY DOG.

HEY!

YOU ARE HERE, SANGO, BECAUSE LORD INU-YASHA REFUSED TO LEAVE YOU BEHIND IN YOUR INJURED STATE.

ELDER MYŌGA...

I'M GOING TO SPEED UP!

HWOOOO

NARAKU... WILL NOT... ESCAPE!!

SHHF SHHF

HEH HEH HEH...

WHY SO ASTONISHED, MONK?

SSHHHH

RIIIP

UNKH!

RIIIP

WHIP

SHPLATT

GLOB GLOB

BLLLSSH

AARGH!

EVEN WHEN I SEVER THEM, THEY FLOW BACK INTO ONE!

DWOK

DWOK

WHOA!

SHWRRRRR

KRAK KRAK

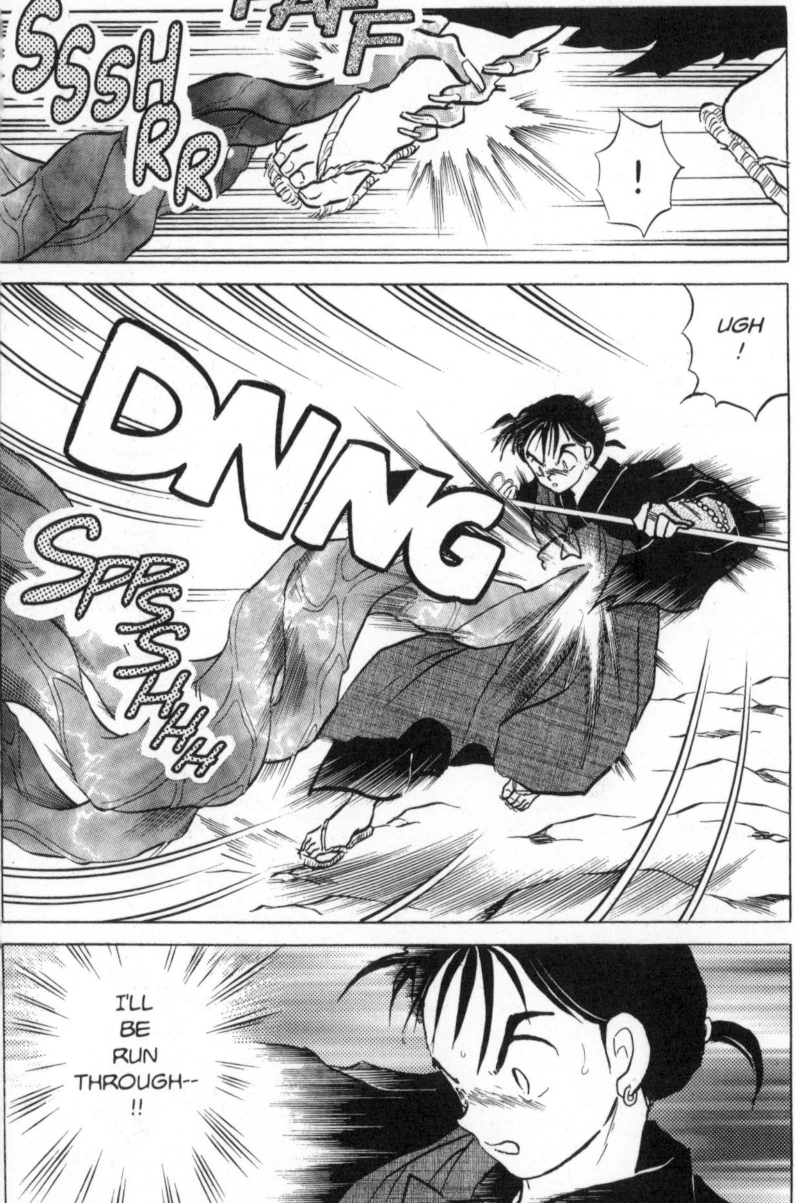
SSSH
RR
PAFF
!
UGH
!
DNNG
SPPSSHHH
I'LL BE RUN THROUGH-- !!

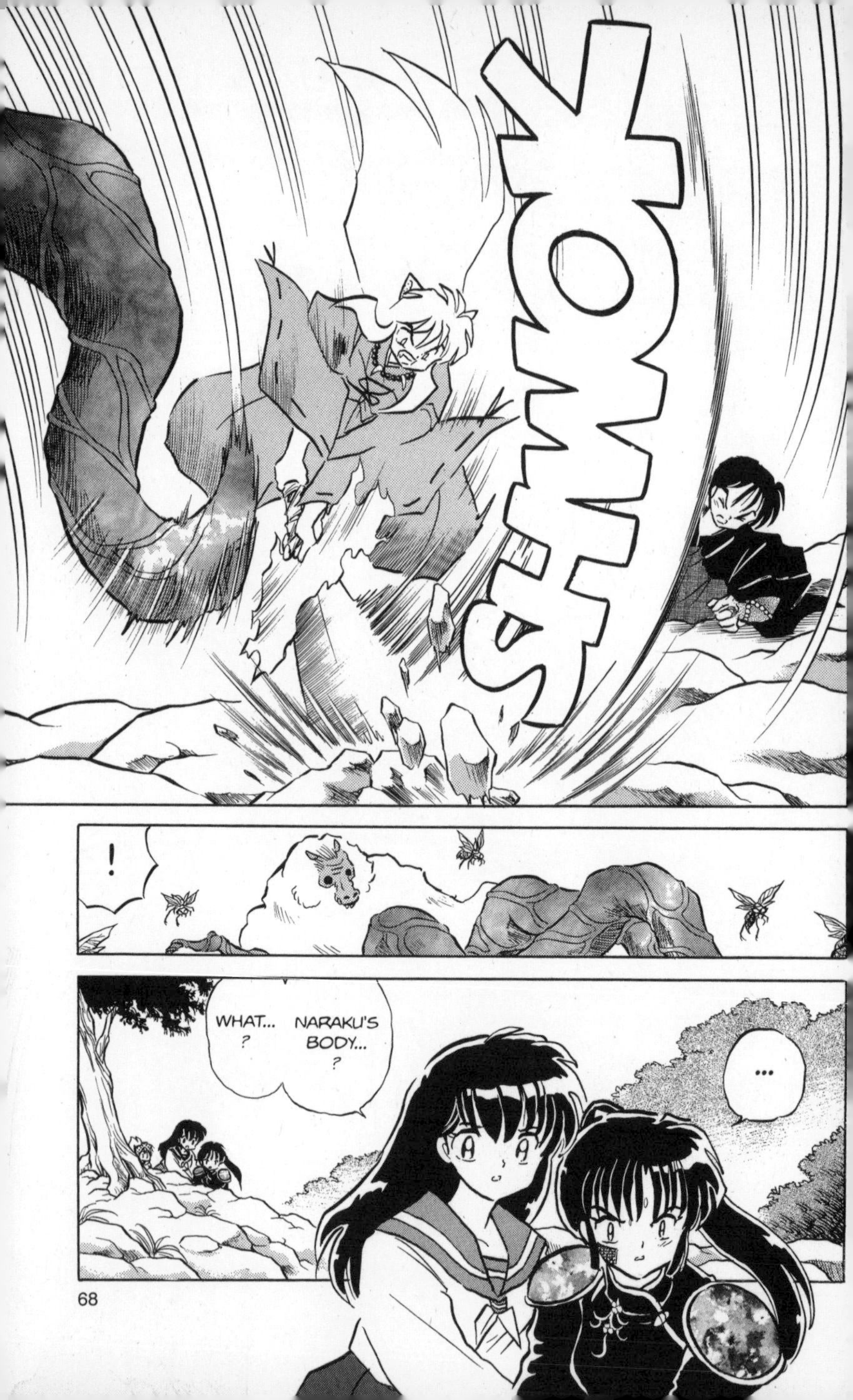
SHWOK
!
WHAT... ?
NARAKU'S BODY... ?
...

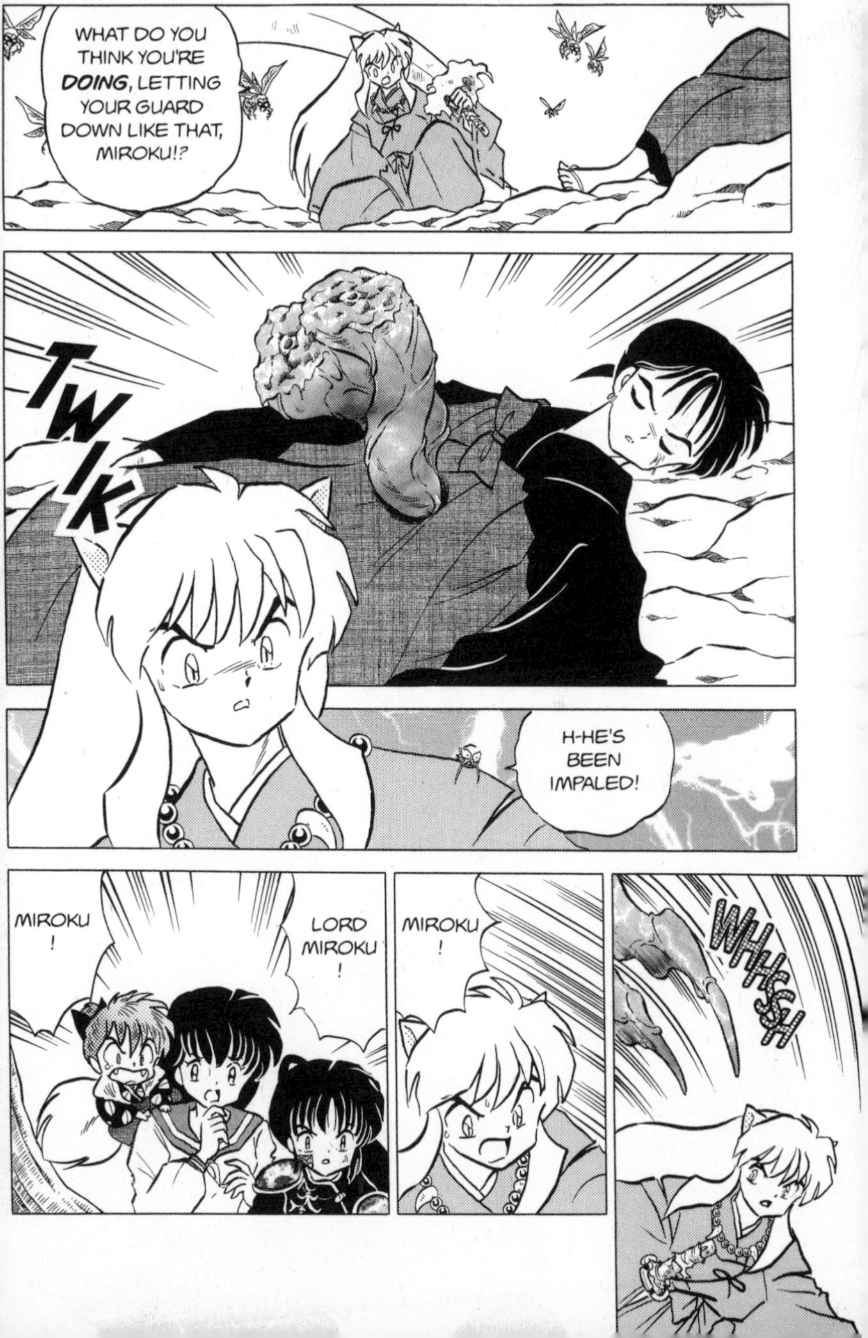
WHAT DO YOU THINK YOU'RE *DOING*, LETTING YOUR GUARD DOWN LIKE THAT, MIROKU!?
TWIK
H-HE'S BEEN IMPALED!
MIROKU!
LORD MIROKU!
MIROKU!
WHHSSH

WHOA!

MIROKU! DON'T YOU *DARE* DIE!

DAMN...

IF I'D JUST SPEEDED UP EARLIER....

WHEW...

I THOUGHT I WAS GOING TO DIE!

HUH?!

OH...!

SHLLLLIP

HUH--?

THERE'S NOT EVEN A HOLE!

NOW *THAT* WAS CLOSE...

WHAT'S THE IDEA OF COLLAPSING WITH THAT *DEAD* LOOK ON YOUR FACE!?

MOOSH

YOU'RE THE ONE WHO DECIDED I LOOKED DEAD!

SO, INU-YASHA... YOU STILL LIVE....

KRII KRII

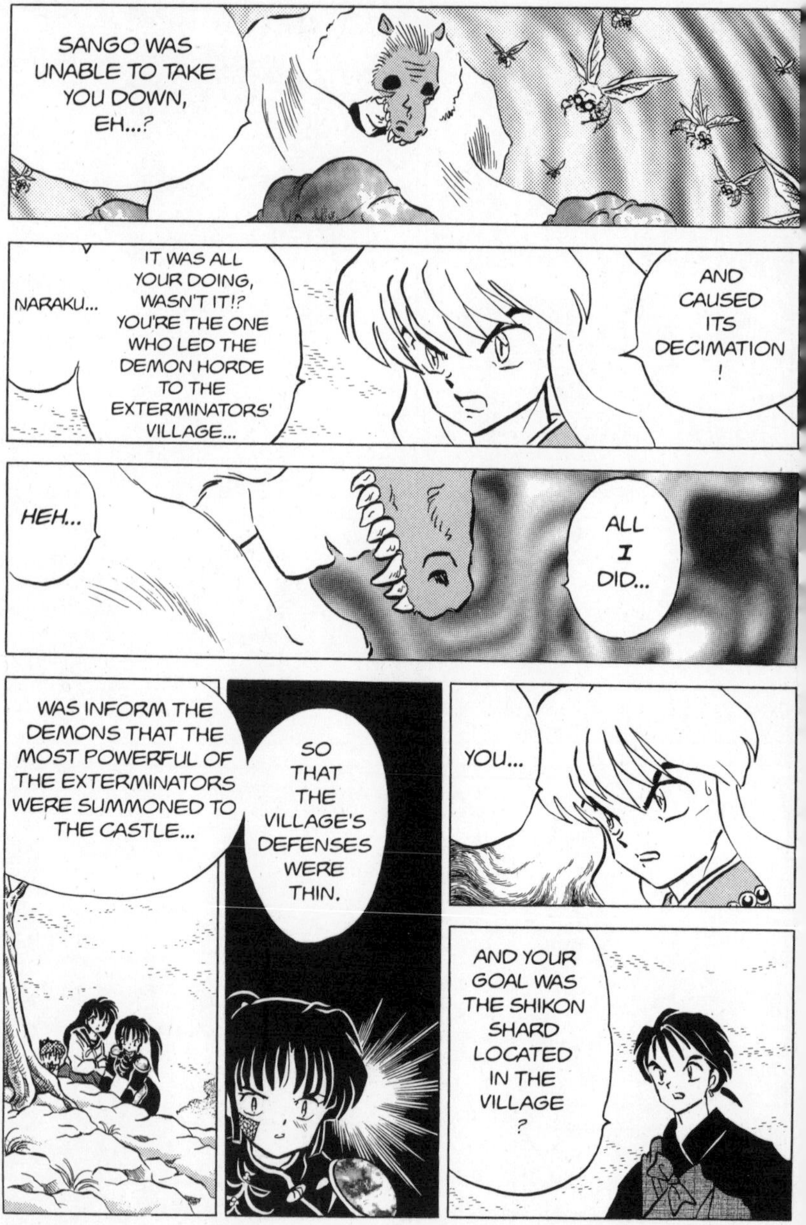
SANGO WAS UNABLE TO TAKE YOU DOWN, EH...?
NARAKU...
IT WAS ALL YOUR DOING, WASN'T IT!? YOU'RE THE ONE WHO LED THE DEMON HORDE TO THE EXTERMINATORS' VILLAGE...
AND CAUSED ITS DECIMATION!
HEH...
ALL I DID...
WAS INFORM THE DEMONS THAT THE MOST POWERFUL OF THE EXTERMINATORS WERE SUMMONED TO THE CASTLE...
SO THAT THE VILLAGE'S DEFENSES WERE THIN.
YOU...
AND YOUR GOAL WAS THE SHIKON SHARD LOCATED IN THE VILLAGE?

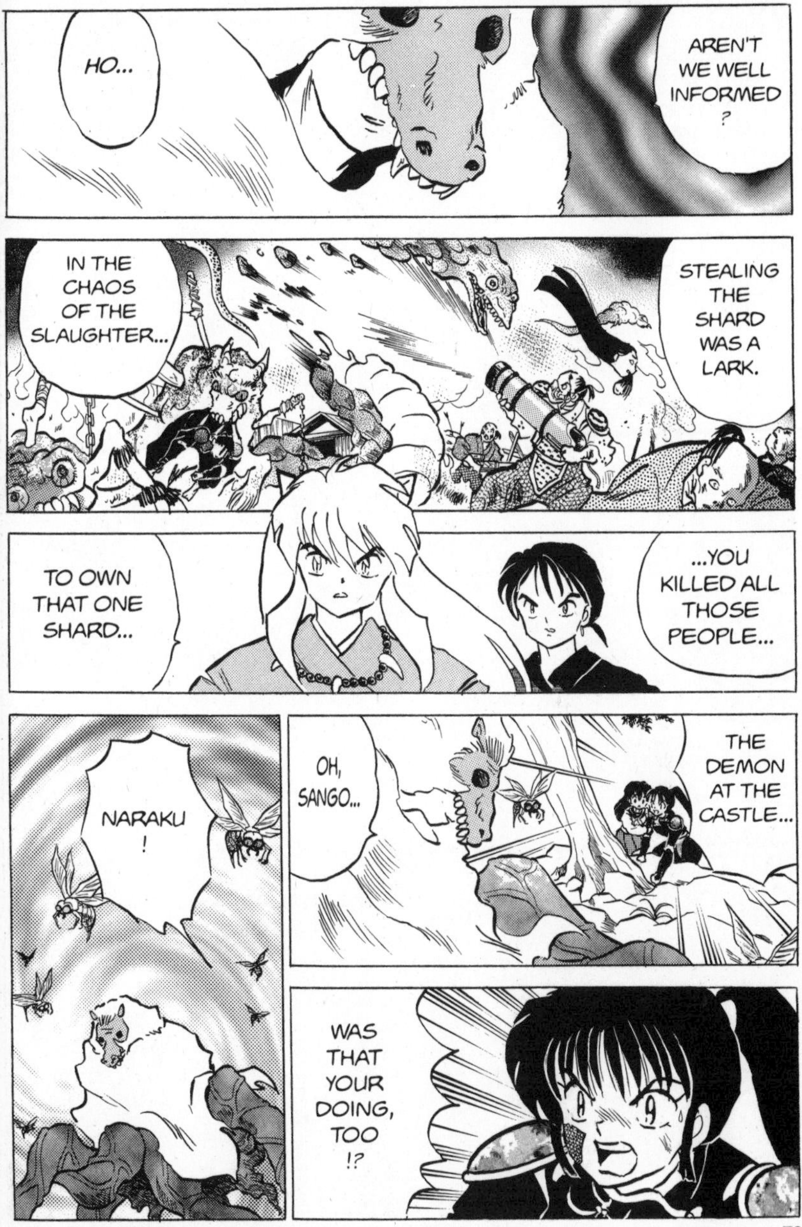
HO...
AREN'T WE WELL INFORMED ?
IN THE CHAOS OF THE SLAUGHTER...
STEALING THE SHARD WAS A LARK.
TO OWN THAT ONE SHARD...
...YOU KILLED ALL THOSE PEOPLE...
NARAKU !
OH, SANGO...
THE DEMON AT THE CASTLE...
WAS THAT YOUR DOING, TOO !?

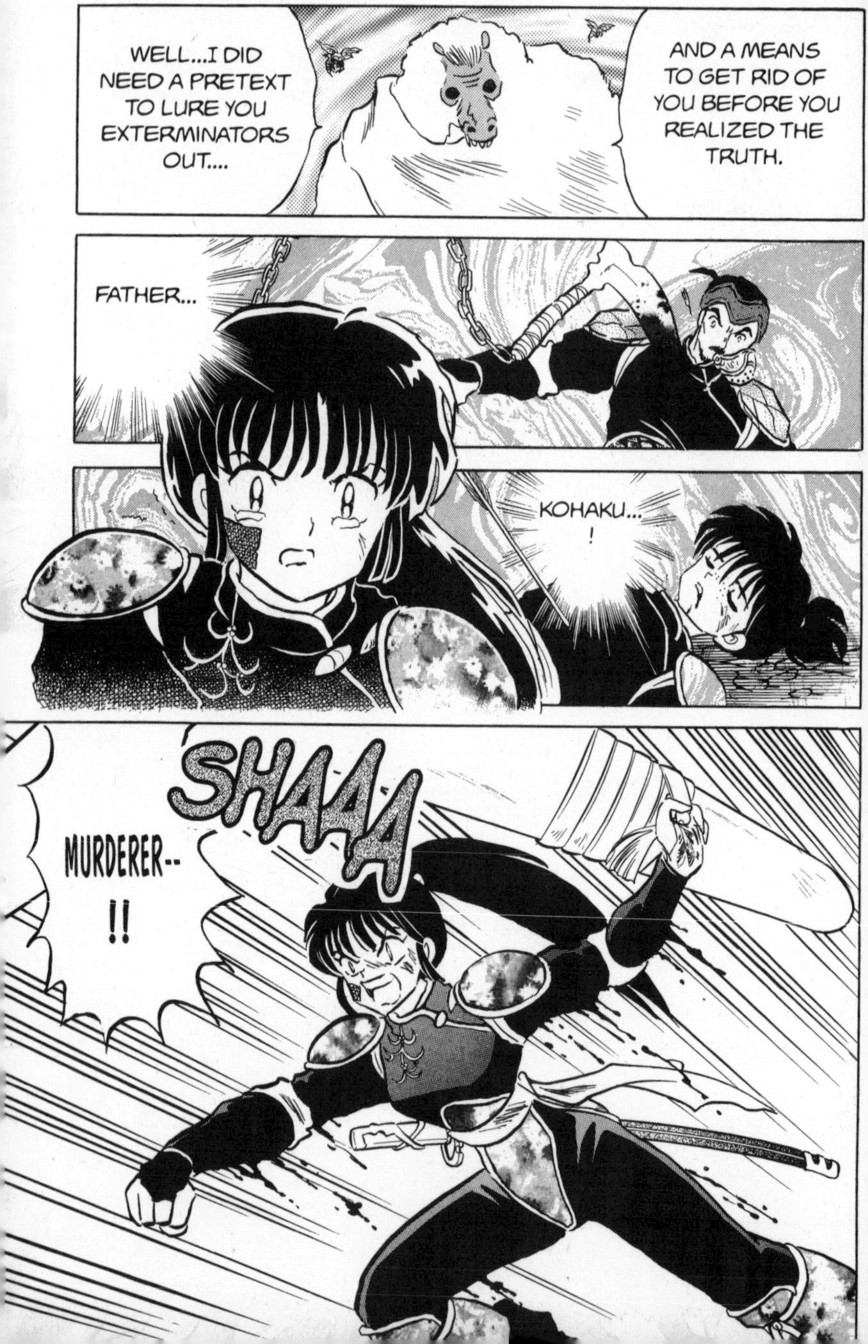
WELL...I DID NEED A PRETEXT TO LURE YOU EXTERMINATORS OUT....
AND A MEANS TO GET RID OF YOU BEFORE YOU REALIZED THE TRUTH.
FATHER...
KOHAKU... !
SHAAA
MURDERER-- !!

AAUGH!

SHHHKK

KIIINNNN

STAGGER

SANGO!

NNNNN NNN

THE SHIKON SHARD THAT WAS SUPPRESSING HER PAIN POPPED OUT...!

AAAARRH!

HEH...

YOU'D HAVE BEEN BETTER OFF DYING SATISFIED THAT YOU'D FULFILLED YOUR VENGEANCE AGAINST INU-YASHA...

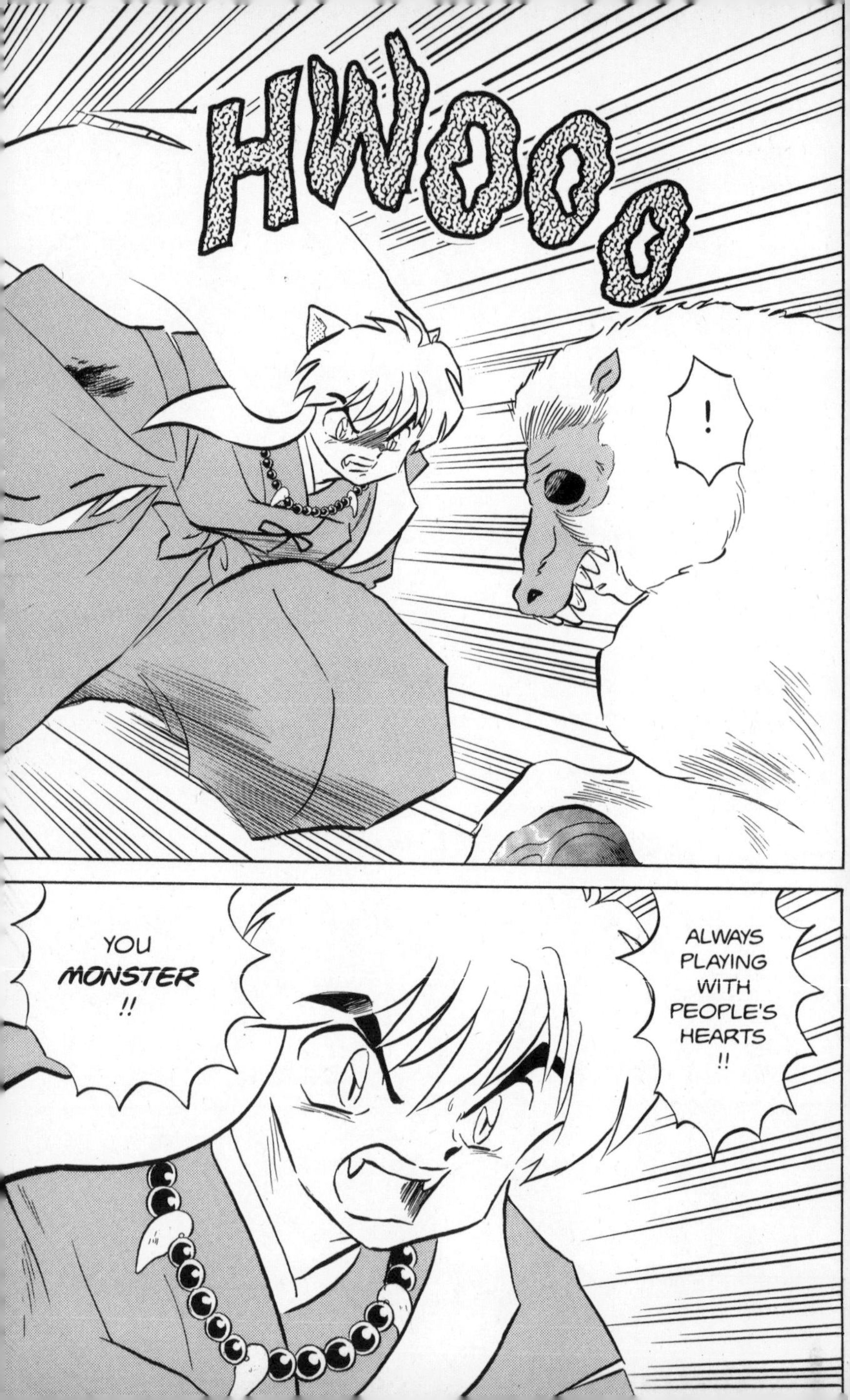
HWOOO
!
YOU MONSTER !!
ALWAYS PLAYING WITH PEOPLE'S HEARTS !!

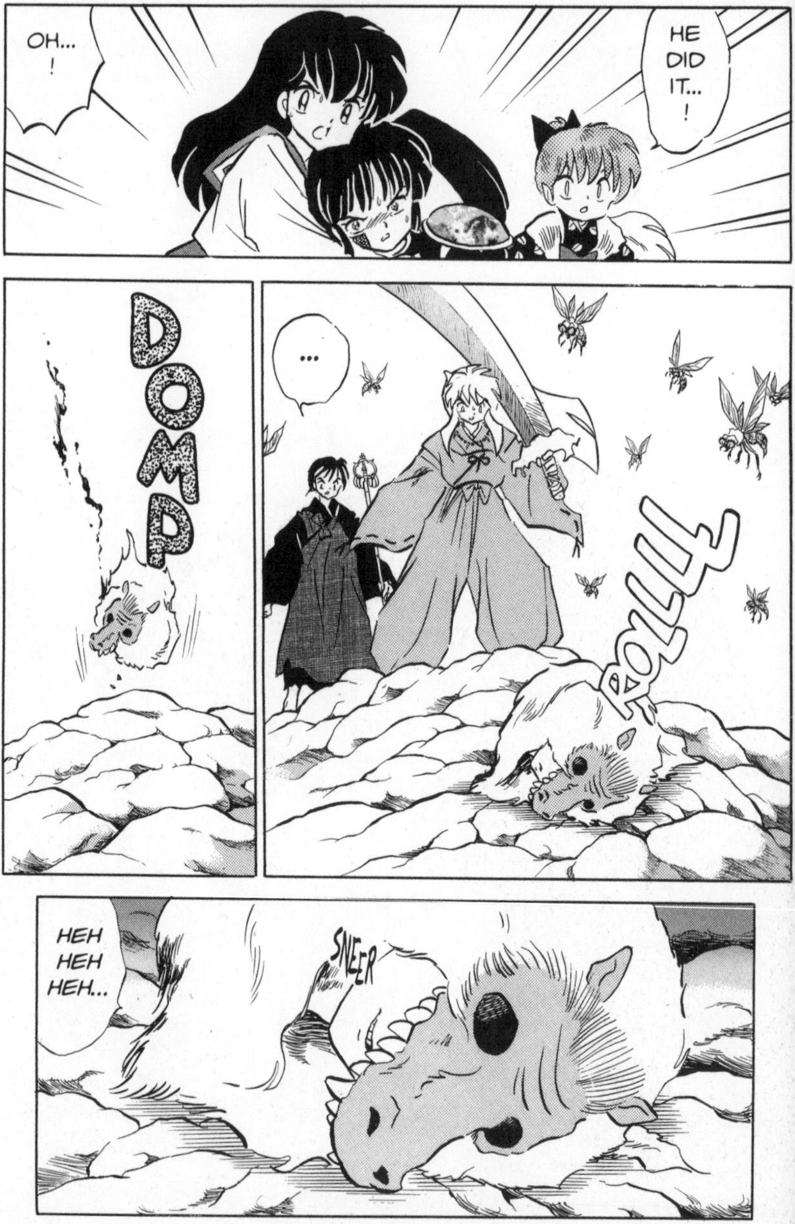
OH...
!
HE
DID
IT...
!
DOMP
...
ROLLLL
HEH
HEH
HEH...
SNEER

SCROLL FIVE
GOLEM

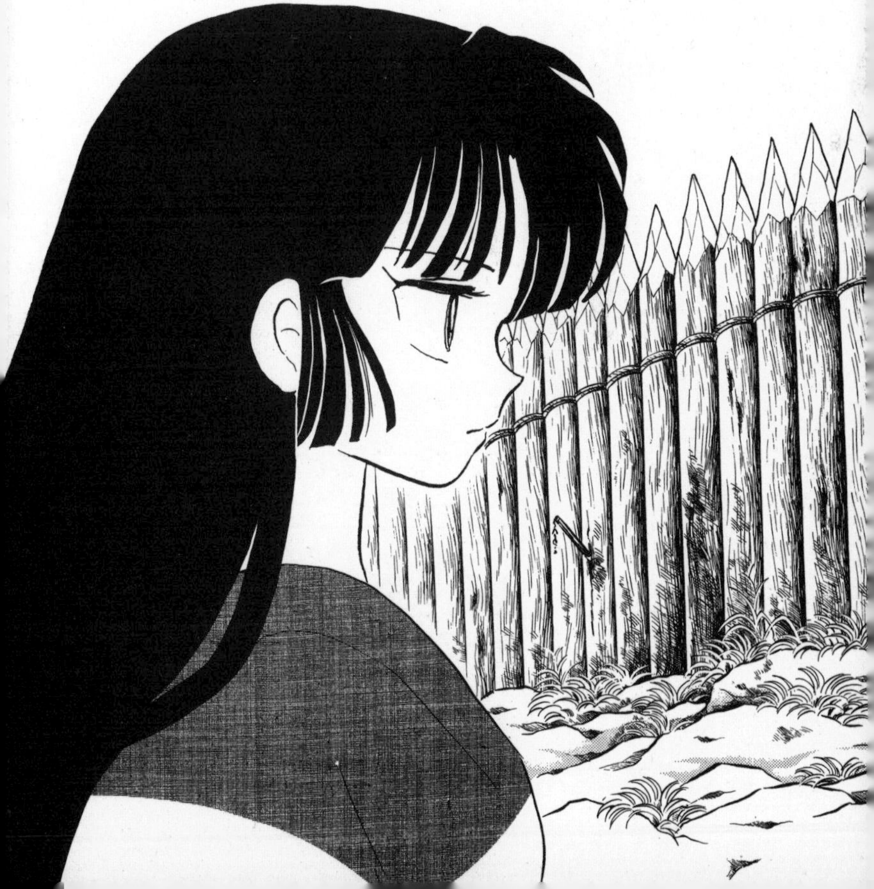

HWOOOOO...

WE DID IT... AT LAST...

NARAKU... IS FINALLY... DEAD.

IT'S OVER, LADY SANGO... HE'S GONE.

...

THAT WAS ALMOST TOO EASY...

WAS THIS REALLY THE NARAKU THAT I'VE BEEN PURSUING ALL THIS TIME...?

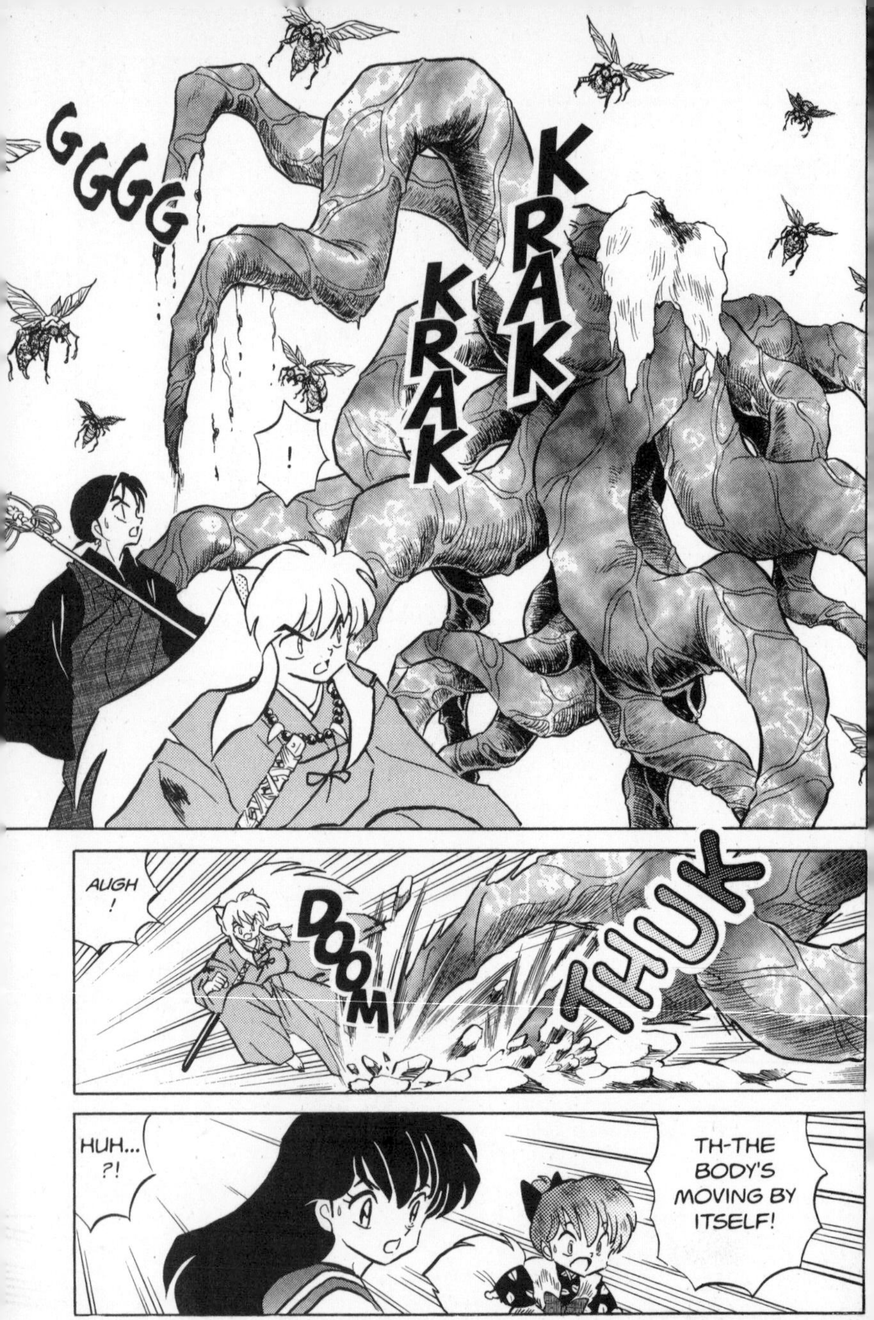
GGGG
KRAK
KRAK
!
AUGH
!
DOOM
THUK
HUH...
?!
TH-THE
BODY'S
MOVING BY
ITSELF!

HEH... HEH... HEH...

DID YOU THINK...I COULD DIE?

THE HEAD'S STILL ALIVE TOO...?!

GRROOOP

SOMETHING ELSE STRANGE....

DESPITE THIS TRICK....

NARAKU'S EVIL AURA WHEN WE FACED HIM LAST...

...WAS FAR MORE POWERFUL THAN THIS!

SSSHHHH

GUHH!

BWOK
BWOK

PPCH
PPCH

HE'S BECOMING WHOLE AGAIN...!

IS IT THE SHIKON SHARD'S DEMON POWER?!

BUT NO-- IT'S NOT!

OTHER-WISE IT WOULD HAVE DISSOLVED MORE--!

GLEAM

HOW COULD I HAVE BEEN SUCH A FOOL ?!

I CAN'T BELIEVE I TRAVELED WITH THAT WRETCHED DEMON...

...AND NEVER SENSED A GLIMMER OF AN EVIL AURA!

BUT EVEN NOW... I STILL DON'T... !

HE'S **STILL** NOT EMANATING ANY DEMONIC POWER!

WHAT CAN HE **BE...?**

KRIII
KRIII

HWOOOO

THAT'S IT-- I SEE IT NOW!

HE'S...

TARGET THE IMMOBILE PART!!

TARGET HIS CHEST !!

HIS **CHEST** ?!

SO...

YOU'VE CAUGHT ON....

HGGH!

SHLLAAAGGG

IF YOU SAY SO!!

THHHHOK

A DOLL...

A *DOLL*... YOU SAID ?!

WITH A STRAND OF HAIR WRAPPED AROUND IT.

THIS IS A GOLEM SPELL.

THIS HAIR MUST BE NARAKU'S....

WE'VE BEEN BATTLING A CONSTRUCT OF MUD AND MAGIC...

FLAP FLAP

THE REAL NARAKU IS MOST LIKELY HOLED UP SOMEWHERE... MANIPULATING THIS THING FROM A SAFE DISTANCE...

ZHZHHH

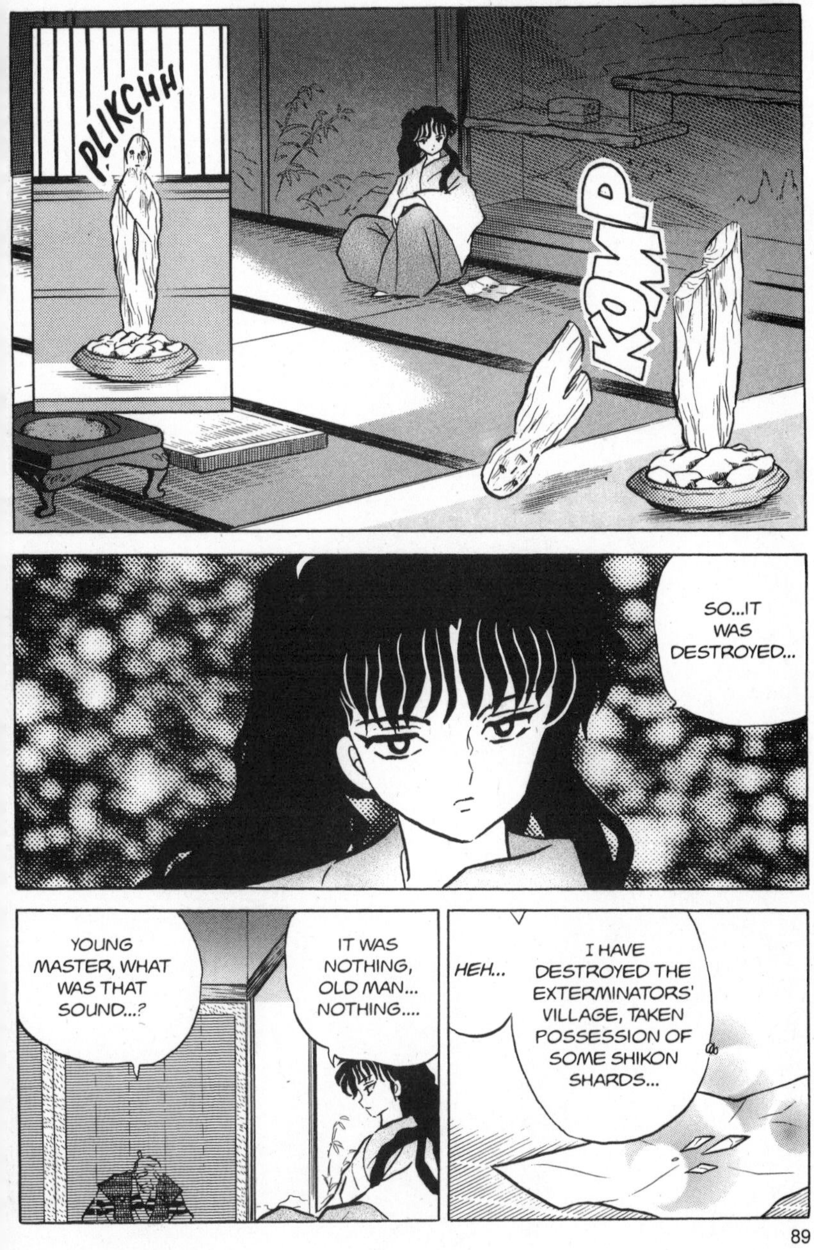
PLIKCHH
KOMP
SO...IT WAS DESTROYED...
YOUNG MASTER, WHAT WAS THAT SOUND...?
IT WAS NOTHING, OLD MAN... NOTHING....
HEH...
I HAVE DESTROYED THE EXTERMINATORS' VILLAGE, TAKEN POSSESSION OF SOME SHIKON SHARDS...

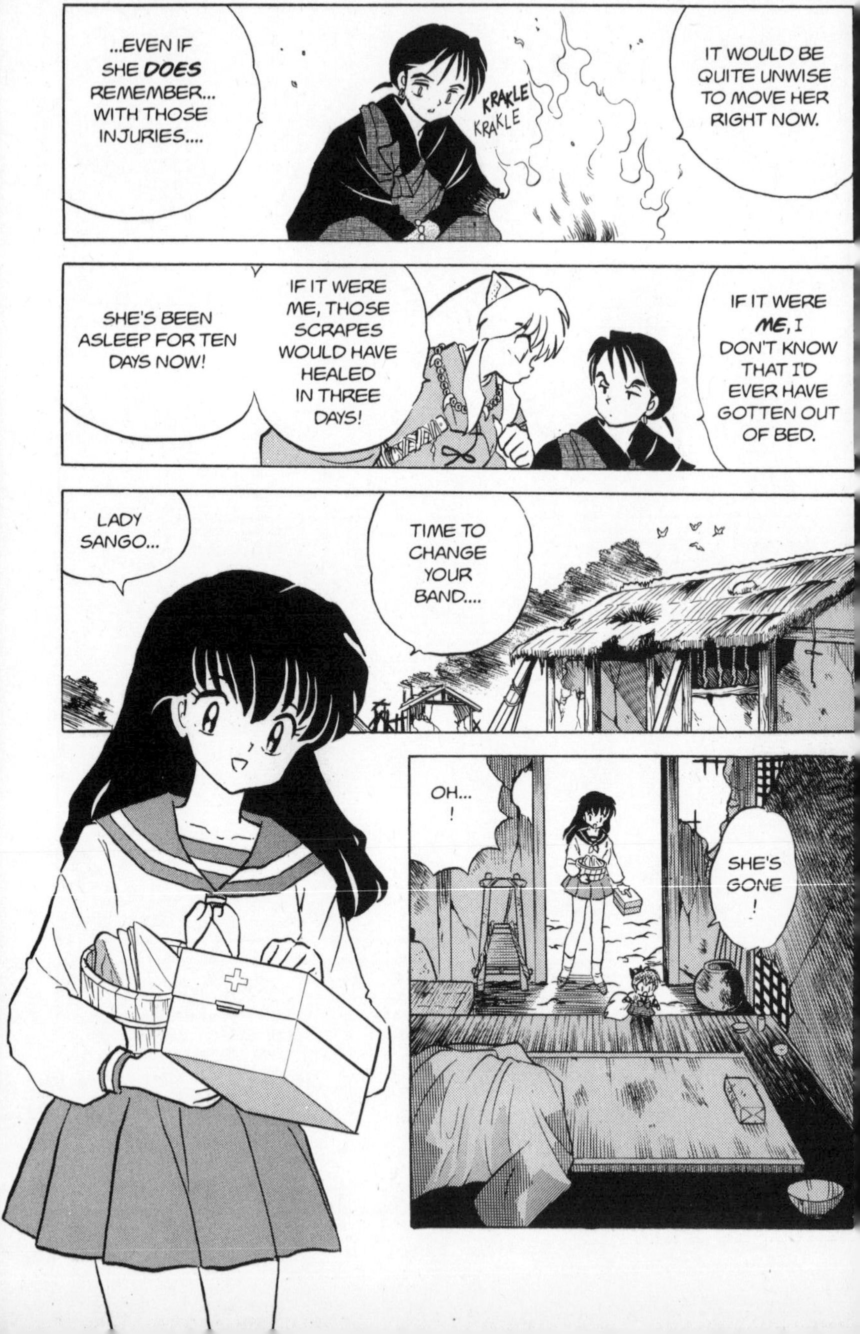
...EVEN IF SHE DOES REMEMBER... WITH THOSE INJURIES....
KRAKLE KRAKLE
IT WOULD BE QUITE UNWISE TO MOVE HER RIGHT NOW.
SHE'S BEEN ASLEEP FOR TEN DAYS NOW!
IF IT WERE ME, THOSE SCRAPES WOULD HAVE HEALED IN THREE DAYS!
IF IT WERE ME, I DON'T KNOW THAT I'D EVER HAVE GOTTEN OUT OF BED.
LADY SANGO...
TIME TO CHANGE YOUR BAND....
OH...!
SHE'S GONE!

HYUUUUUU

LADY SANGO, PLEASE...YOU SHOULDN'T BE MOVING AROUND YET...

THESE GRAVES...

WHAT...?

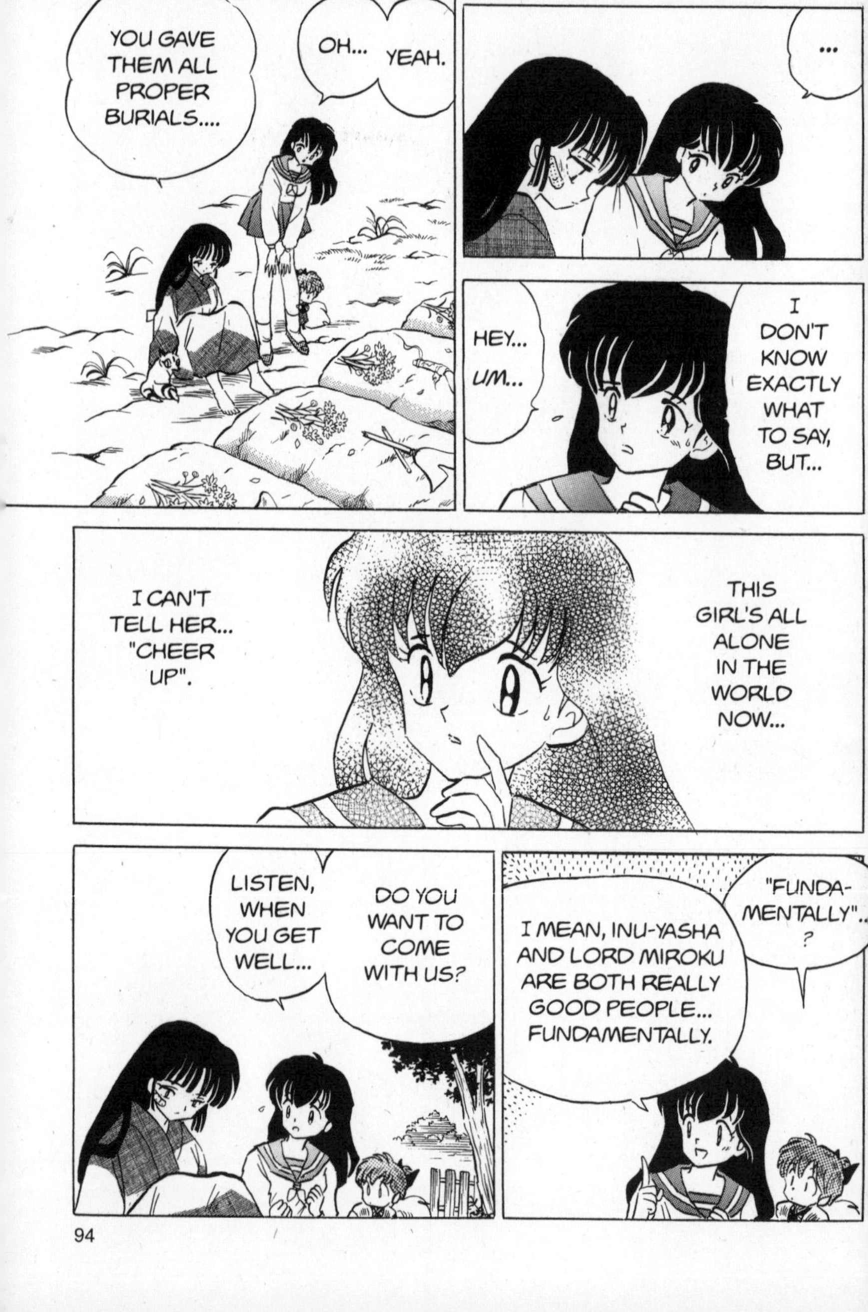
YOU GAVE THEM ALL PROPER BURIALS....
OH... YEAH.
...
HEY... UM...
I DON'T KNOW EXACTLY WHAT TO SAY, BUT...
I CAN'T TELL HER... "CHEER UP".
THIS GIRL'S ALL ALONE IN THE WORLD NOW...
LISTEN, WHEN YOU GET WELL...
DO YOU WANT TO COME WITH US?
I MEAN, INU-YASHA AND LORD MIROKU ARE BOTH REALLY GOOD PEOPLE... FUNDAMENTALLY.
"FUNDA-MENTALLY"... ?

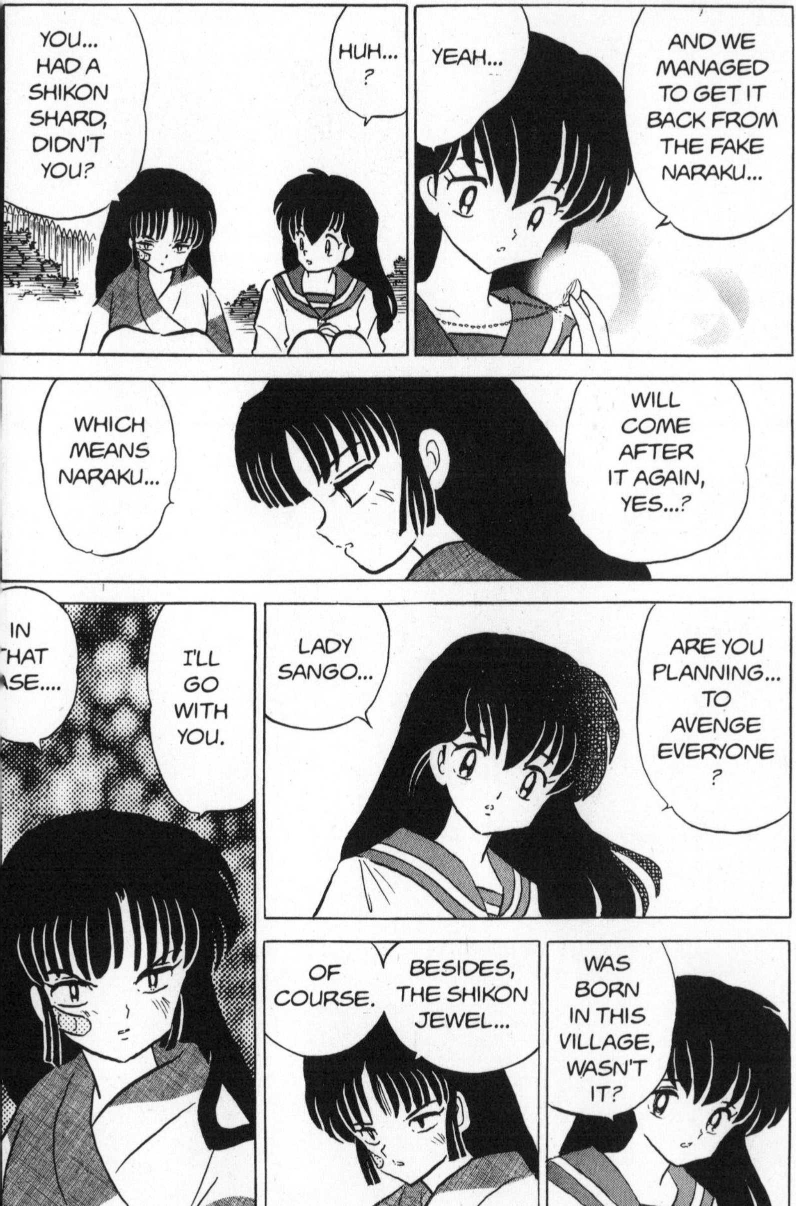
YOU... HAD A SHIKON SHARD, DIDN'T YOU?
HUH... ?
YEAH...
AND WE MANAGED TO GET IT BACK FROM THE FAKE NARAKU...
WHICH MEANS NARAKU...
WILL COME AFTER IT AGAIN, YES...?
IN HAT SE....
I'LL GO WITH YOU.
LADY SANGO...
ARE YOU PLANNING... TO AVENGE EVERYONE ?
OF COURSE.
BESIDES, THE SHIKON JEWEL...
WAS BORN IN THIS VILLAGE, WASN'T IT?

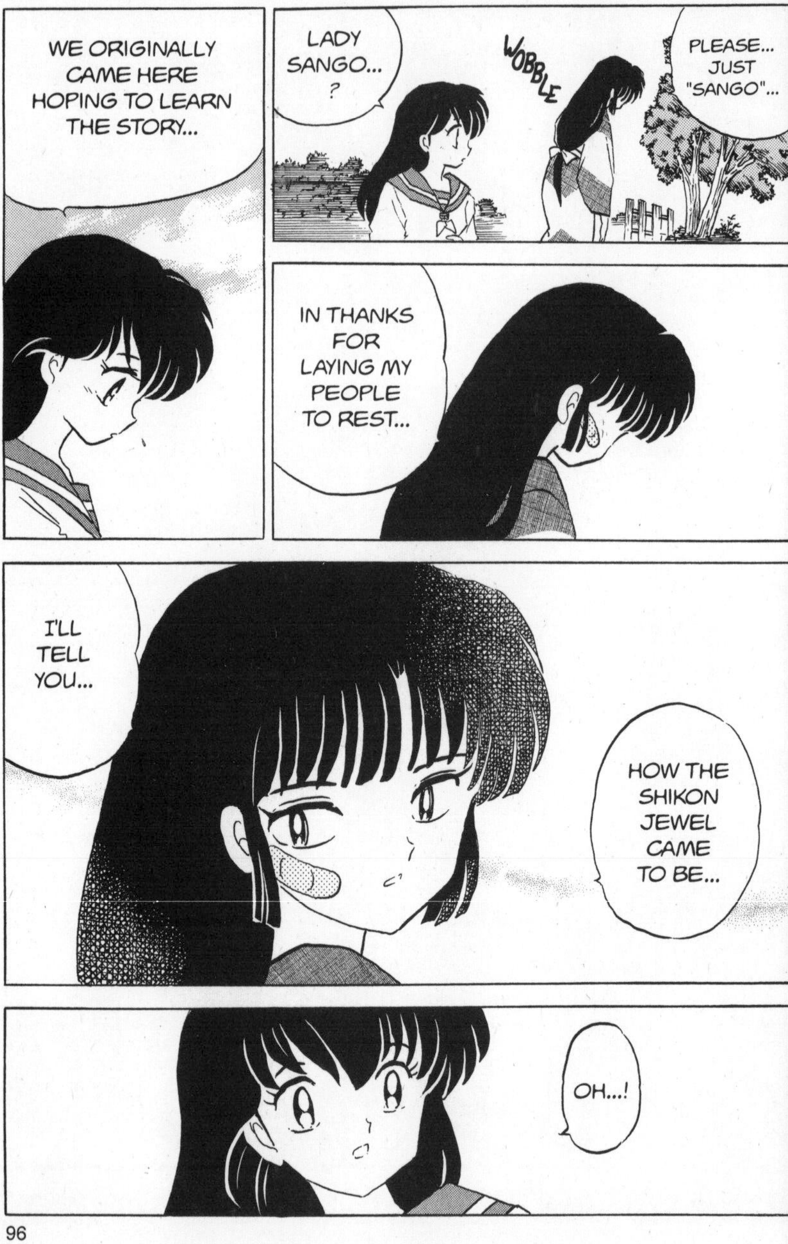
WE ORIGINALLY CAME HERE HOPING TO LEARN THE STORY...
LADY SANGO... ?
WOBBLE
PLEASE... JUST "SANGO"...
IN THANKS FOR LAYING MY PEOPLE TO REST...
I'LL TELL YOU...
HOW THE SHIKON JEWEL CAME TO BE...
OH...!

SCROLL SIX

THE BIRTH OF THE JEWEL

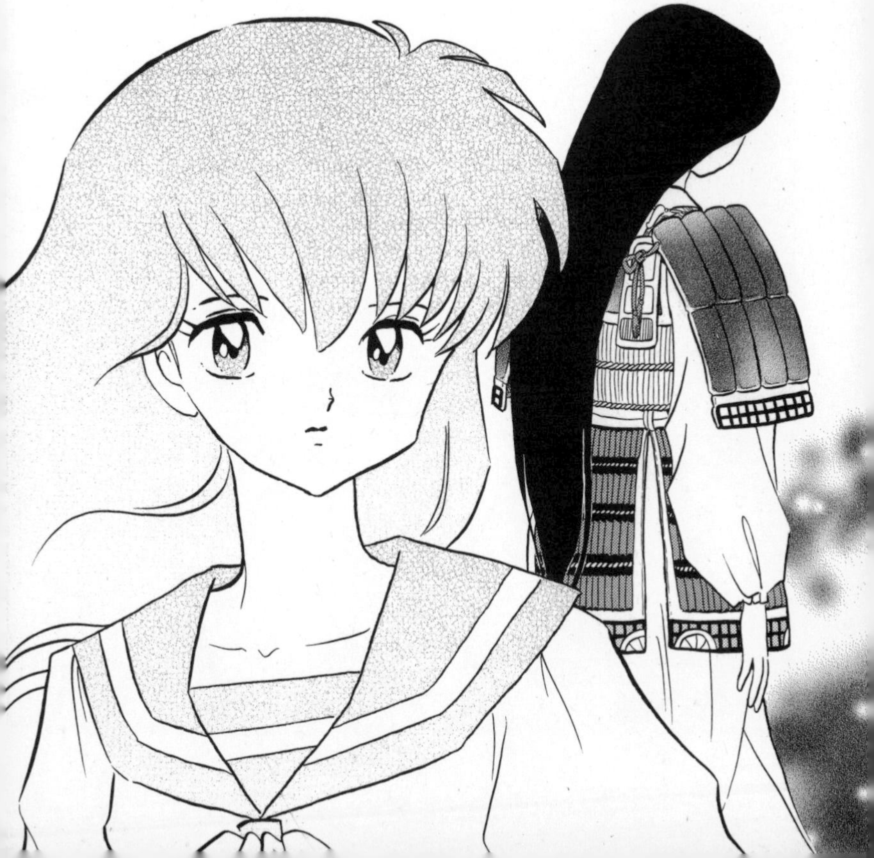

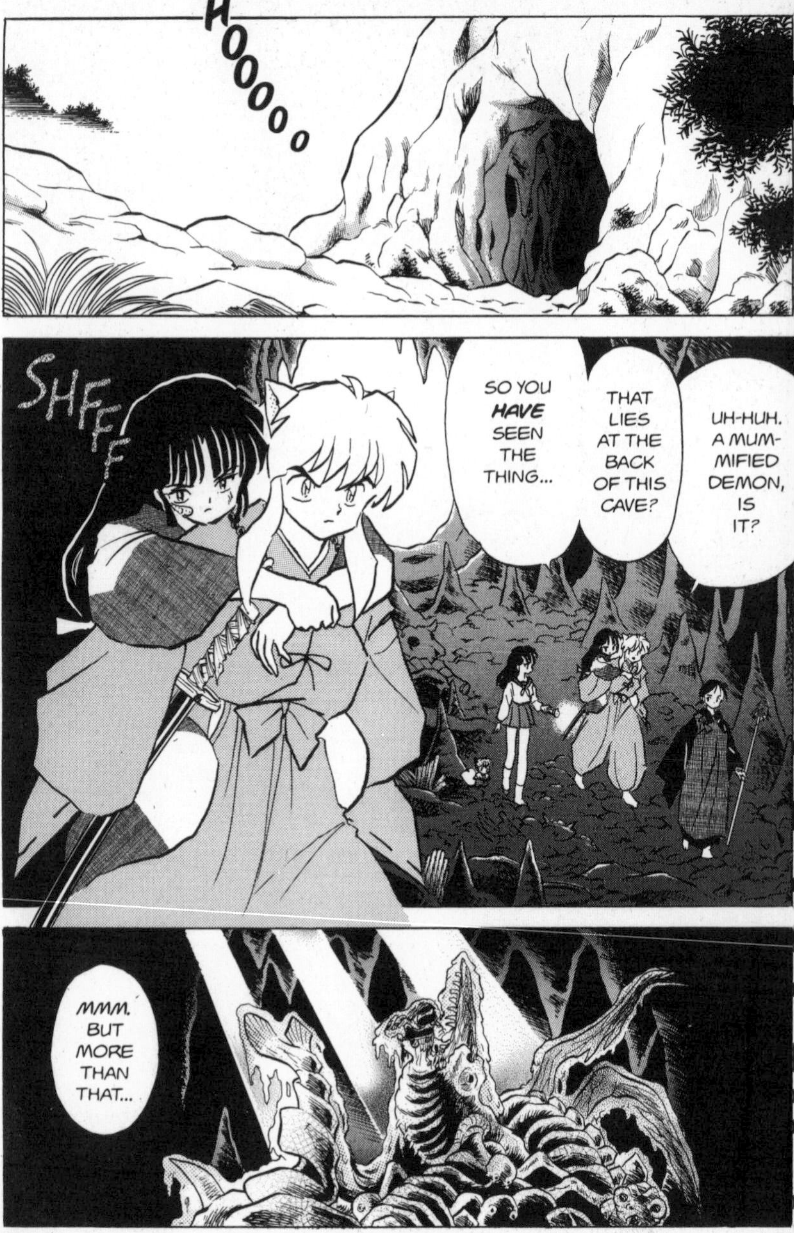
HOOOOOO
SHFFFF
SO YOU *HAVE* SEEN THE THING...
THAT LIES AT THE BACK OF THIS CAVE?
UH-HUH. A MUMMIFIED DEMON, IS IT?
MMM. BUT MORE THAN THAT...

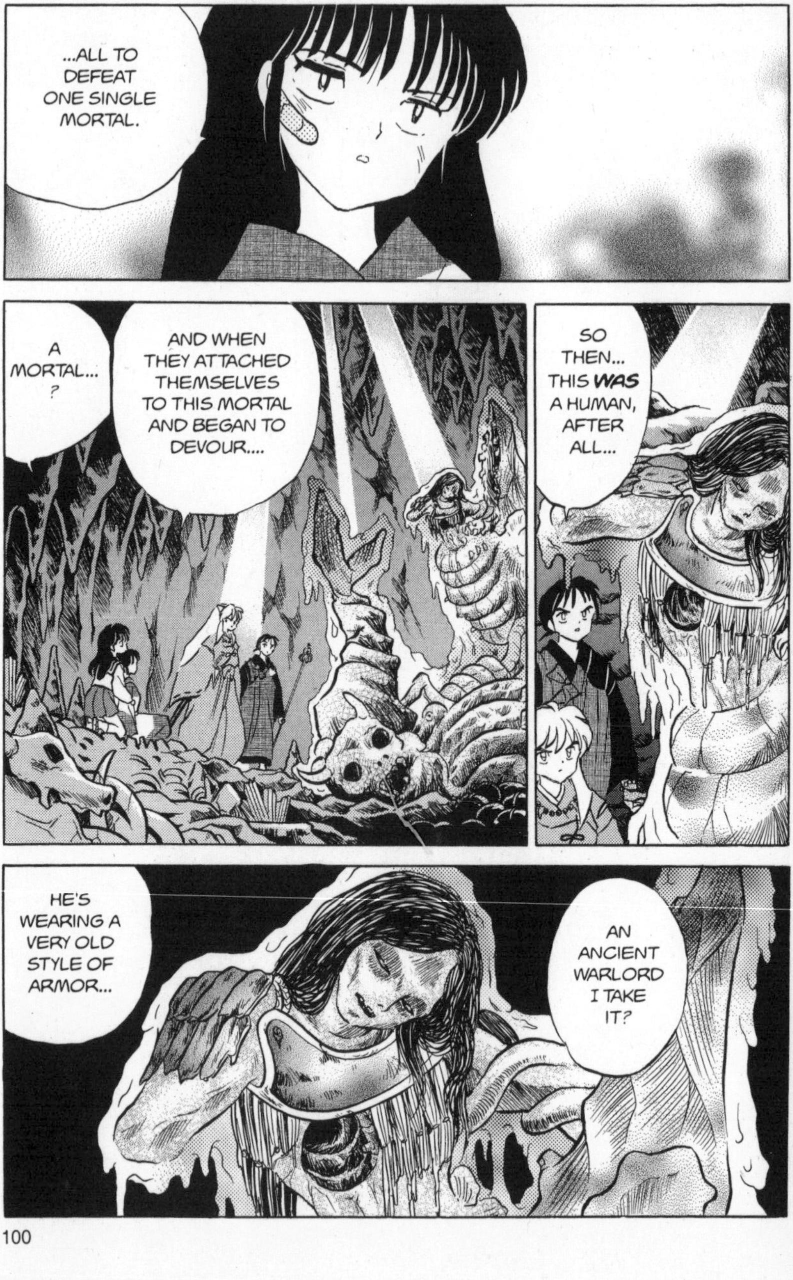
...ALL TO DEFEAT ONE SINGLE MORTAL.
A MORTAL...?
AND WHEN THEY ATTACHED THEMSELVES TO THIS MORTAL AND BEGAN TO DEVOUR....
SO THEN... THIS **WAS** A HUMAN, AFTER ALL...
HE'S WEARING A VERY OLD STYLE OF ARMOR...
AN ANCIENT WARLORD I TAKE IT?

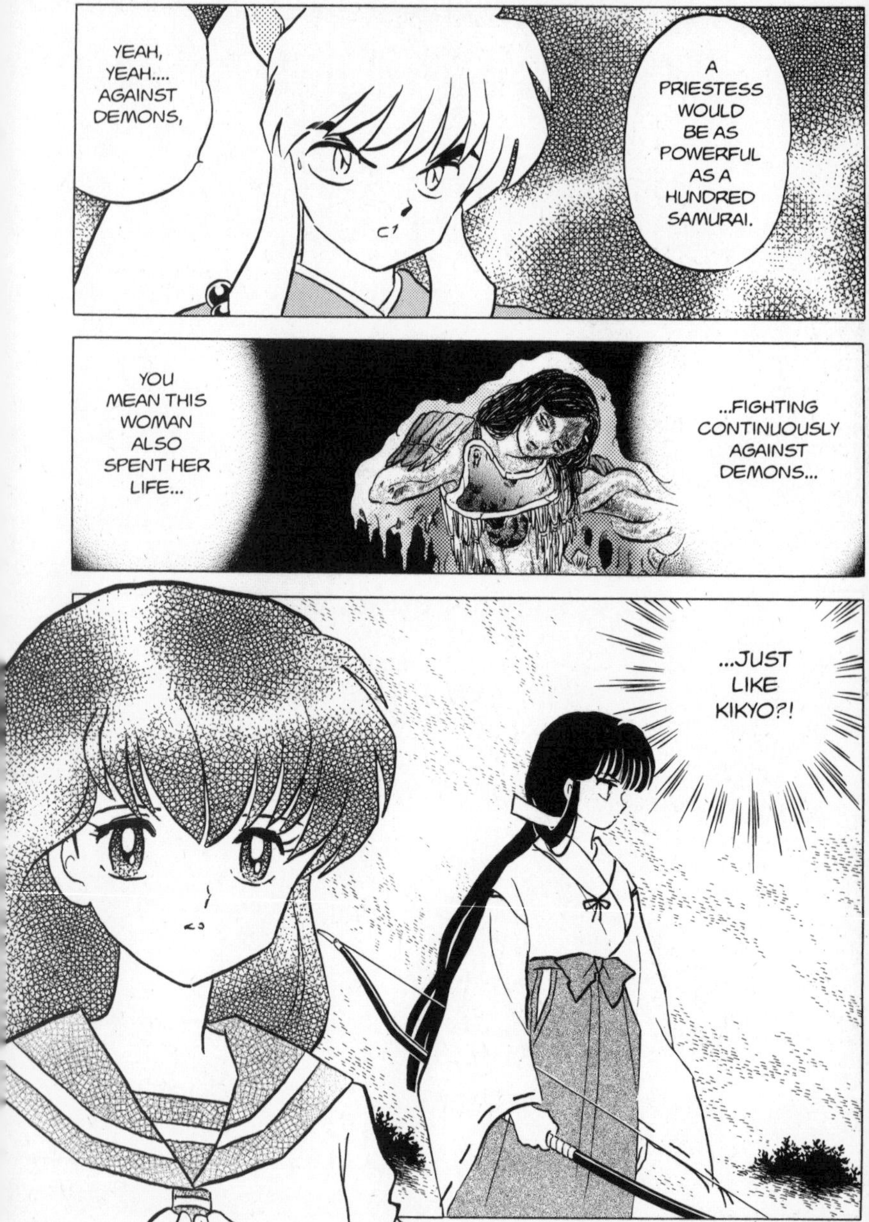
YEAH, YEAH.... AGAINST DEMONS,
A PRIESTESS WOULD BE AS POWERFUL AS A HUNDRED SAMURAI.
YOU MEAN THIS WOMAN ALSO SPENT HER LIFE...
...FIGHTING CONTINUOUSLY AGAINST DEMONS...
...JUST LIKE KIKYO?!

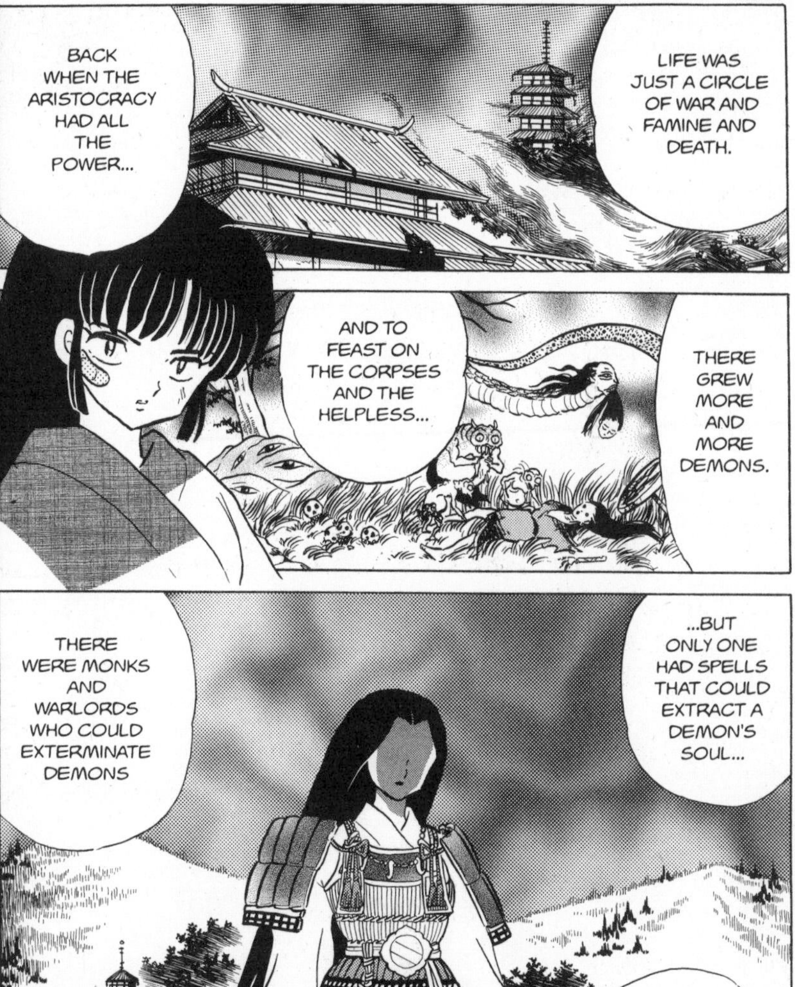
BACK WHEN THE ARISTOCRACY HAD ALL THE POWER...
LIFE WAS JUST A CIRCLE OF WAR AND FAMINE AND DEATH.
AND TO FEAST ON THE CORPSES AND THE HELPLESS...
THERE GREW MORE AND MORE DEMONS.
THERE WERE MONKS AND WARLORDS WHO COULD EXTERMINATE DEMONS
...BUT ONLY ONE HAD SPELLS THAT COULD EXTRACT A DEMON'S SOUL...
...AND CLEANSE IT UTTERLY. THE PRIESTESS NAMED MIDORIKO.

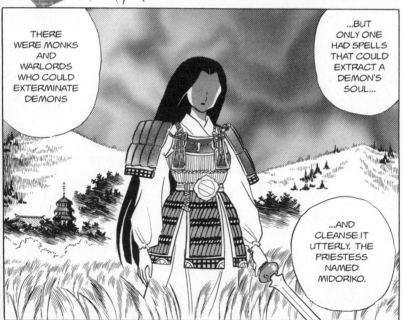

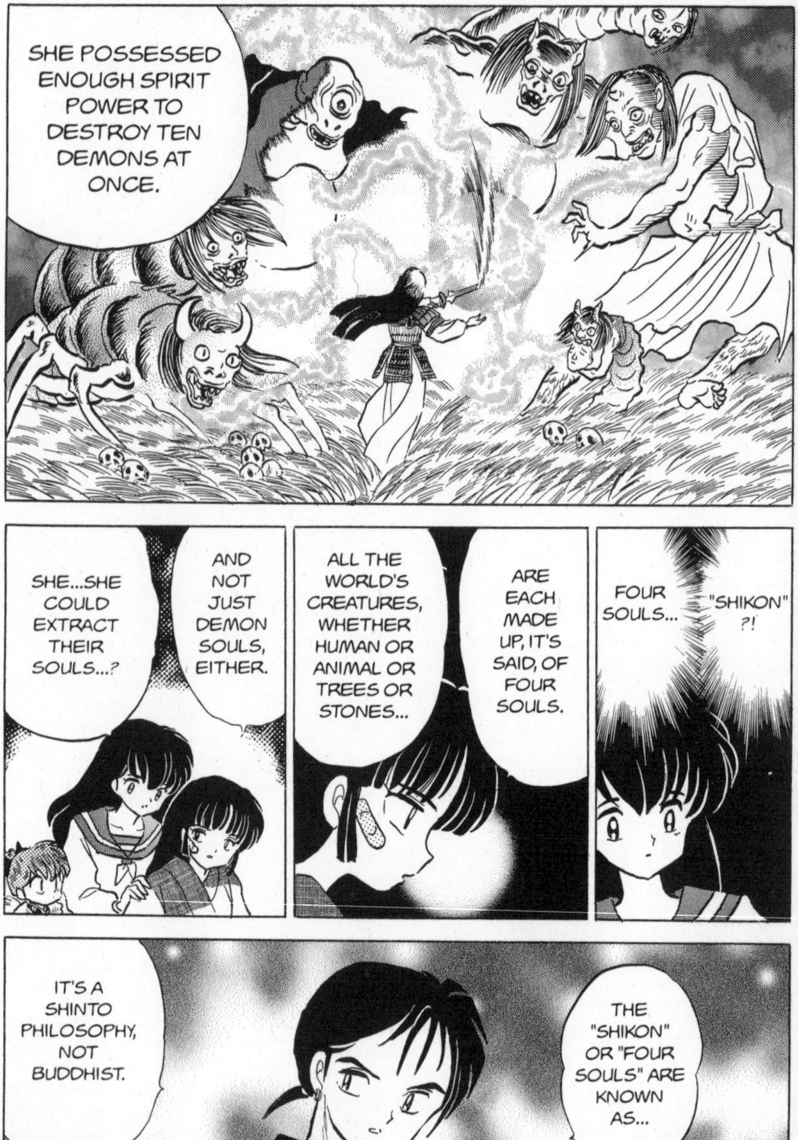
SHE POSSESSED ENOUGH SPIRIT POWER TO DESTROY TEN DEMONS AT ONCE.
SHE...SHE COULD EXTRACT THEIR SOULS...?
AND NOT JUST DEMON SOULS, EITHER.
ALL THE WORLD'S CREATURES, WHETHER HUMAN OR ANIMAL OR TREES OR STONES...
ARE EACH MADE UP, IT'S SAID, OF FOUR SOULS.
FOUR SOULS...
"SHIKON" ?!
IT'S A SHINTO PHILOSOPHY, NOT BUDDHIST.
THE "SHIKON" OR "FOUR SOULS" ARE KNOWN AS...

ARAMI-TAMA, NIGIMI-TAMA, KUSHIMI-TAMA AND SAKIMI-TAMA.

TOGETHER THOSE SPIRITS ARE HOUSED IN A PHYSICAL BODY AS ITS SOUL OR "HEART."

THE ARAMI-TAMA PRESIDES OVER VALOR, NIGIMI-TAMA HARMONY, KUSHIMI-TAMA MIRACLES, AND SAKIMI-TAMA LOVE.

A SOUL IN WHICH THESE FOUR ASPECTS ARE COMBINED AND BALANCED IS CALLED A "NAOHI." A "TRUE" SPIRIT.

GAPE

FOR THAT PERSON IT IS EASY TO REMAIN ON A TRUE PATH.

I DON'T GET THIS AT ALL.

IT IS KINDA OVER-WHELMING TO HEAR IT ALL AT ONCE...

AND...?

IF AN EVIL DEED IS COMMITTED, THEN THE FOUR ASPECTS ARE UNBALANCED... THE SOUL BECOMES A "MAGATSUHI"...A "TWISTED SPIRIT." AND THE PERSON WILL TURN ONTO THE WRONG PATH.

...

WHICH MEANS...?

DO YOU WANT ME TO REPEAT IT...?

ALL IT MEANS IS THAT THE SAME SOUL CAN BE EITHER GOOD **OR** EVIL.

RIGHT.

MIDORIKO MASTERED A SPELL TO PULL THE FOUR ASPECTS...

...INTO A PROPER BALANCE...AND THUS NULLIFY DEMON-SOULS.

SO THE DEMONS FEARED MIDORIKO

AND BEGAN TO TARGET HER FOR DEATH.

BUT THEY KNEW THAT IF THEY ATTACKED HER, THEY WOULD PROBABLY BE CLEANSED INTO NOTHINGNESS.

AND SO THEY DECIDED TO CONCOCT A WICKED SOUL, ONE SO EVIL, SO POWERFUL, SO **HUGE** THAT IT COULD STAND UP TO MIDORIKO'S ENORMOUS SPIRIT POWER.

THAT'S WHY THE DEMONS MERGED INTO ONE...?

BUT HOW...

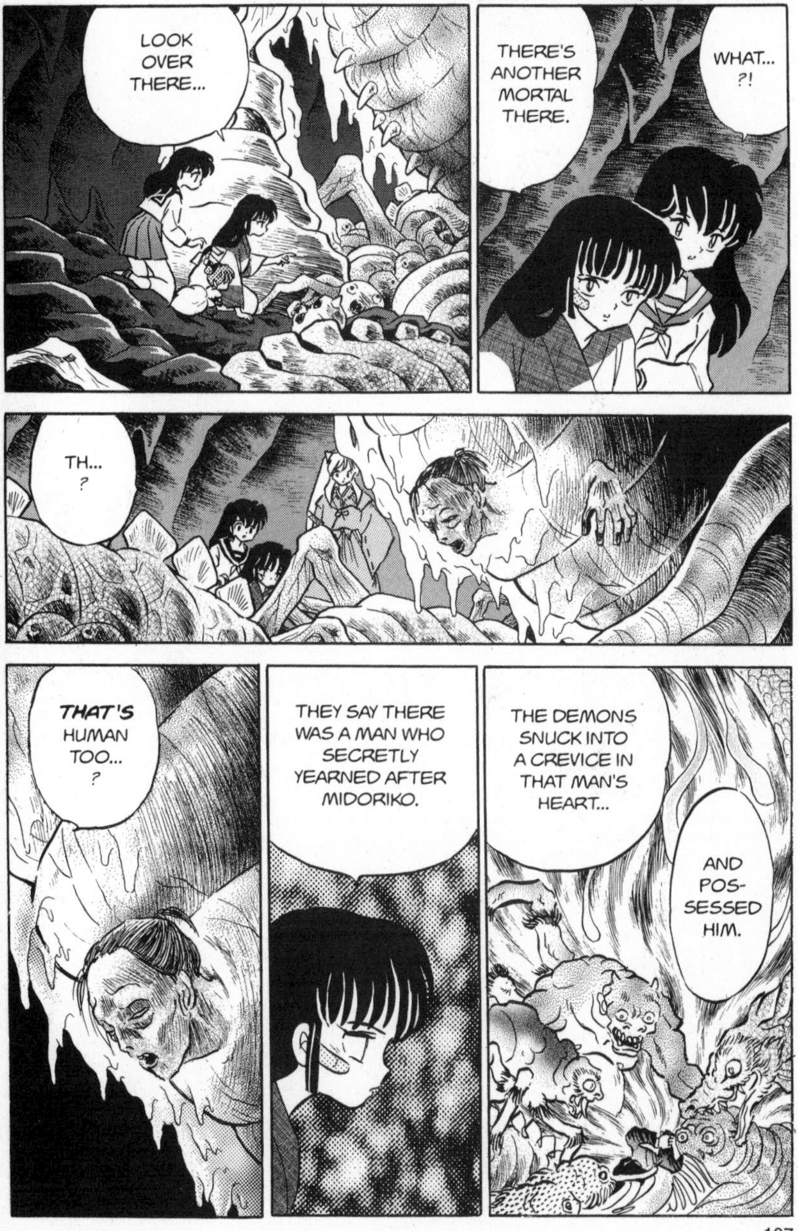
LOOK OVER THERE...
THERE'S ANOTHER MORTAL THERE.
WHAT... ?!
TH... ?
THAT'S HUMAN TOO... ?
THEY SAY THERE WAS A MAN WHO SECRETLY YEARNED AFTER MIDORIKO.
THE DEMONS SNUCK INTO A CREVICE IN THAT MAN'S HEART...
AND POSSESSED HIM.

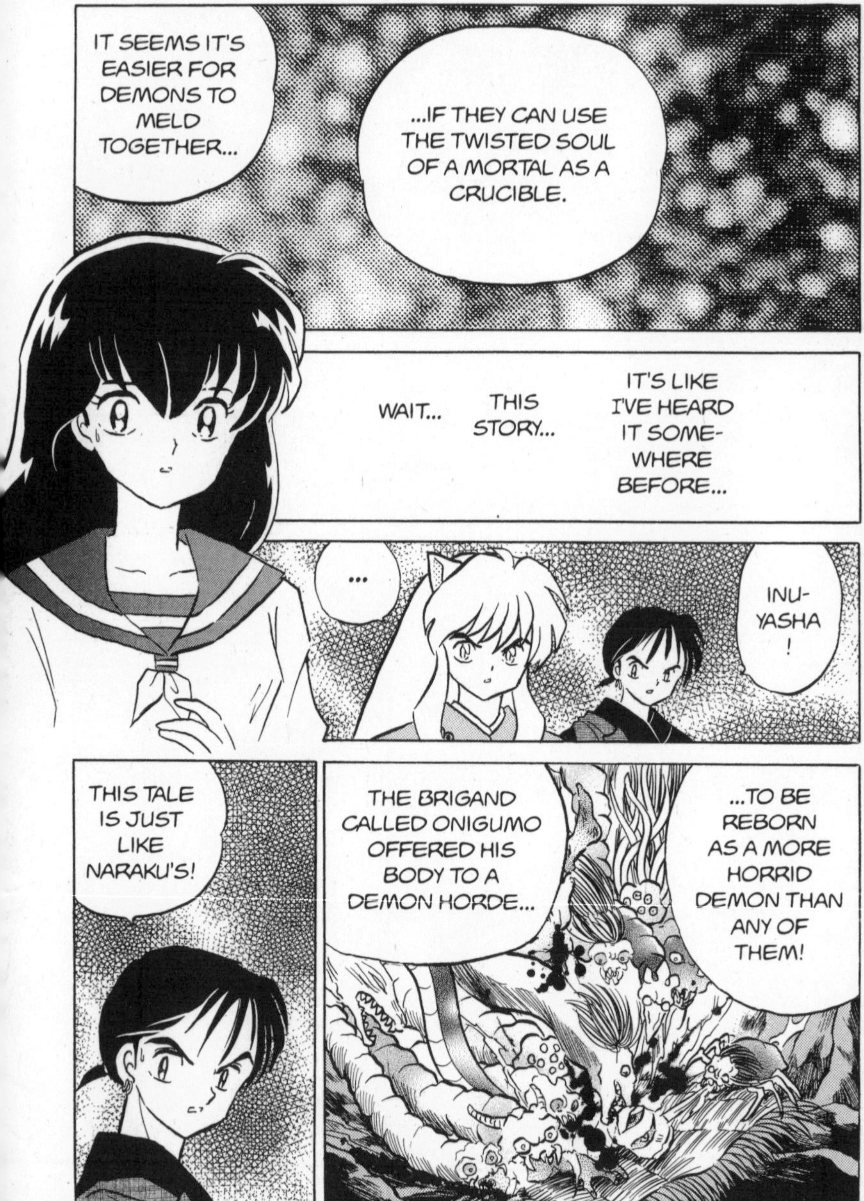
IT SEEMS IT'S EASIER FOR DEMONS TO MELD TOGETHER...
...IF THEY CAN USE THE TWISTED SOUL OF A MORTAL AS A CRUCIBLE.
WAIT...
THIS STORY...
IT'S LIKE I'VE HEARD IT SOMEWHERE BEFORE...
...
INU-YASHA!
THIS TALE IS JUST LIKE NARAKU'S!
THE BRIGAND CALLED ONIGUMO OFFERED HIS BODY TO A DEMON HORDE...
...TO BE REBORN AS A MORE HORRID DEMON THAN ANY OF THEM!

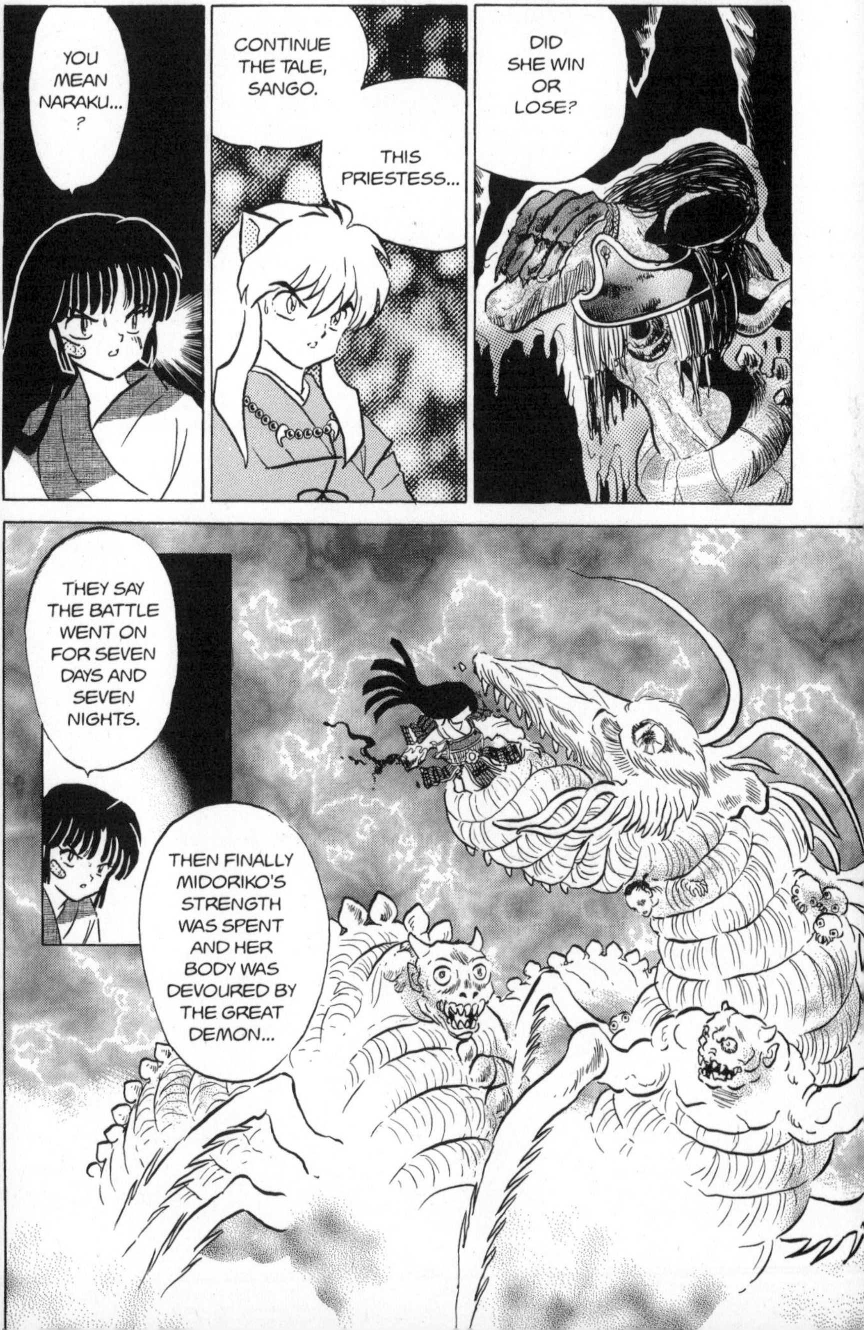
YOU MEAN NARAKU...?
CONTINUE THE TALE, SANGO.
THIS PRIESTESS...
DID SHE WIN OR LOSE?
THEY SAY THE BATTLE WENT ON FOR SEVEN DAYS AND SEVEN NIGHTS.
THEN FINALLY MIDORIKO'S STRENGTH WAS SPENT AND HER BODY WAS DEVOURED BY THE GREAT DEMON...

WHEN HER SOUL WAS ABOUT TO BE SUCKED OUT OF HER...

IN THAT MOMENT, MIDORIKO USED THE LAST OF **HER** ENERGY TO STEAL THE DEMON'S SOUL...

...TO TAKE IT INTO HER OWN SOUL...

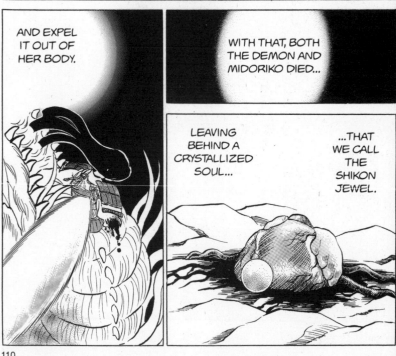

AND EXPEL IT OUT OF HER BODY.

WITH THAT, BOTH THE DEMON AND MIDORIKO DIED...

LEAVING BEHIND A CRYSTALLIZED SOUL...

...THAT WE CALL THE SHIKON JEWEL.

BUT EVEN THOUGH THEIR PHYSICAL BODIES HAVE PERISHED...

INSIDE THE SHIKON JEWEL, THEY SAY, THE SOULS OF MIDORIKO AND THE DEMON-OF-DEMONS ARE STILL BATTLING EACH OTHER...

HUH...?

AND SO THE SHIKON JEWEL CAN BECOME AS GOOD *OR* AS EVIL AS THE SOUL OF WHOEVER POSSESSES IT.

IN THE HANDS OF A DEMON THE STAIN OF CORRUPTION WILL GROW WITHIN IT...

...BUT IN THE HANDS OF A PURE-SOULED BEING, IT WILL BECOME PURIFIED.

111

THEN IT WAS BECAUSE KIKYO PURIFIED THE JEWEL...

MOST LIKELY, YES.

NARAKU WANTED TO DEFILE THE JEWEL.

...THAT NARAKU WAS CREATED?

HE WANTED TO CORRUPT LADY KIKYO'S HEART WITH HATRED, AND HAVE THE SHIKON JEWEL STEEP IN THE BLOOD OF HER BITTERNESS...

THEN THE JEWEL...

...IS PLAYING ITS LIFE OVER AGAIN.

KIKYO CARRIED THE JEWEL WITH HER TO HER DEATH!

SHE WAS TRYING TO END THE CYCLE ONCE AND FOR ALL!

BUT IN THE END...

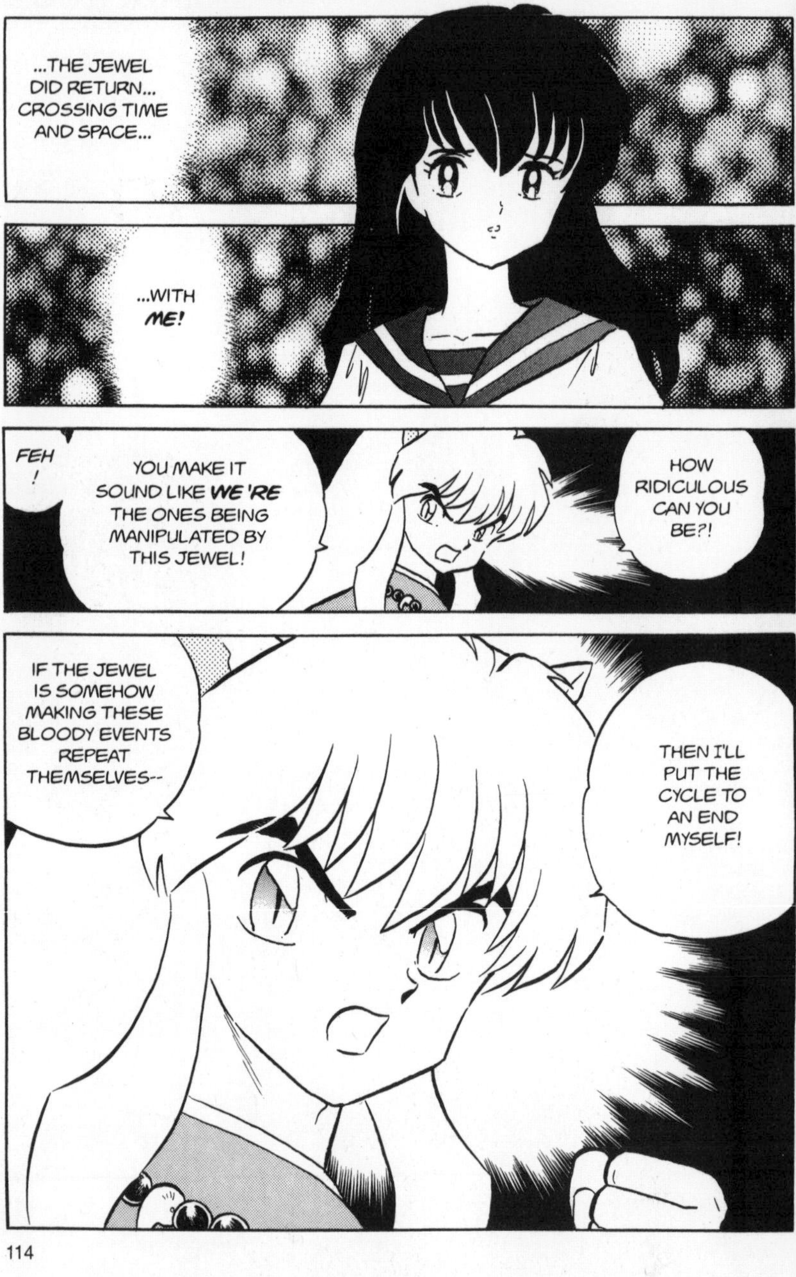
...THE JEWEL DID RETURN... CROSSING TIME AND SPACE...
...WITH *ME!*
FEH!
YOU MAKE IT SOUND LIKE *WE'RE* THE ONES BEING MANIPULATED BY THIS JEWEL!
HOW RIDICULOUS CAN YOU BE?!
IF THE JEWEL IS SOMEHOW MAKING THESE BLOODY EVENTS REPEAT THEMSELVES--
THEN I'LL PUT THE CYCLE TO AN END MYSELF!

SCROLL SEVEN

THE WATER GOD

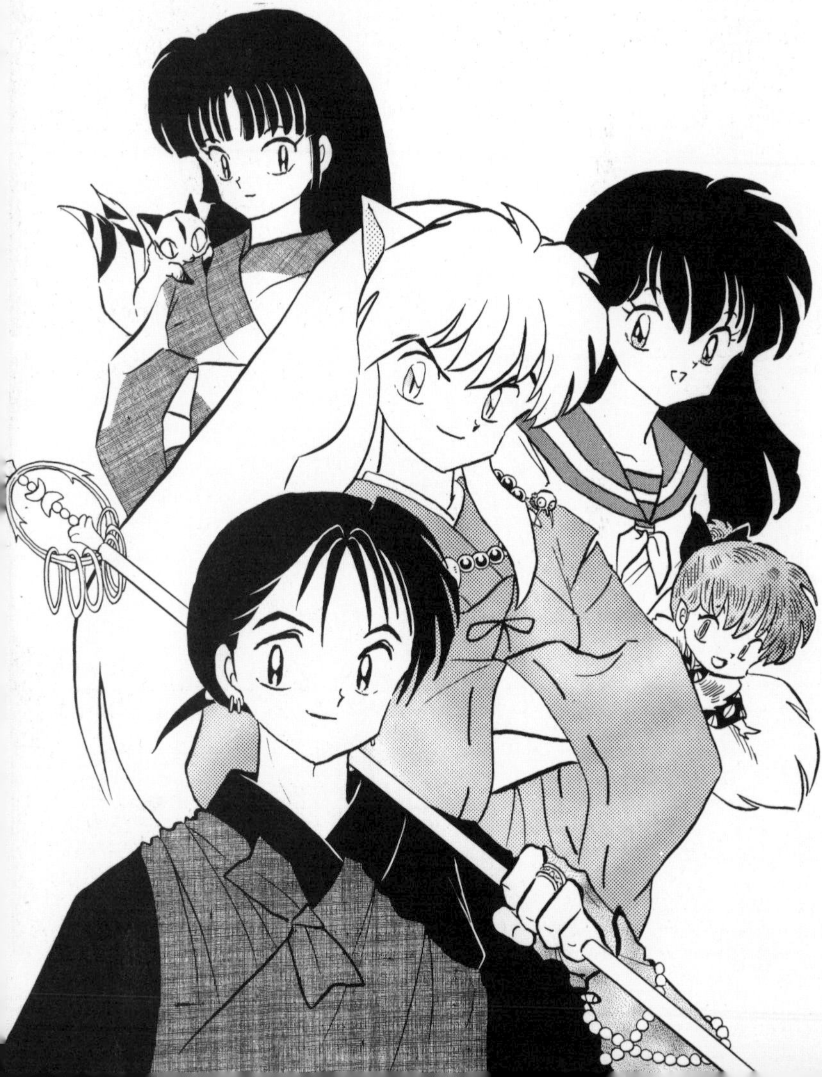

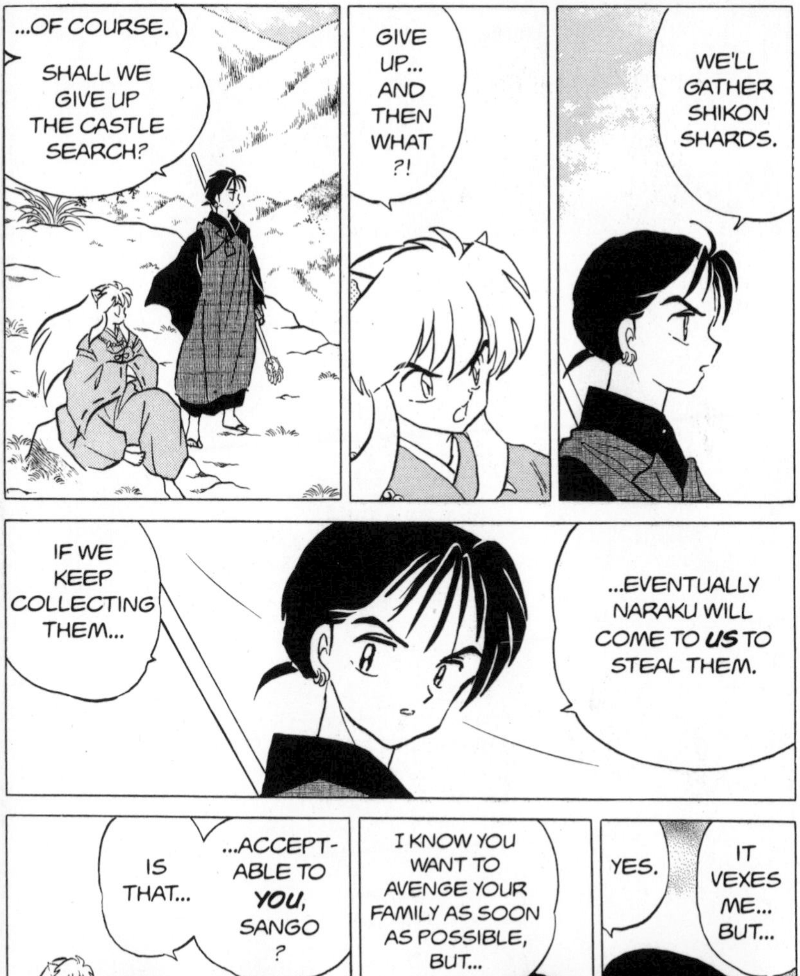
...OF COURSE.
SHALL WE GIVE UP THE CASTLE SEARCH?
GIVE UP... AND THEN WHAT ?!
WE'LL GATHER SHIKON SHARDS.
IF WE KEEP COLLECTING THEM...
...EVENTUALLY NARAKU WILL COME TO *US* TO STEAL THEM.
IS THAT...
...ACCEPT-ABLE TO *YOU*, SANGO ?
TP
I KNOW YOU WANT TO AVENGE YOUR FAMILY AS SOON AS POSSIBLE, BUT...
YES.
IT VEXES ME... BUT...

I DO FEEL YOUR *PAIN*, SANGO.

MMMM

OH REALLY...?

WELL... I'M SURE YOU FEEL MY *KNEES*, AT LEAST!

SKWEEN

I CAN'T *BELIEVE* THAT SLEAZY MONK....

HE HELD BACK UNTIL HER WOUNDS WERE HEALED, ANYWAY...

AAAH...

THE SACRIFICIAL PALANQUIN PASSES THROUGH....

GONNNG

LET US HOPE THIS ONE STAUNCHES THE FLOODS.

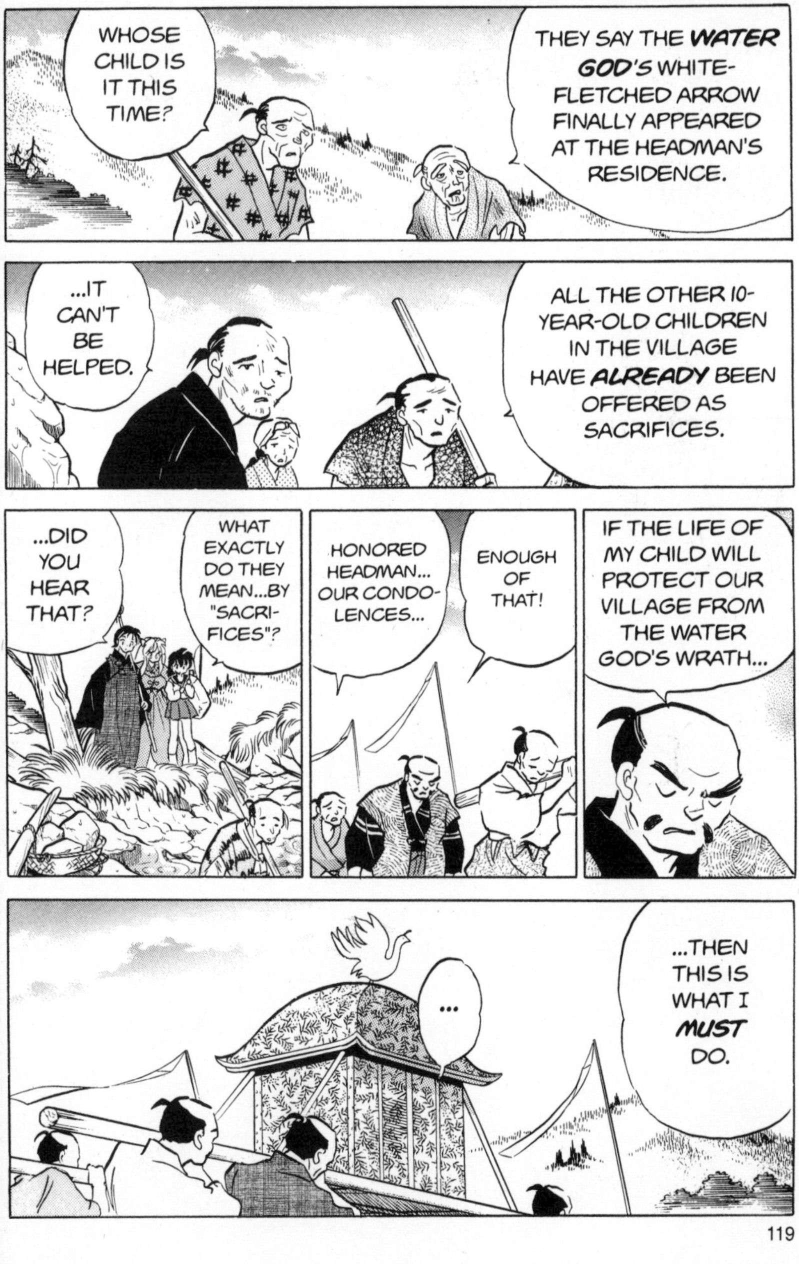
WHOSE CHILD IS IT THIS TIME?
THEY SAY THE WATER GOD'S WHITE-FLETCHED ARROW FINALLY APPEARED AT THE HEADMAN'S RESIDENCE.
...IT CAN'T BE HELPED.
ALL THE OTHER 10-YEAR-OLD CHILDREN IN THE VILLAGE HAVE ALREADY BEEN OFFERED AS SACRIFICES.
...DID YOU HEAR THAT?
WHAT EXACTLY DO THEY MEAN...BY "SACRIFICES"?
HONORED HEADMAN... OUR CONDOLENCES...
ENOUGH OF THAT!
IF THE LIFE OF MY CHILD WILL PROTECT OUR VILLAGE FROM THE WATER GOD'S WRATH...
...
...THEN THIS IS WHAT I MUST DO.

THIS "WATER GOD" OF YOURS--

--ARE YOU SURE IT'S NOT JUST A *DEMON*?!

WHA...?!

WHO IS *HE*...?

PLEASE! YOU NEED NOT FEAR US!

WE MERELY HAPPENED TO OVERHEAR YOUR TALE.

TOOM

IF YOU WOULD LIKE, WE CAN EXORCISE THIS CREATURE FOR YOU.

C-CAN YOU REALLY DO THAT, LORD MONK?!

NU! DON'T BE FOOLED BY HIM! IT'S A TRICK!

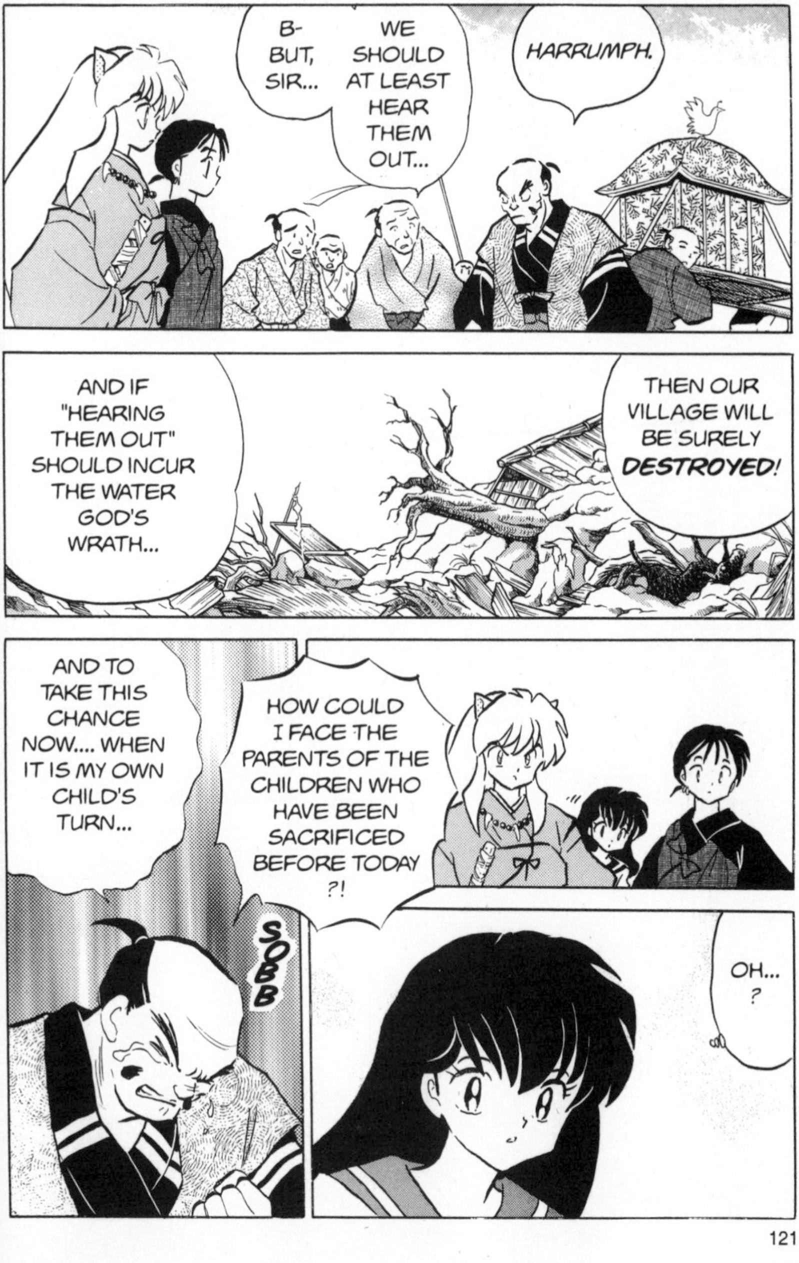
B- BUT, SIR...
WE SHOULD AT LEAST HEAR THEM OUT...
HARRUMPH.
AND IF "HEARING THEM OUT" SHOULD INCUR THE WATER GOD'S WRATH...
THEN OUR VILLAGE WILL BE SURELY DESTROYED!
AND TO TAKE THIS CHANCE NOW.... WHEN IT IS MY OWN CHILD'S TURN...
HOW COULD I FACE THE PARENTS OF THE CHILDREN WHO HAVE BEEN SACRIFICED BEFORE TODAY ?!
SOBB
OH... ?

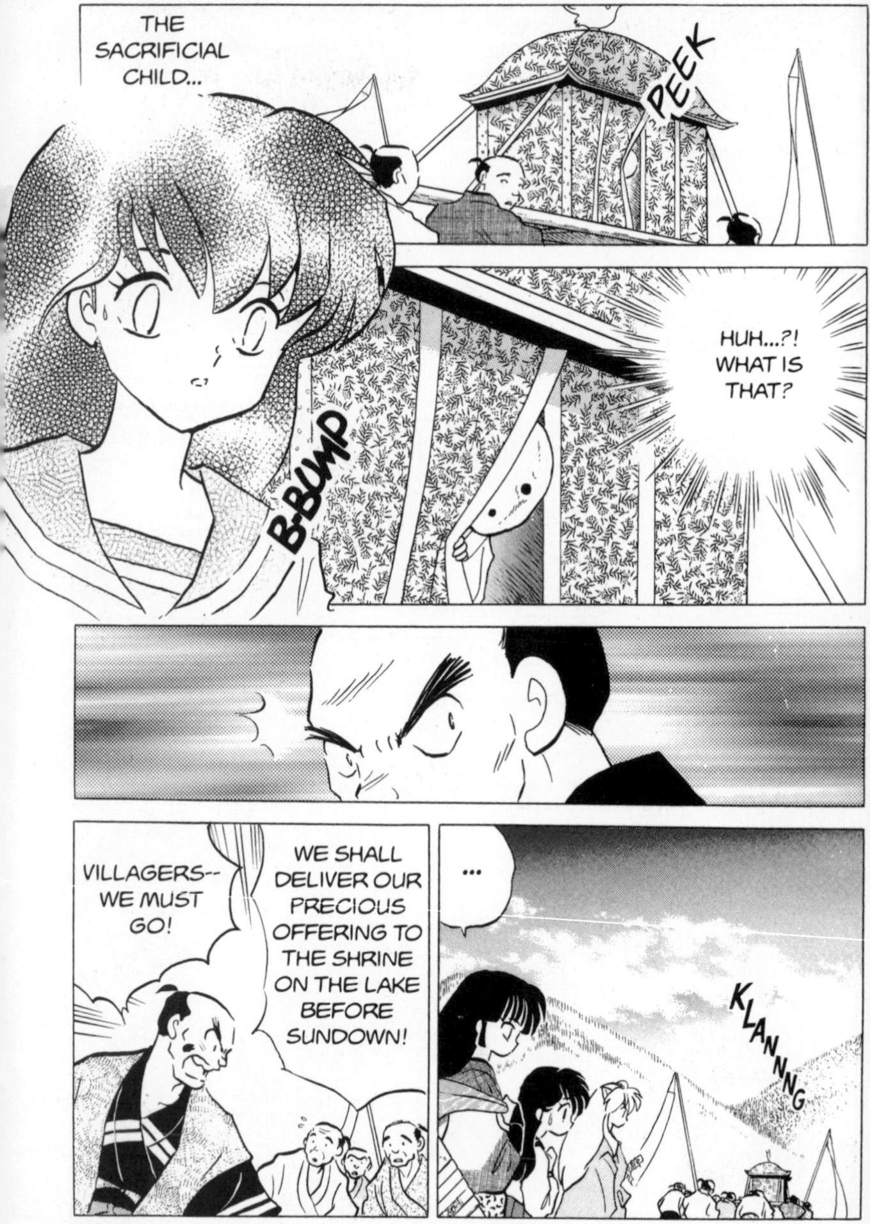
THE SACRIFICIAL CHILD...
PEEK
B-BUMP
HUH...?! WHAT IS THAT?
VILLAGERS-- WE MUST GO!
WE SHALL DELIVER OUR PRECIOUS OFFERING TO THE SHRINE ON THE LAKE BEFORE SUNDOWN!
...
KLANNNNG

I'D SAY THIS VILLAGE SHOULD HAVE ITS HEADMAN EXAMINED....

HE ALMOST ACTED LIKE HE *WANTED* TO SACRIFICE HIS OWN CHILD...

HE DID SEEM TO FIND US QUITE AN INTRUSION, DIDN'T HE?

UM... I KNOW THIS MIGHT SOUND KINDA *BIZARRE*... BUT...

INSIDE THAT... THAT THING...

YES?

I SAW SOMETHING.... WEIRD...

A...

A MASK ?!

MOST LIKELY A PART OF THE SACRIFICIAL RITE.

OH... PHEW!

OH, THAT...

SOME SORT OF MASK, NO DOUBT.

hmph

123

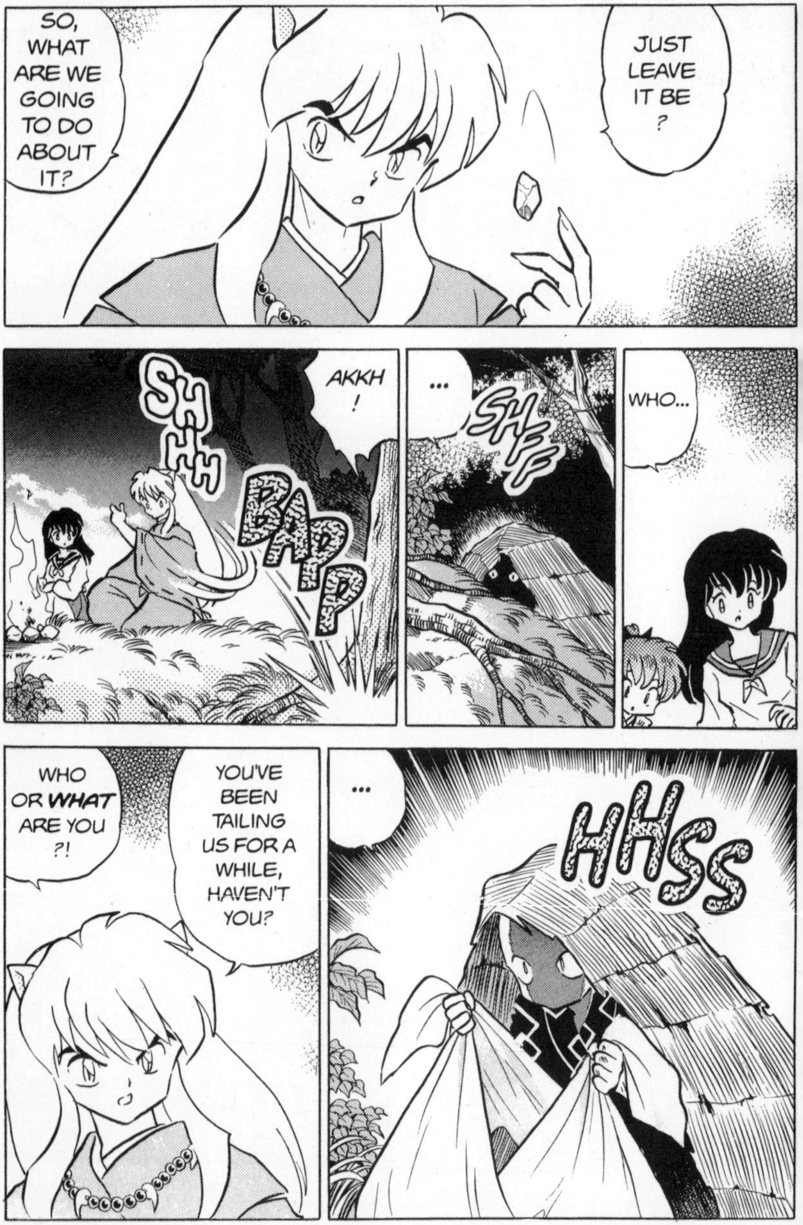
SO, WHAT ARE WE GOING TO DO ABOUT IT?
JUST LEAVE IT BE ?
SHHHH
BADDP
AKKH !
...
SHFF
WHO...
WHO OR WHAT ARE YOU ?!
YOU'VE BEEN TAILING US FOR A WHILE, HAVEN'T YOU?
...
HHSS

HERE !

TAKE IT!

I'LL **GIVE** IT TO YOU !!

A KID...?

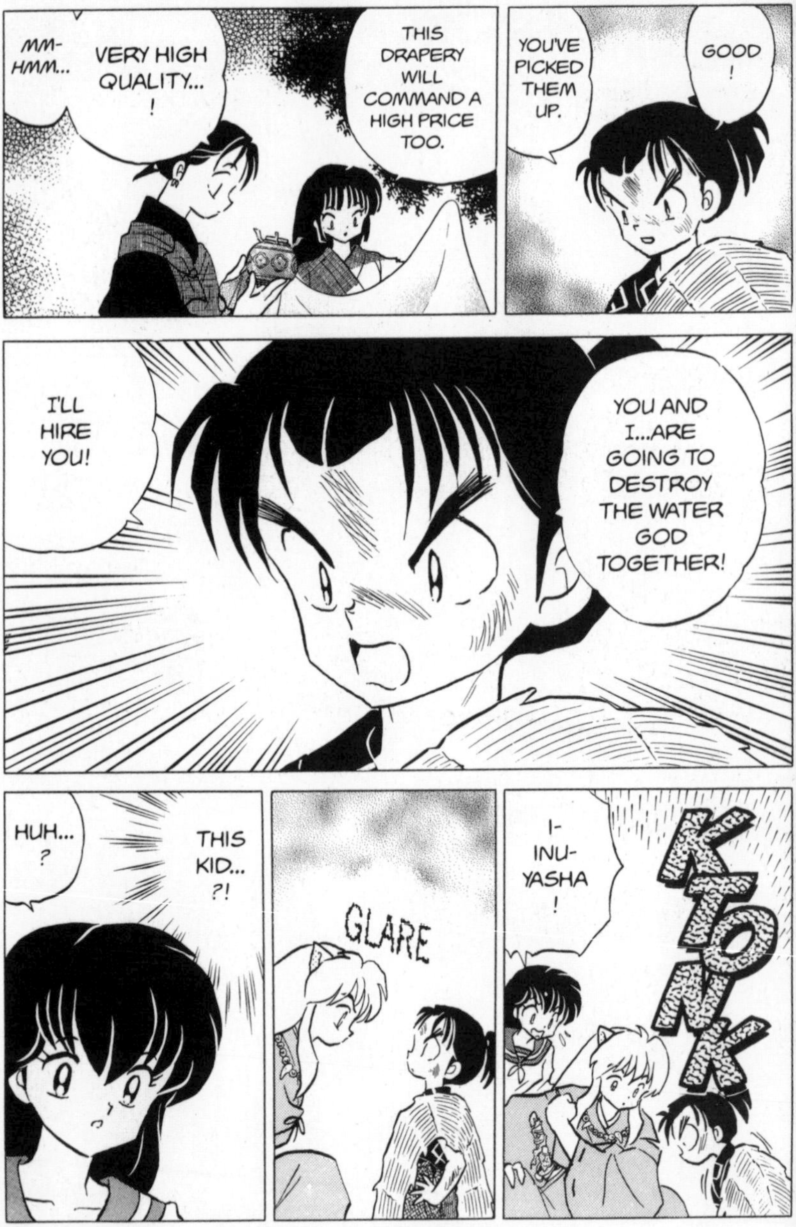
MM-HMM...
VERY HIGH QUALITY... !
THIS DRAPERY WILL COMMAND A HIGH PRICE TOO.
YOU'VE PICKED THEM UP.
GOOD !
I'LL HIRE YOU!
YOU AND I...ARE GOING TO DESTROY THE WATER GOD TOGETHER!
HUH... ?
THIS KID... ?!
GLARE
I-INU-YASHA !
KTONK

HE'S JUST A KID--!

WE HAVE TO LET HIM KNOW WHO'S BOSS!

LOOKS LIKE WE'LL BE APOLOGIZING FOR DOG-BOY YET AGAIN...

GRRN GRRN

FLAIL FLAIL

SHH

SSHHH...

...

127

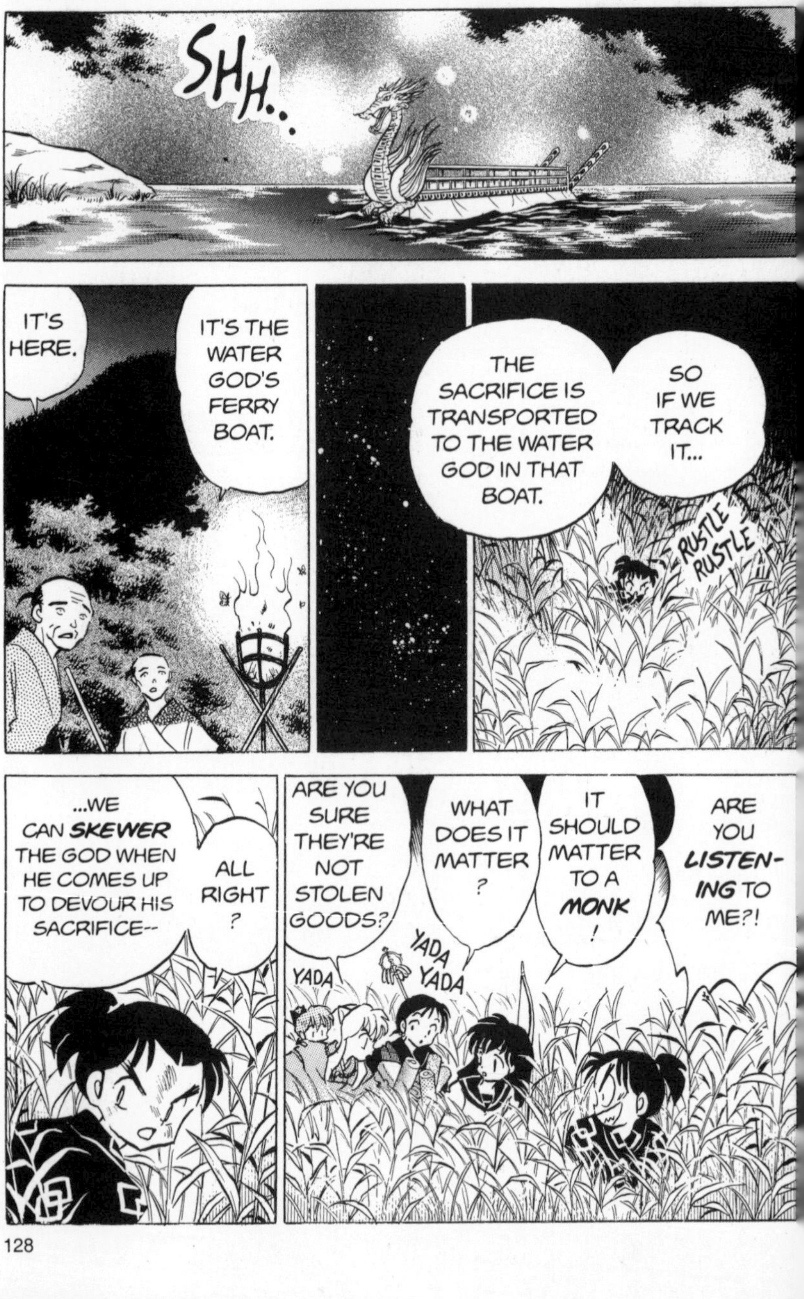
SHH...
IT'S HERE.
IT'S THE WATER GOD'S FERRY BOAT.
THE SACRIFICE IS TRANSPORTED TO THE WATER GOD IN THAT BOAT.
SO IF WE TRACK IT...
RUSTLE RUSTLE
...WE CAN SKEWER THE GOD WHEN HE COMES UP TO DEVOUR HIS SACRIFICE--
ALL RIGHT?
ARE YOU SURE THEY'RE NOT STOLEN GOODS?
YADA
YADA YADA
WHAT DOES IT MATTER?
IT SHOULD MATTER TO A MONK!
ARE YOU LISTENING TO ME?!

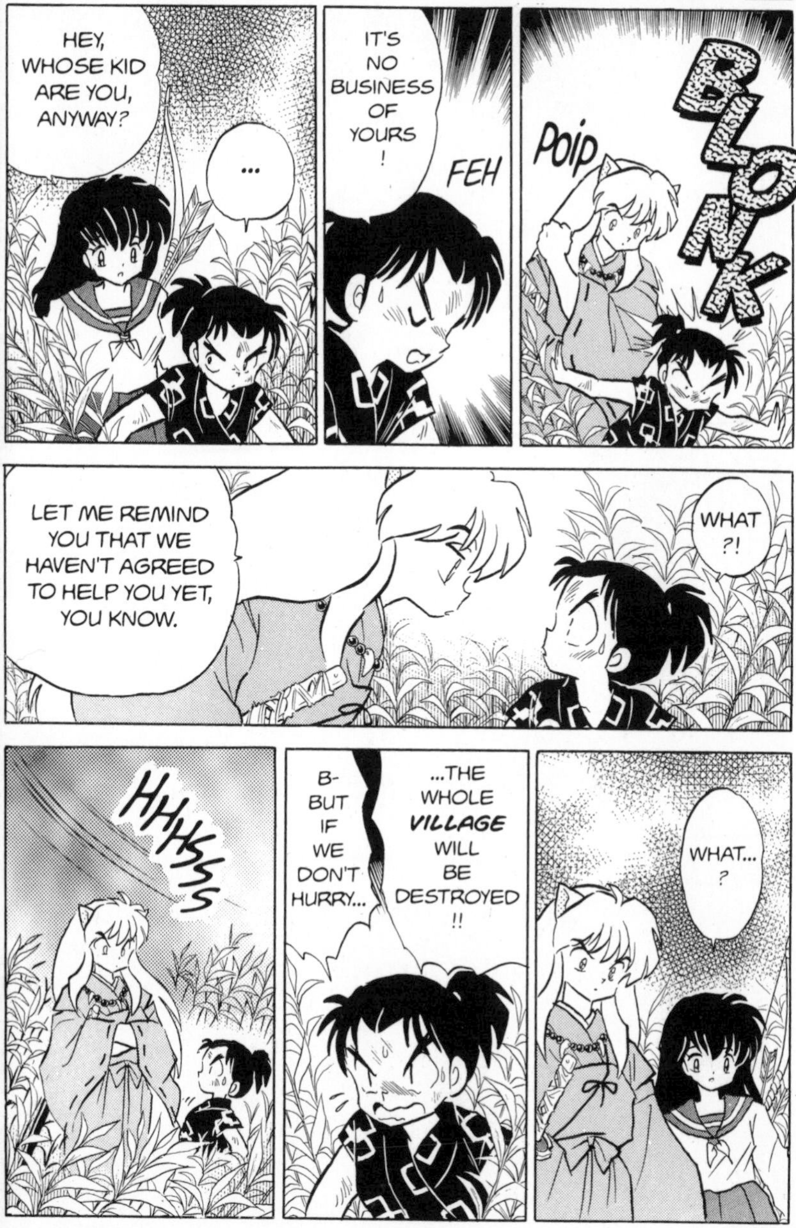
HEY, WHOSE KID ARE YOU, ANYWAY?
...
IT'S NO BUSINESS OF YOURS!
FEH
Poip
BLONK
LET ME REMIND YOU THAT WE HAVEN'T AGREED TO HELP YOU YET, YOU KNOW.
WHAT?!
HHHSSS
B-BUT IF WE DON'T HURRY...
...THE WHOLE VILLAGE WILL BE DESTROYED!!
WHAT...?

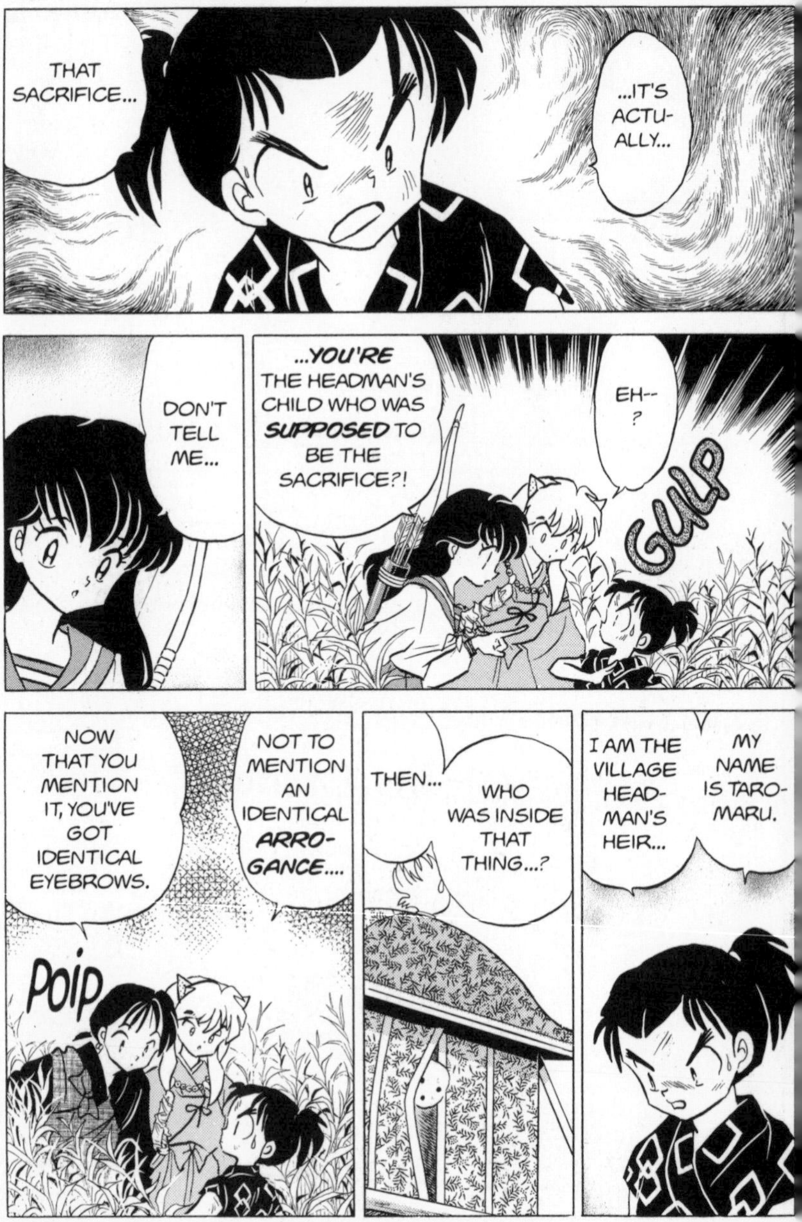
THAT SACRIFICE...
...IT'S ACTUALLY...
DON'T TELL ME...
...*YOU'RE* THE HEADMAN'S CHILD WHO WAS *SUPPOSED* TO BE THE SACRIFICE?!
EH-- ?
GULP
NOW THAT YOU MENTION IT, YOU'VE GOT IDENTICAL EYEBROWS.
NOT TO MENTION AN IDENTICAL *ARROGANCE*....
POIP
THEN...
WHO WAS INSIDE THAT THING...?
I AM THE VILLAGE HEADMAN'S HEIR...
MY NAME IS TAROMARU.

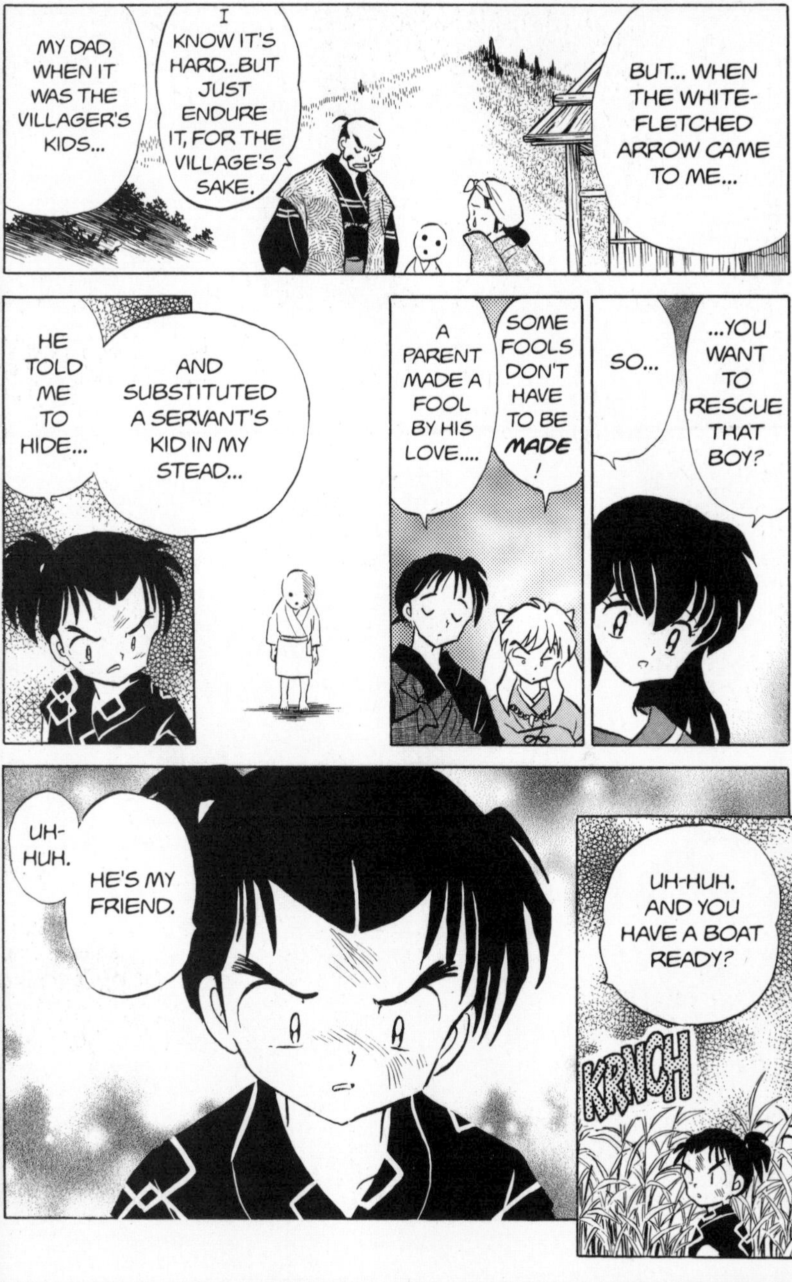
MY DAD, WHEN IT WAS THE VILLAGER'S KIDS...
I KNOW IT'S HARD...BUT JUST ENDURE IT, FOR THE VILLAGE'S SAKE.
BUT... WHEN THE WHITE-FLETCHED ARROW CAME TO ME...
HE TOLD ME TO HIDE...
AND SUBSTITUTED A SERVANT'S KID IN MY STEAD...
A PARENT MADE A FOOL BY HIS LOVE....
SOME FOOLS DON'T HAVE TO BE *MADE*!
SO...
...YOU WANT TO RESCUE THAT BOY?
UH-HUH.
HE'S MY FRIEND.
UH-HUH. AND YOU HAVE A BOAT READY?
KRNCH

SCROLL EIGHT
THE HOLY RELIC

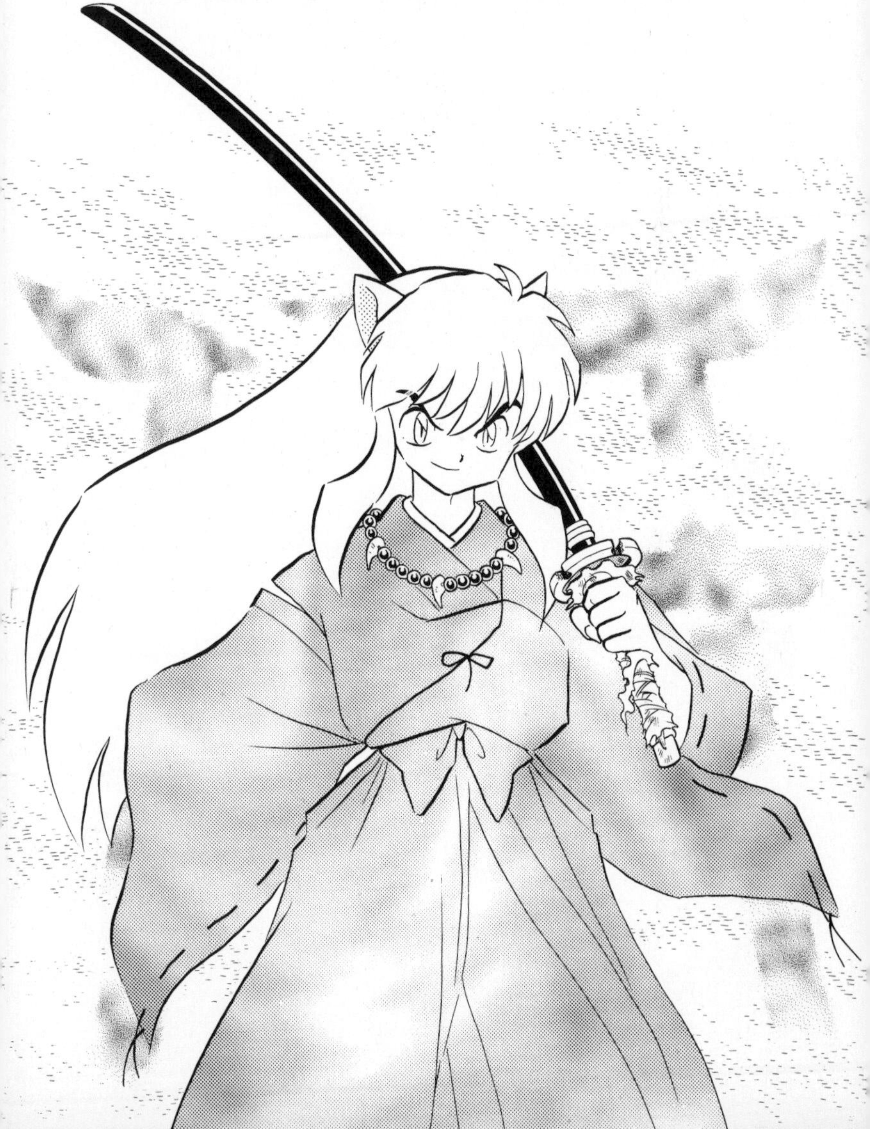

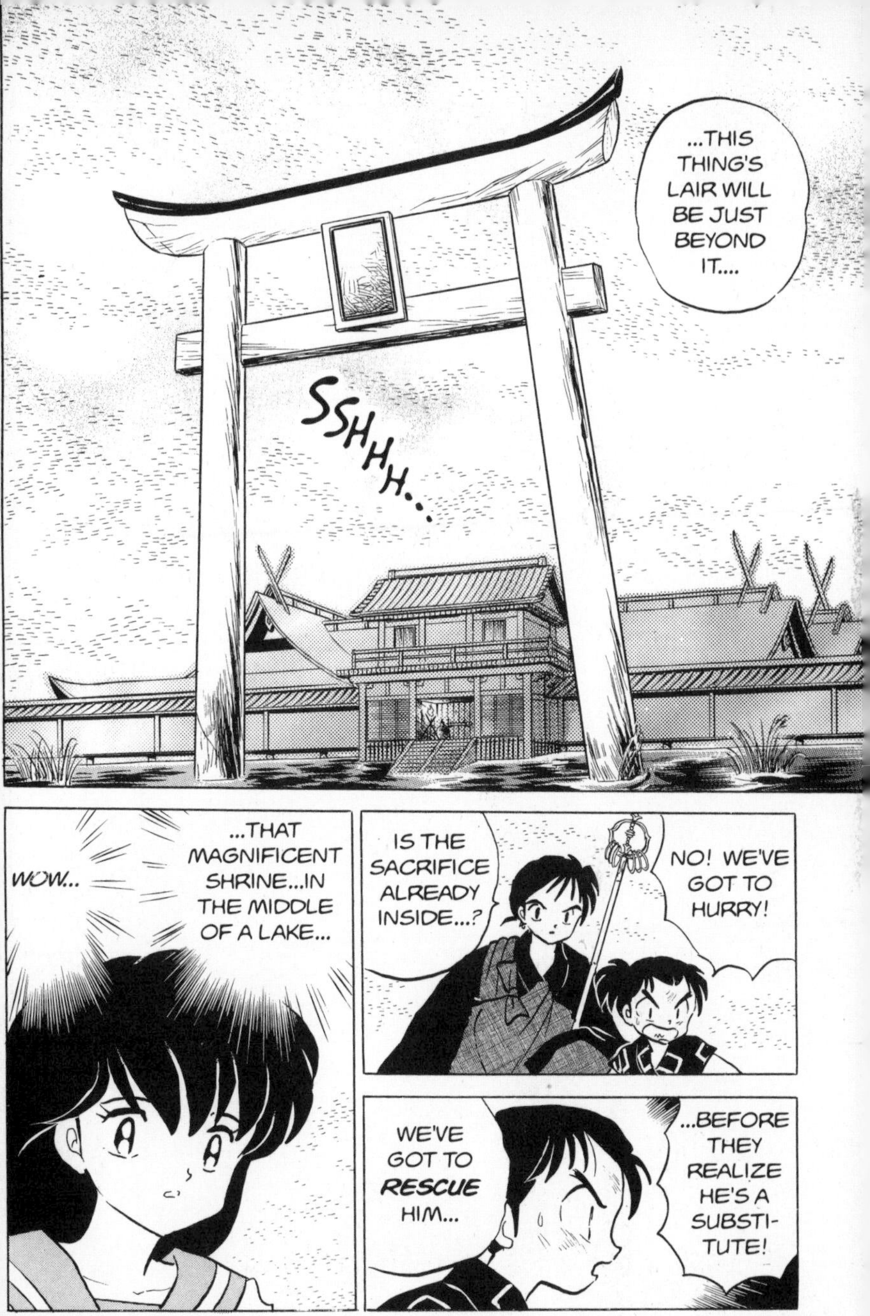
...THIS THING'S LAIR WILL BE JUST BEYOND IT....
SSHHH...
WOW...
...THAT MAGNIFICENT SHRINE...IN THE MIDDLE OF A LAKE...
IS THE SACRIFICE ALREADY INSIDE...?
NO! WE'VE GOT TO HURRY!
WE'VE GOT TO *RESCUE* HIM...
...BEFORE THEY REALIZE HE'S A SUBSTI-TUTE!

136

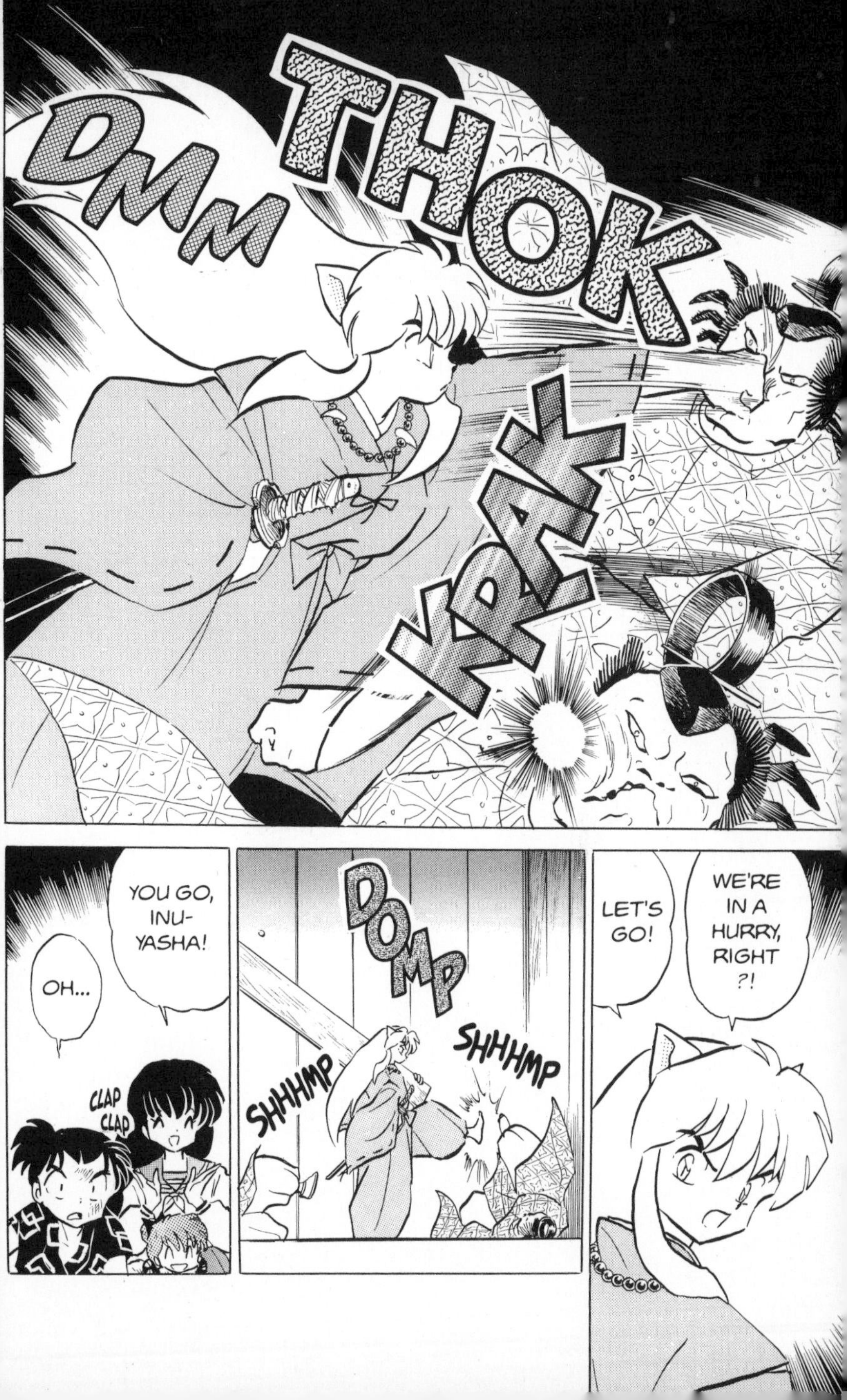
DMM
THOK
KRAK
YOU GO, INU-YASHA!
OH...
CLAP CLAP
DOMP
SHHHMP
SHHHMP
LET'S GO!
WE'RE IN A HURRY, RIGHT?!

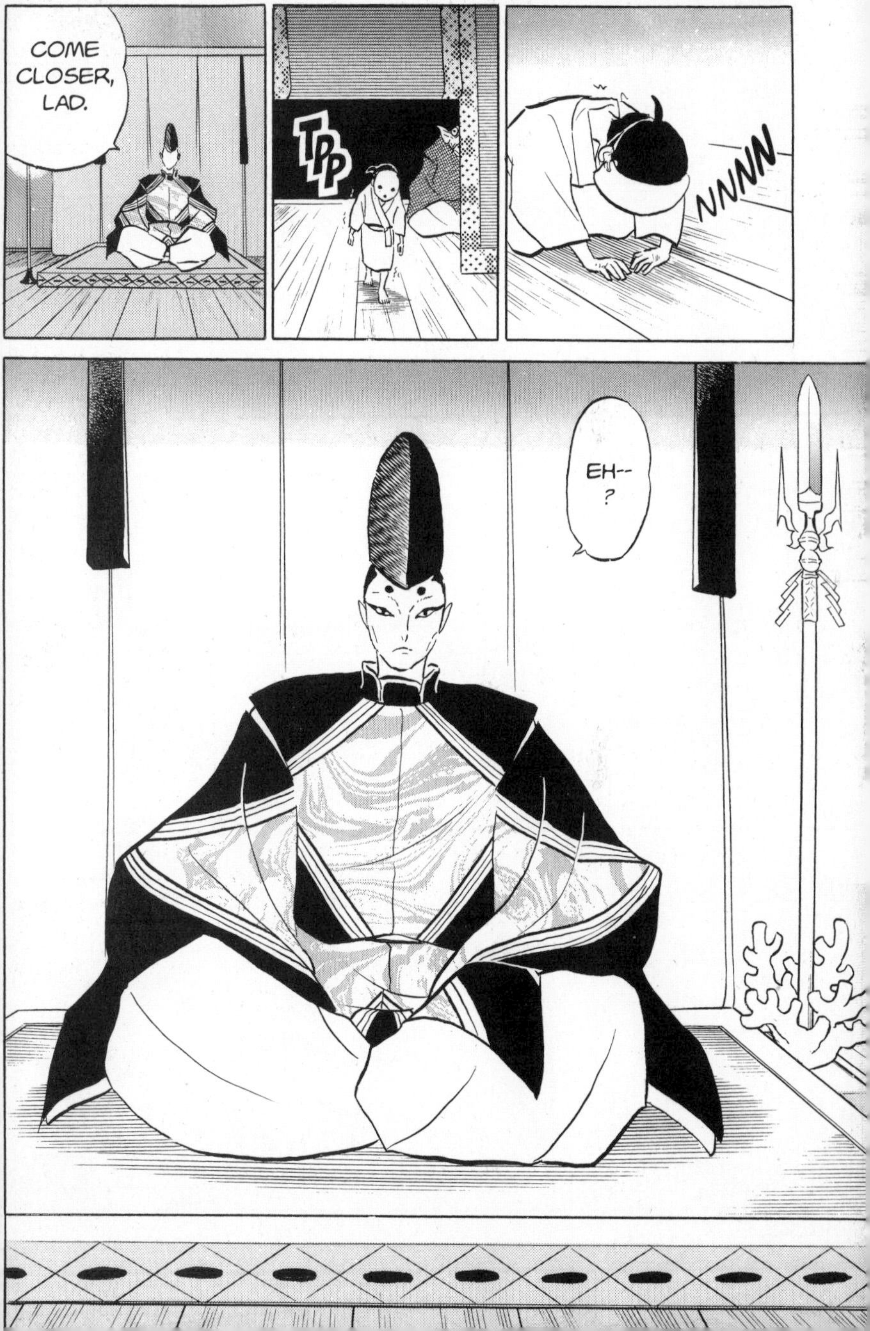
COME CLOSER, LAD.
TPP
NNNN
EH--?

THESE FILTHY CORN-ENCRUSTED HANDS...

YOU...

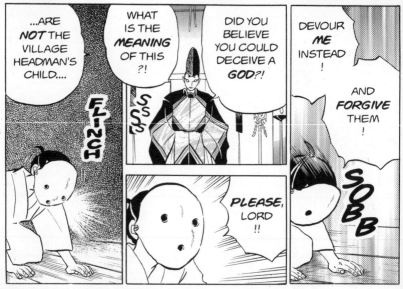

...ARE *NOT* THE VILLAGE HEADMAN'S CHILD....

WHAT IS THE *MEANING* OF THIS ?!

DID YOU BELIEVE YOU COULD DECEIVE A *GOD*?!

DEVOUR *ME* INSTEAD !

AND *FORGIVE* THEM !

FLINCH

SSSS

PLEASE, LORD !!

SOBB

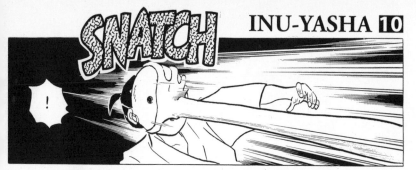

SURELY YOU KNOW THAT I CANNOT FORGIVE *THIS....*

HOW COULD I KEEP MY DIGNITY AS A *GOD?*

DANGLE

SKWRM

SKWRM

...

NNNSH NNNSH

SKWIIISH

THE BLOODY SCRAPS OF YOUR BODY WILL SWIRL IN THE FLOOD I SET LOOSE ON YOUR VILLAGE.

THOK

DM DM DM DM

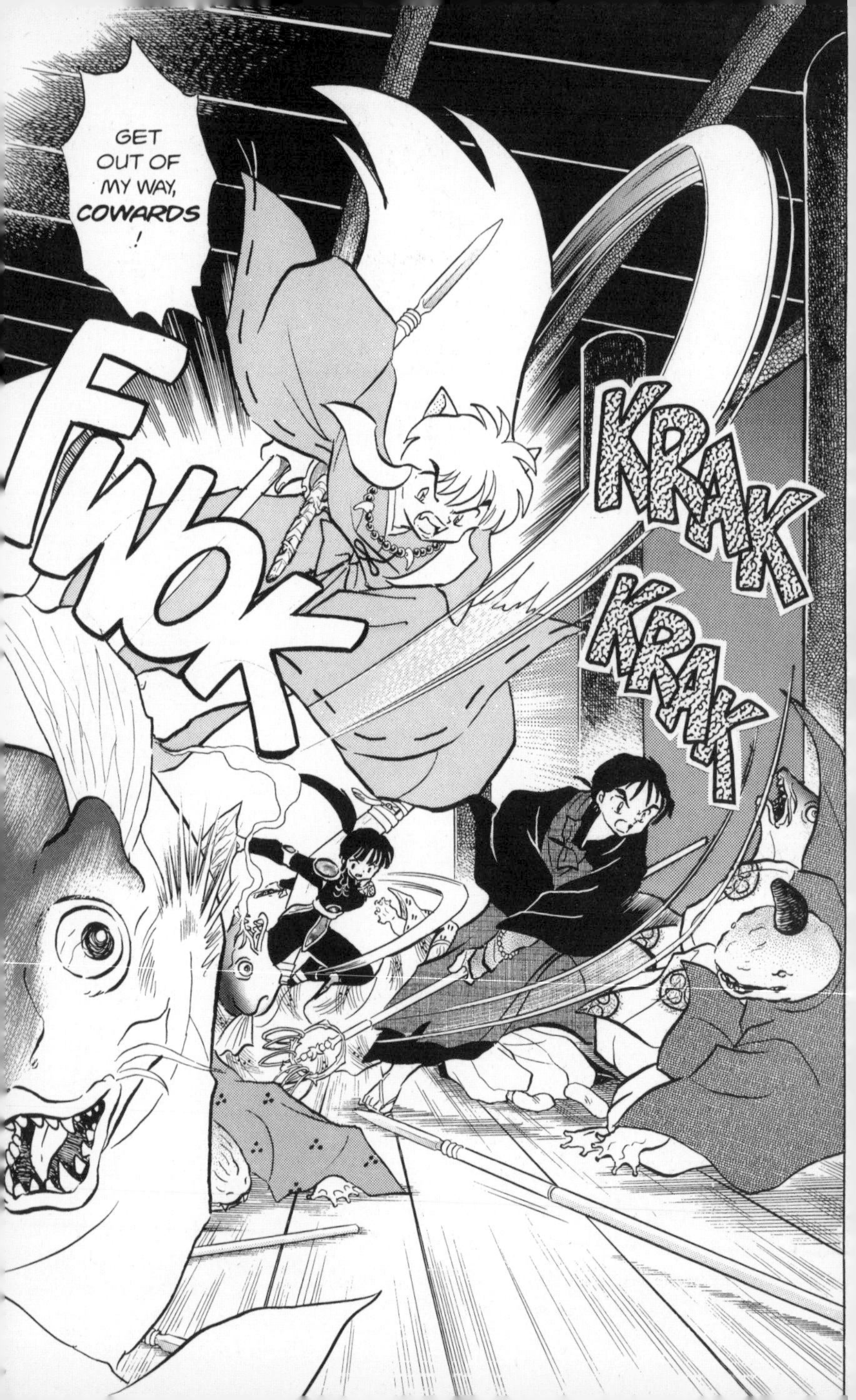
GET OUT OF MY WAY, COWARDS!
FWOK
KRAK
KRAK
KRAK

TH-THIS IS SACRED GROUND!

DM DM DM DM

SHUT UP!

WHOK

SHHMP

WELL! IT LOOKS LIKE WE DON'T NEED TO FIGHT **THESE!**

I'D SAY NOT!

THOK

THEY'RE ALL TRANS-FORMED CARP AND RIVER CRABS!

PLASSH

BLUP BLUP

SKUTLE SKUTLE

143

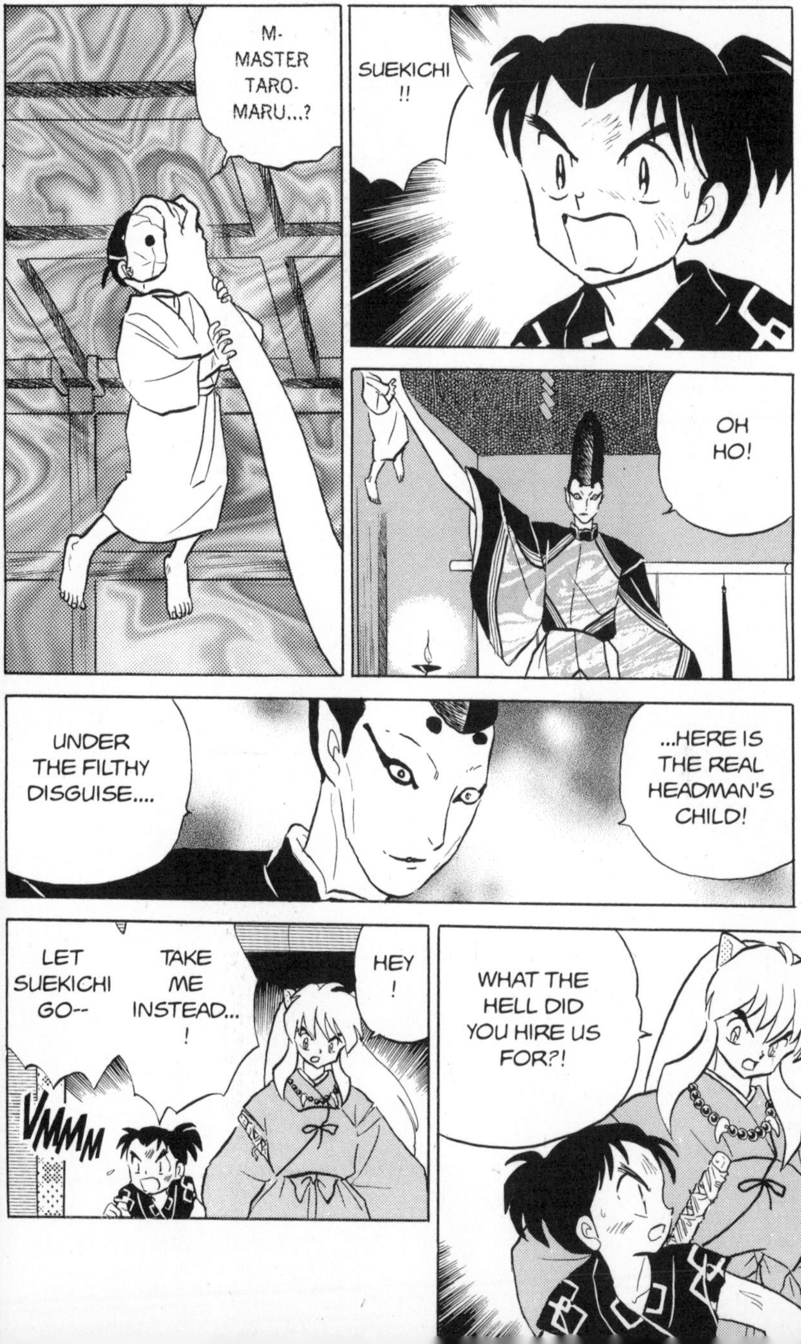
M-MASTER TARO-MARU...?
SUEKICHI !!
OH HO!
UNDER THE FILTHY DISGUISE....
...HERE IS THE REAL HEADMAN'S CHILD!
LET SUEKICHI GO--
TAKE ME INSTEAD... !
HEY !
VMMM
WHAT THE HELL DID YOU HIRE US FOR?!

"WATER GOD"!

WHAT KIND OF DEMON ARE YOU REALLY?!

SHOW YOUR TRUE SELF!!

VMMM

SHHHH

SSSHHH

SNATCH

146

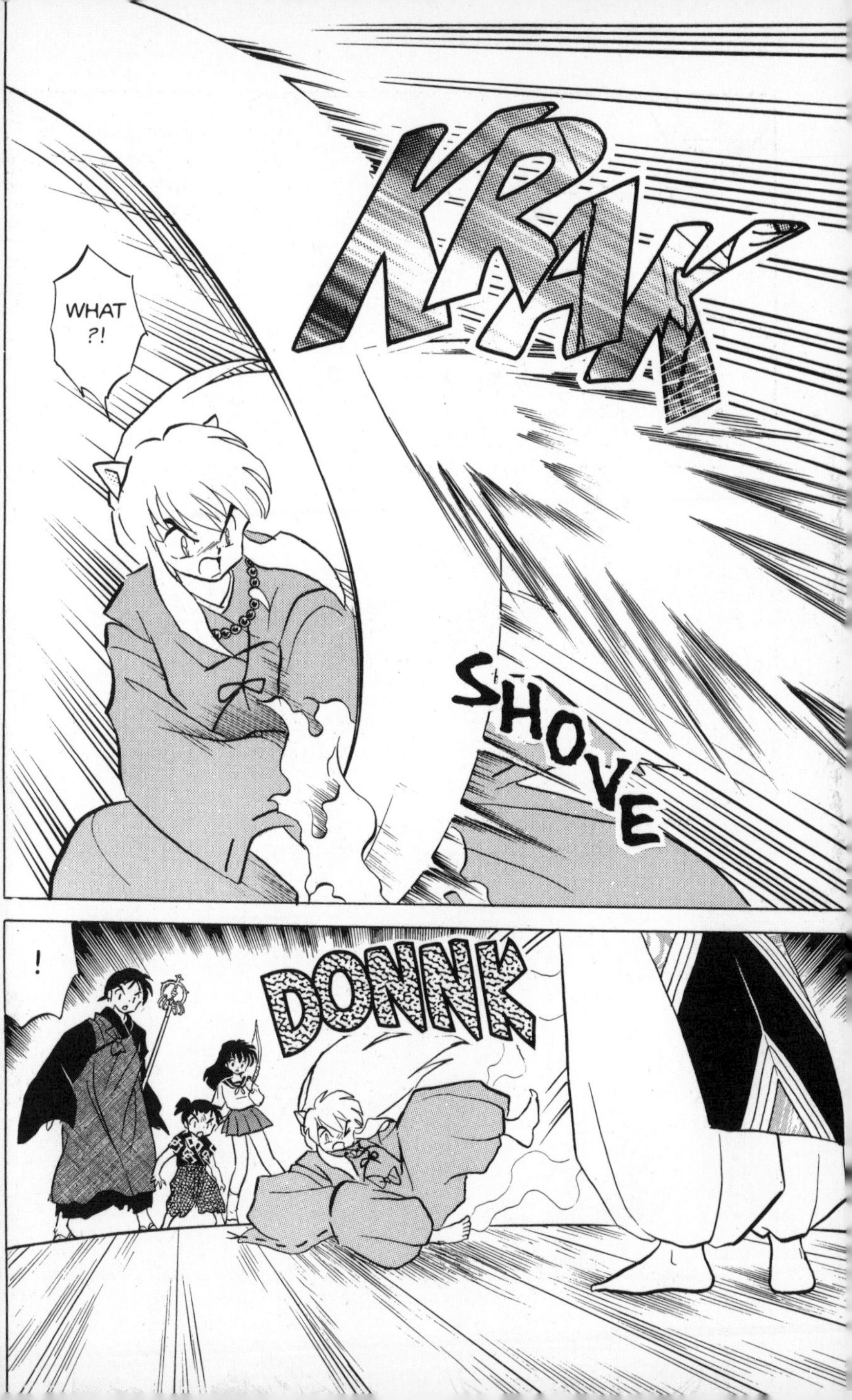
WHAT ?!
KRAK
SHOVE
!
DONNK

WHAT THE...

WOOSH

THE FANG... ITS TRANS-FORMATION WAS UNDONE?!

YOU FOOL...

DID YOU REALLY THINK YOUR DEMON BLADE COULD STAND UP AGAINST THIS HOLY RELIC... THE "AMAKOI HALBERD"?

DON'T MAKE ME LAUGH!

SHHM

WAIT, INU-YASHA!

WOK

WHAT...?!

THIS DOES NOT LOOK GOOD!

FROM HERE... I MUST SAY THAT HALBERD LOOKS LIKE A TRUE HOLY RELIC!

YEAH? SO WHAT?

BUT IF HE HAS A *REAL* HOLY WEAPON...

THEN DOESN'T THAT MEAN HE'S *NOT* A DEMON... THAT HE'S REALLY A GOD...?

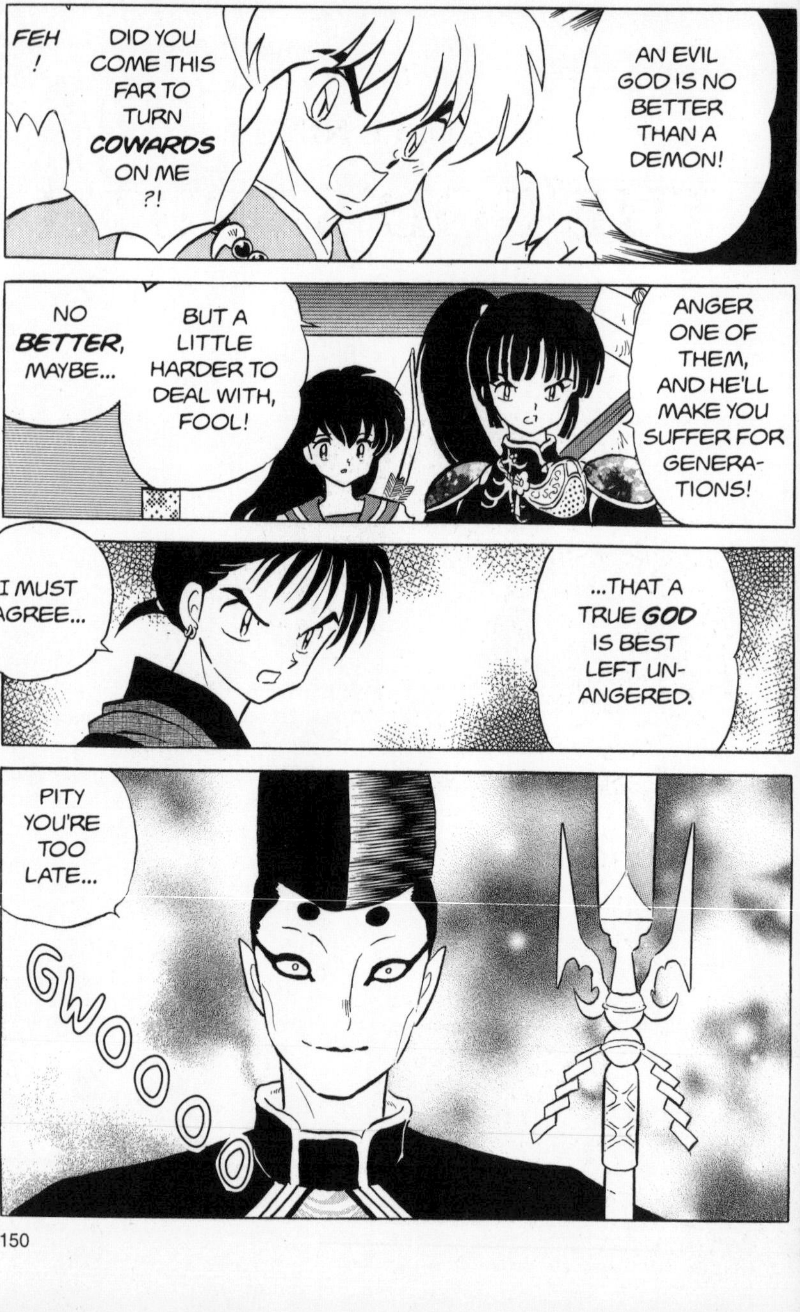
FEH!
DID YOU COME THIS FAR TO TURN COWARDS ON ME?!
AN EVIL GOD IS NO BETTER THAN A DEMON!
NO BETTER, MAYBE...
BUT A LITTLE HARDER TO DEAL WITH, FOOL!
ANGER ONE OF THEM, AND HE'LL MAKE YOU SUFFER FOR GENERA-TIONS!
I MUST AGREE...
...THAT A TRUE GOD IS BEST LEFT UN-ANGERED.
PITY YOU'RE TOO LATE...
GWOOOOO

SCROLL NINE

THE GOD'S TRUTH

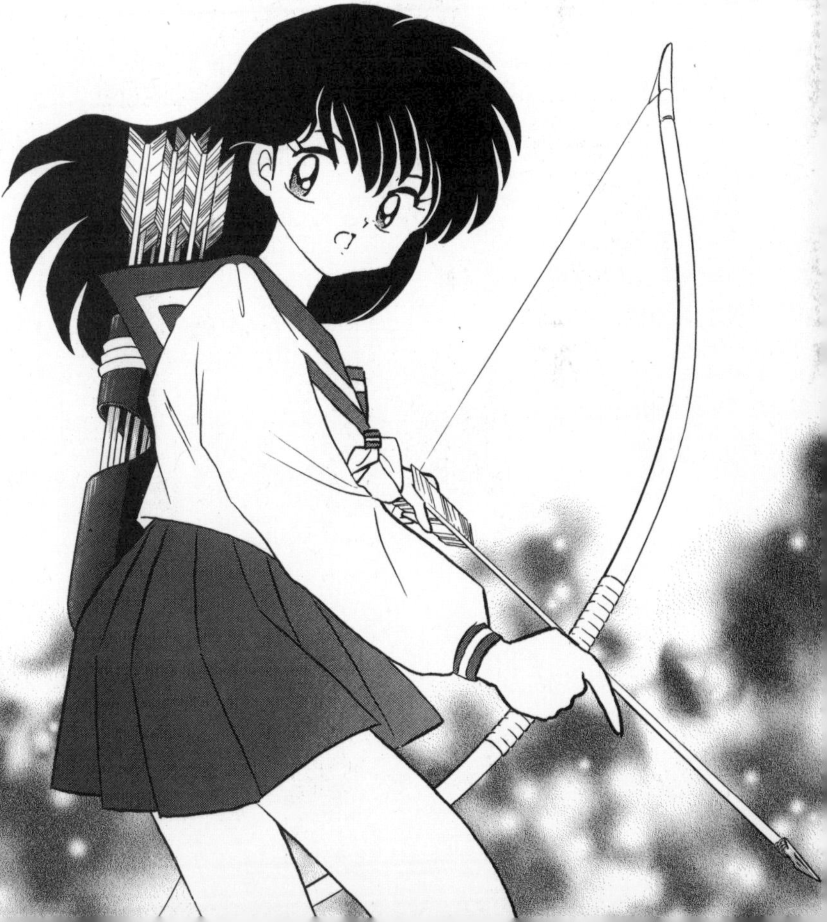

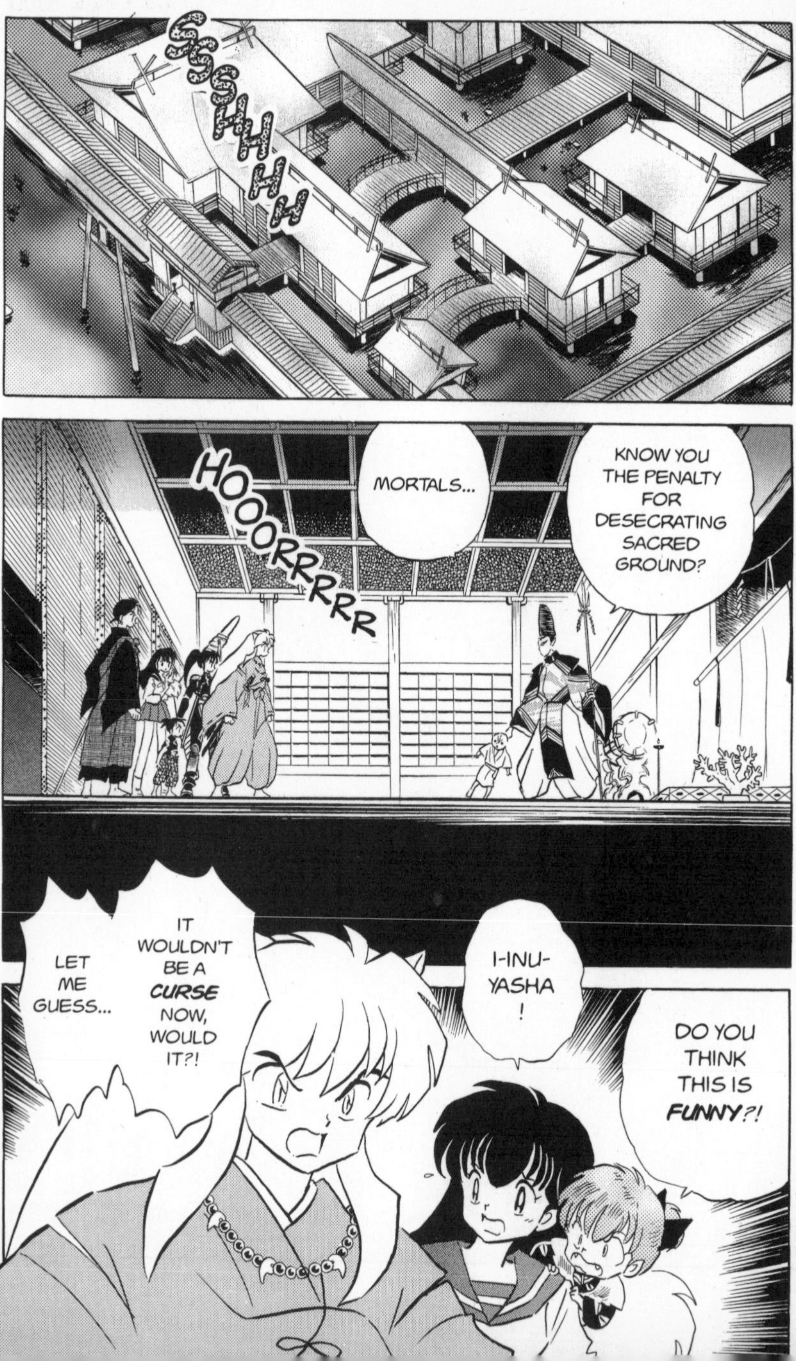
SSSHHHH
HOOORRRRRR
MORTALS...
KNOW YOU THE PENALTY FOR DESECRATING SACRED GROUND?
LET ME GUESS...
IT WOULDN'T BE A *CURSE* NOW, WOULD IT?!
I-INU-YASHA!
DO YOU THINK THIS IS *FUNNY*?!

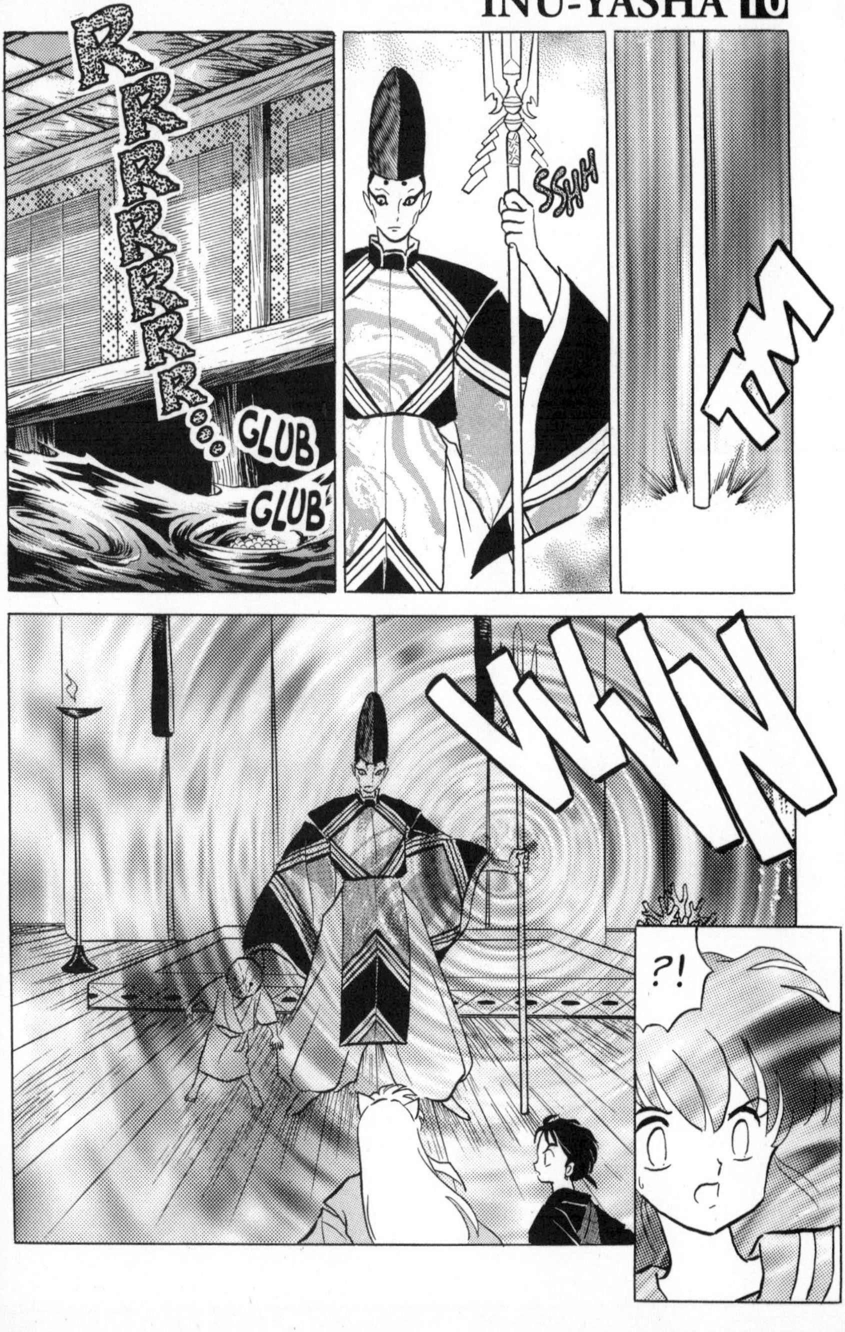
RRRRRRR...
GLUB
GLUB
SSHH
TM
VVVN
?!

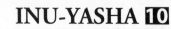

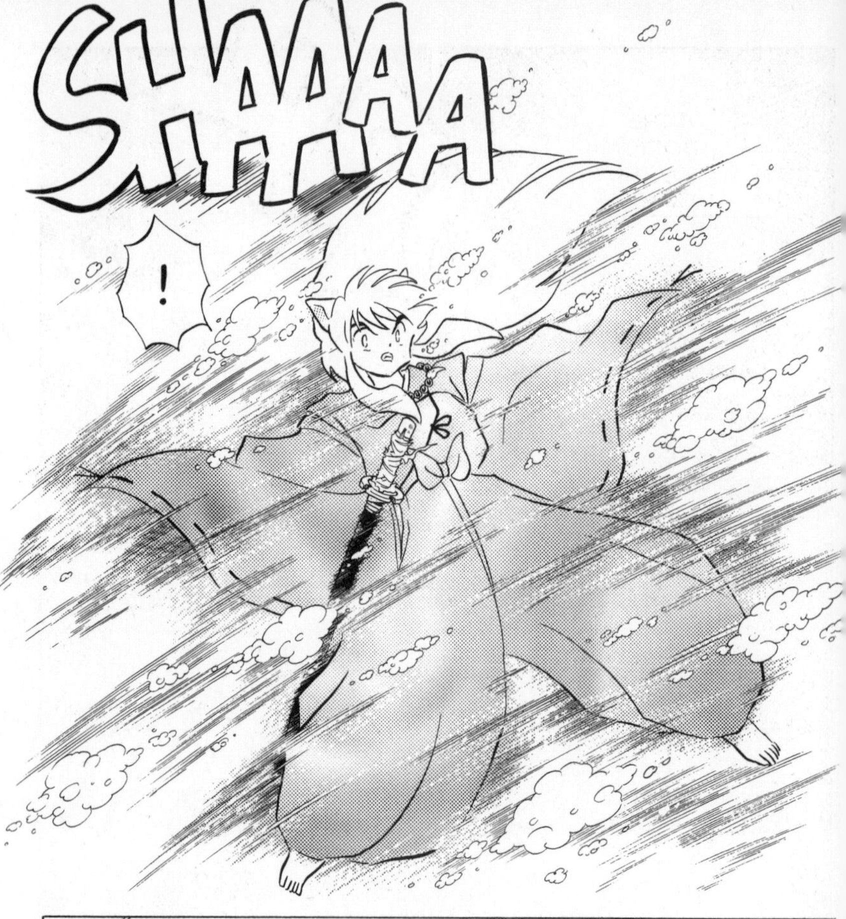
SHAAAA
!

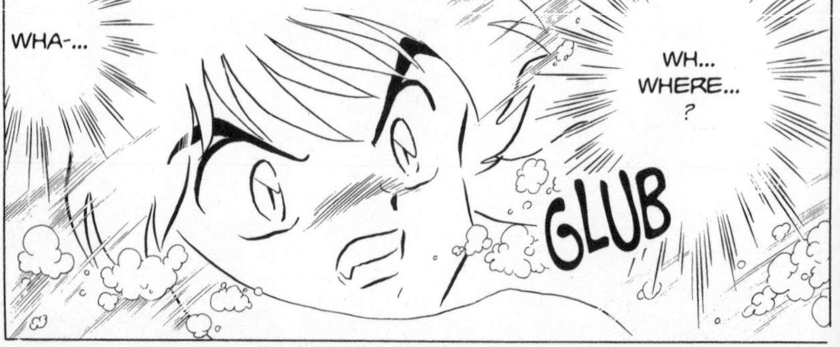
WHA-...
WH... WHERE... ?
GLUB

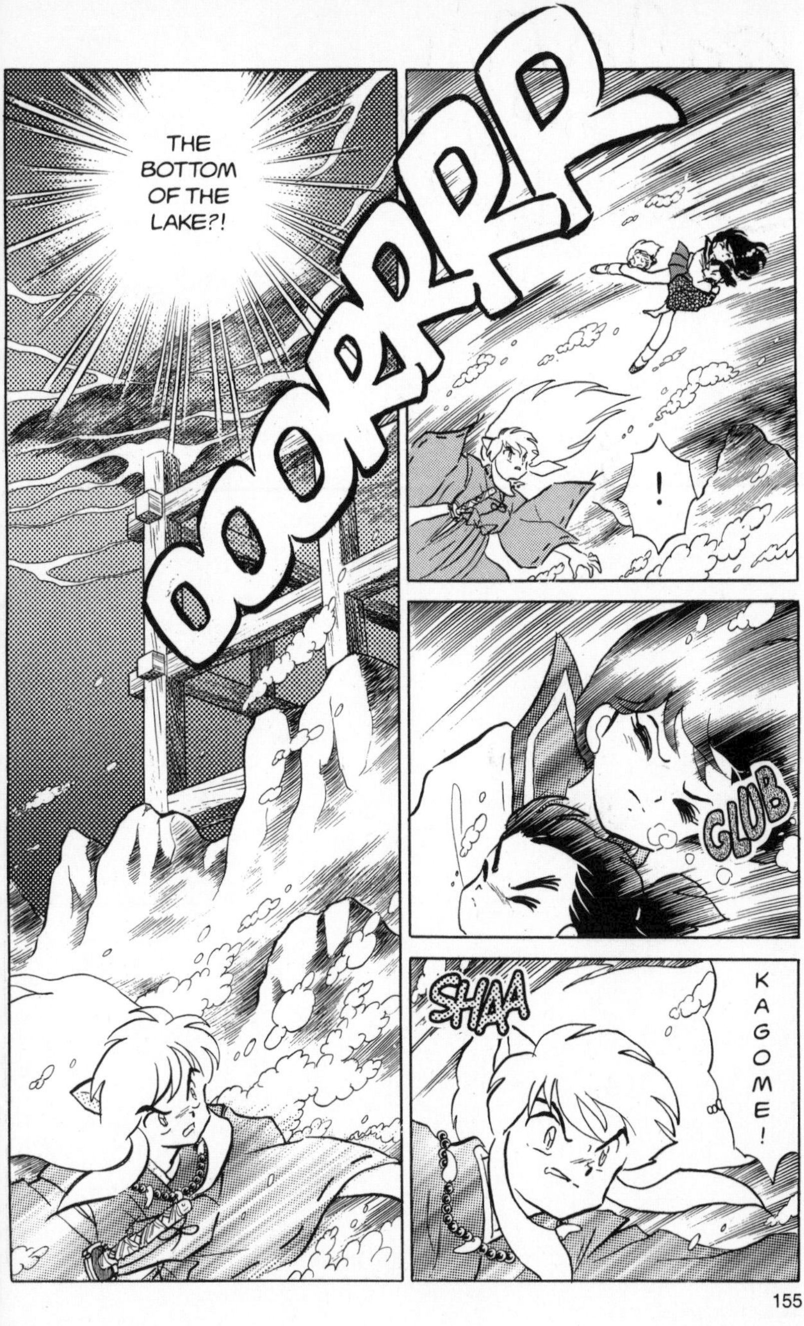
THE BOTTOM OF THE LAKE?!
DOOPPPP
!
GLUB
SHAA
KAGOME!

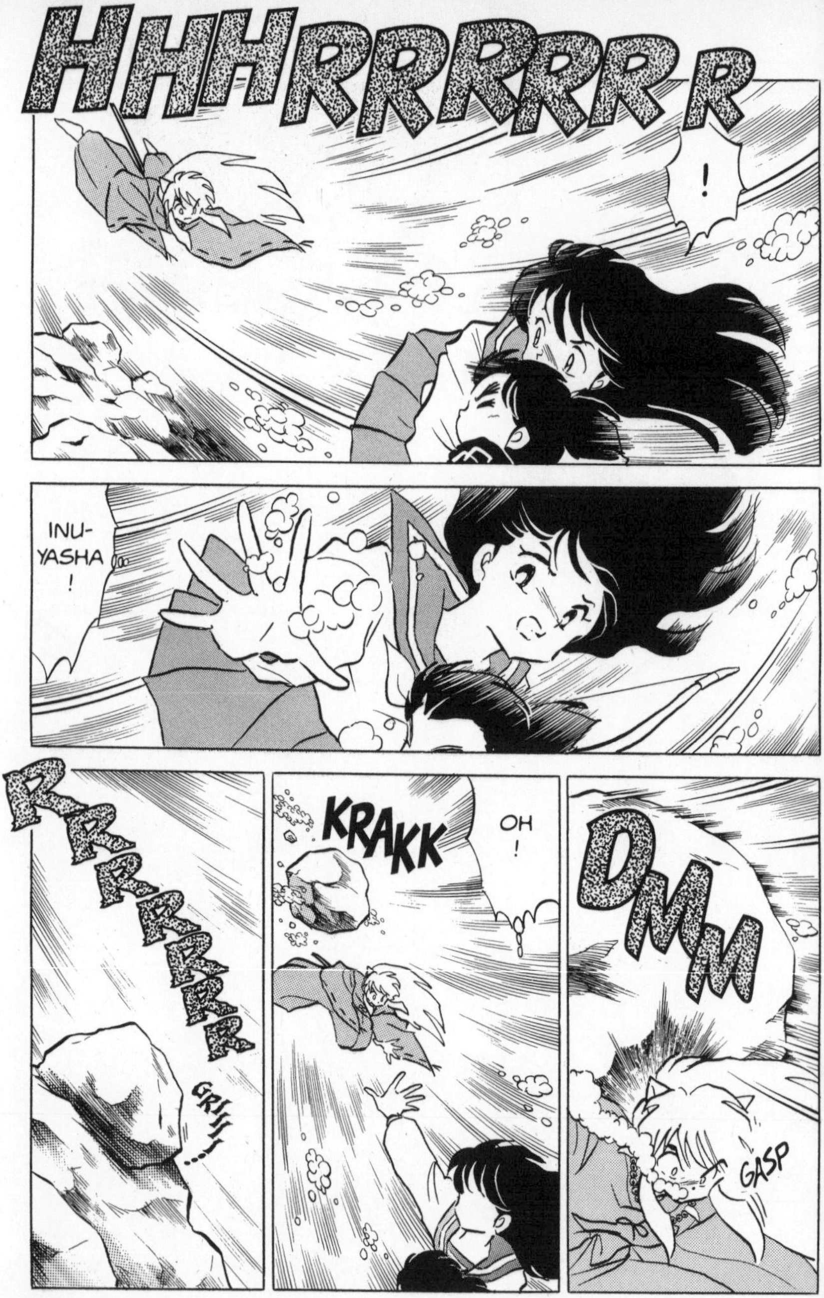
HHHRRRRRRR
!
INU-YASHA!
RRRRRRRRR
GRIIII...
KRAKK
OH!
DMM
GASP

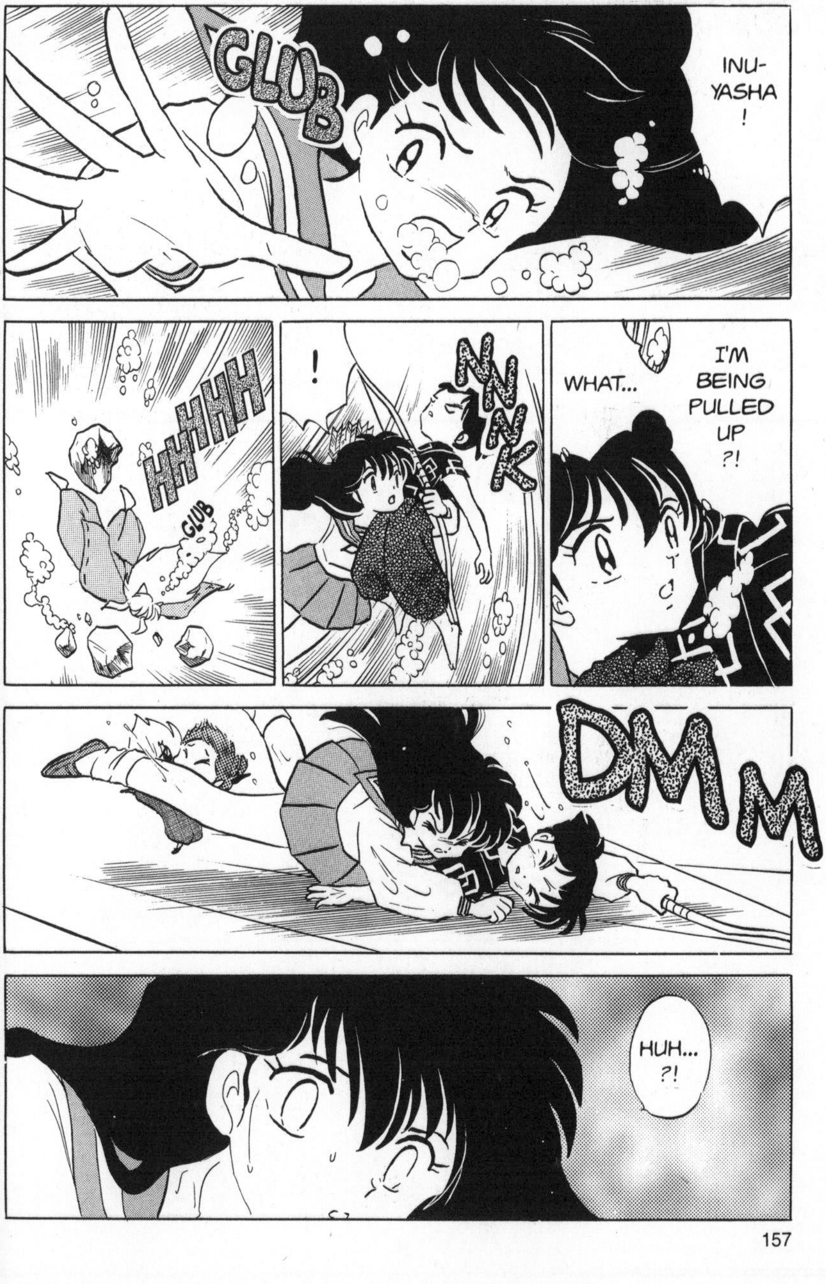
GLUB
INU-YASHA!
HHHHHH
GLUB
!
NNNK
WHAT...
I'M BEING PULLED UP?!
DMMM
HUH...?!

I-I'M BACK... IN THAT ROOM...?

HE'S GOING TO DEVOUR THIS CHILD...!

I'VE GOT TO DO SOME-THING...

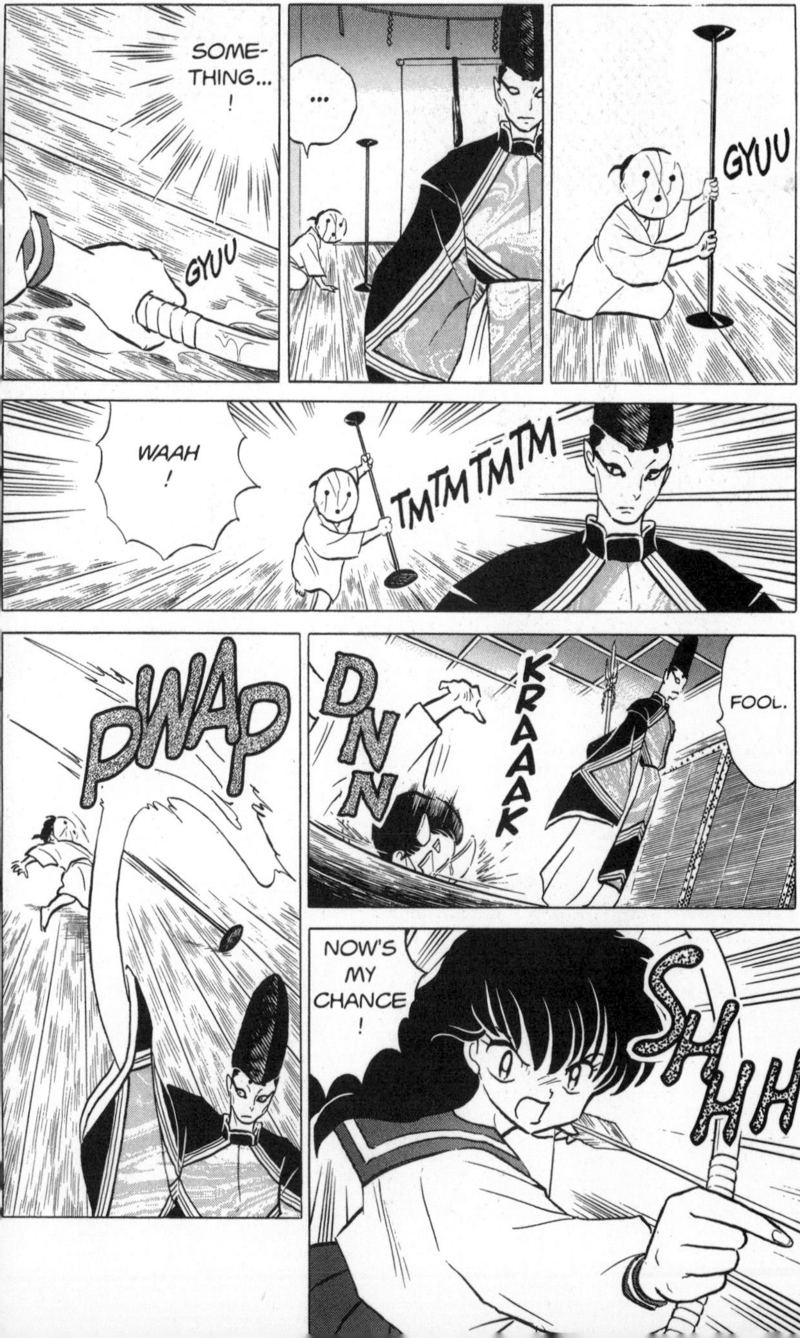
SOME-
THING...
!
GYUU
...
GYUU
WAAH
!
TMTMTMTM
PWAP
DNN
KRAAAK
FOOL.
NOW'S
MY
CHANCE
!
SHHH

IT... CANNOT BE...

THE BODY OF A GOD... AND A MERE ARROW...?!

I DON'T LIKE THE LOOKS OF THIS....

I DIDN'T KNOW IT WOULD BE THAT STRONG...!

CAN YOU RUN?!

Y-YES...

COULD YOU WAKE UP, ALREADY?!

YOU... SHALL... RUE...THIS... DAY....

LET'S GET OUT OF HERE!!

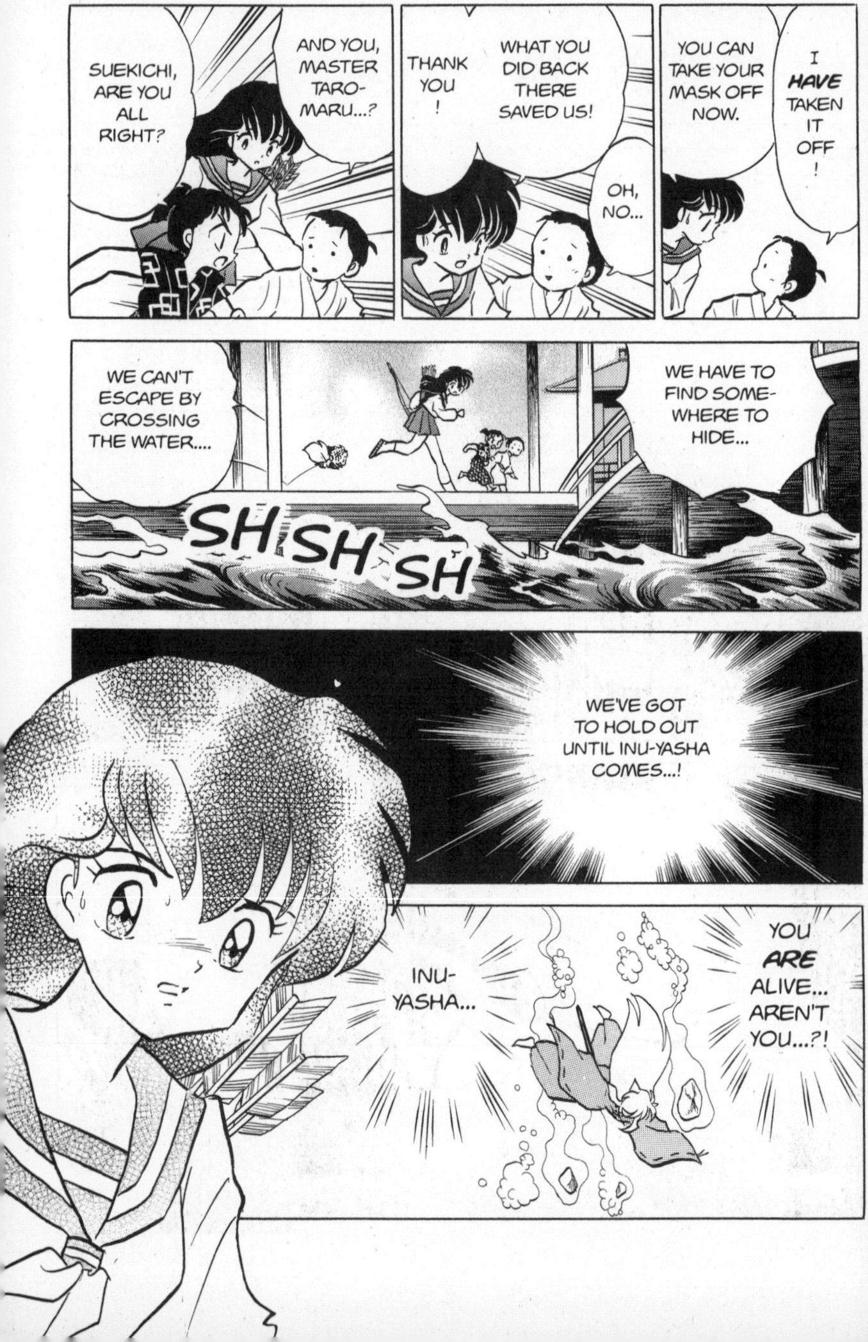
SUEKICHI, ARE YOU ALL RIGHT?
AND YOU, MASTER TARO-MARU...?
THANK YOU !
WHAT YOU DID BACK THERE SAVED US!
OH, NO...
YOU CAN TAKE YOUR MASK OFF NOW.
I *HAVE* TAKEN IT OFF !
WE CAN'T ESCAPE BY CROSSING THE WATER....
WE HAVE TO FIND SOME-WHERE TO HIDE...
SH SH SH
WE'VE GOT TO HOLD OUT UNTIL INU-YASHA COMES...!
INU-YASHA...
YOU *ARE* ALIVE... AREN'T YOU...?!

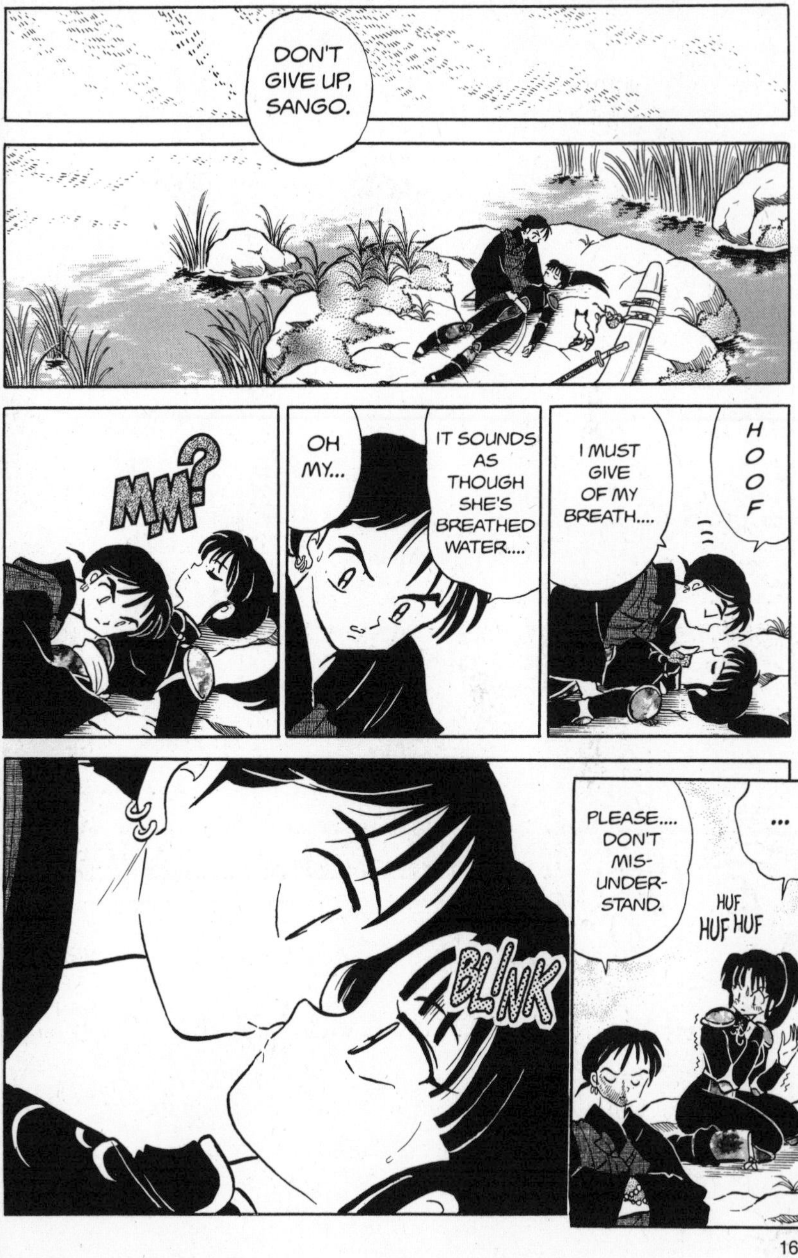
DON'T GIVE UP, SANGO.
MM?
OH MY...
IT SOUNDS AS THOUGH SHE'S BREATHED WATER....
I MUST GIVE OF MY BREATH....
HOOF
BLINK
PLEASE.... DON'T MIS-UNDER-STAND.
...
HUF HUF HUF

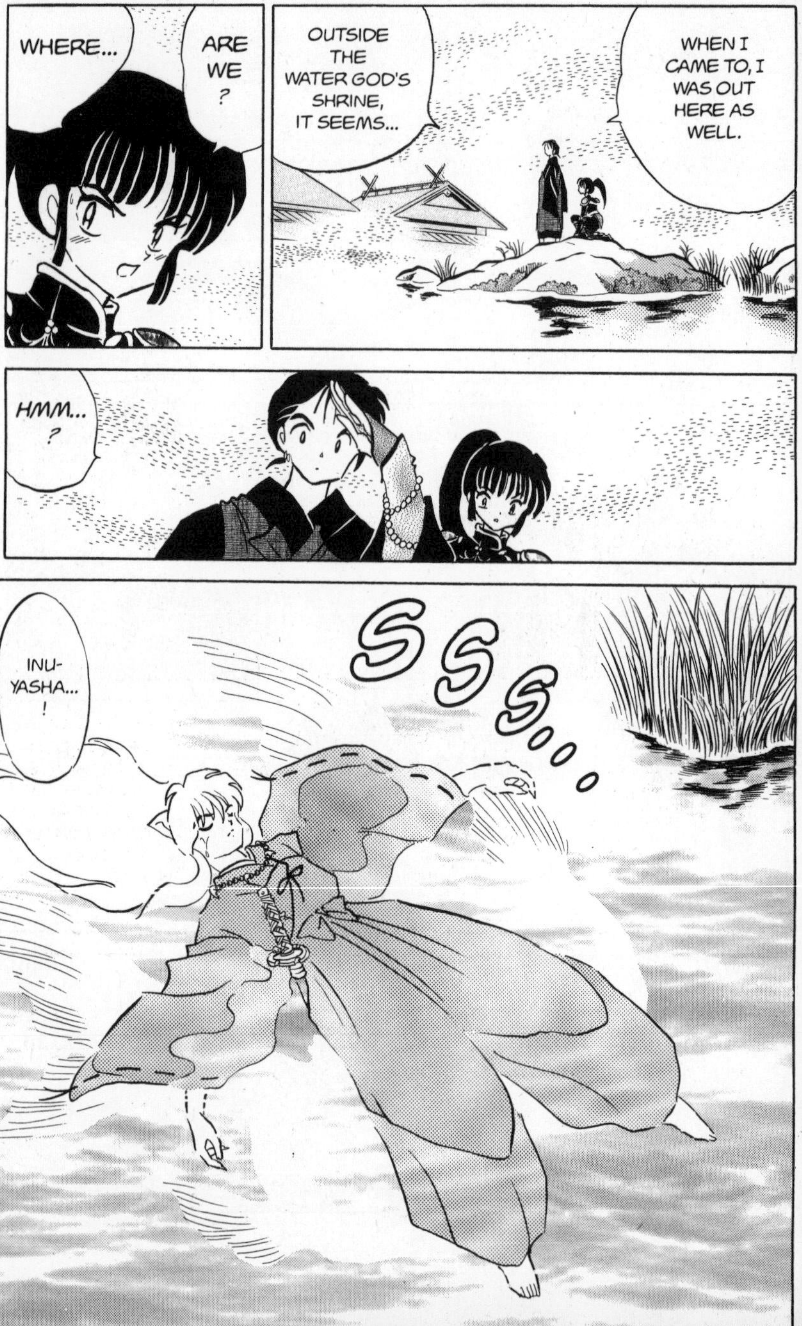
WHERE...
ARE WE ?
OUTSIDE THE WATER GOD'S SHRINE, IT SEEMS...
WHEN I CAME TO, I WAS OUT HERE AS WELL.
HMM... ?
INU-YASHA... !
SSSooo

POP

POP

DID... YOU KIND FOLK RESCUE US...?

SSHH...

WE DID.

ARE YOU SURE YOU SHOULD HAVE DONE THAT?

FROM YOUR APPEARANCE, YOU MUST BE ATTENDANTS OF THE WATER GOD...

THAT "WATER GOD"...

HSST HSST

HSST HSST

...IS A FRAUD.

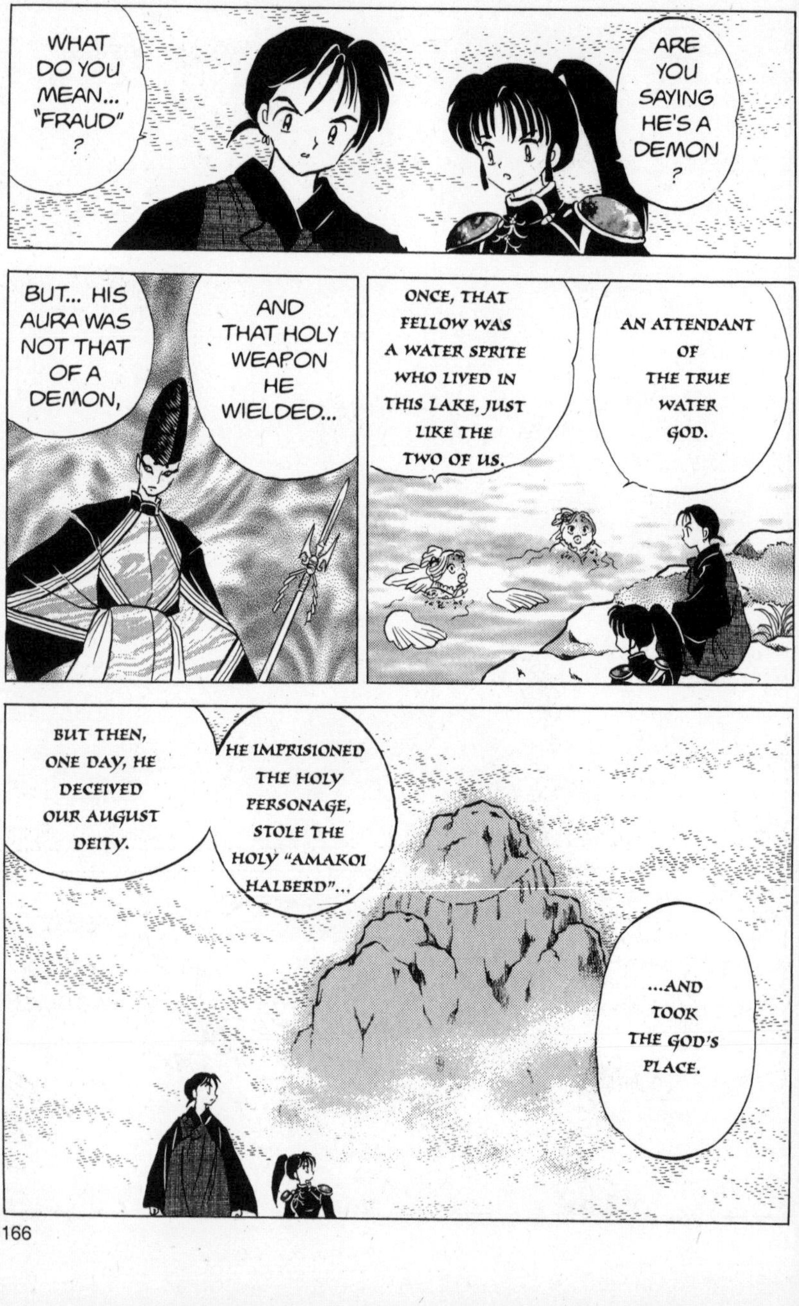
WHAT DO YOU MEAN... "FRAUD"?
ARE YOU SAYING HE'S A DEMON?
BUT... HIS AURA WAS NOT THAT OF A DEMON,
AND THAT HOLY WEAPON HE WIELDED...
ONCE, THAT FELLOW WAS A WATER SPRITE WHO LIVED IN THIS LAKE, JUST LIKE THE TWO OF US.
AN ATTENDANT OF THE TRUE WATER GOD.
BUT THEN, ONE DAY, HE DECEIVED OUR AUGUST DEITY.
HE IMPRISIONED THE HOLY PERSONAGE, STOLE THE HOLY "AMAKOI HALBERD"...
...AND TOOK THE GOD'S PLACE.

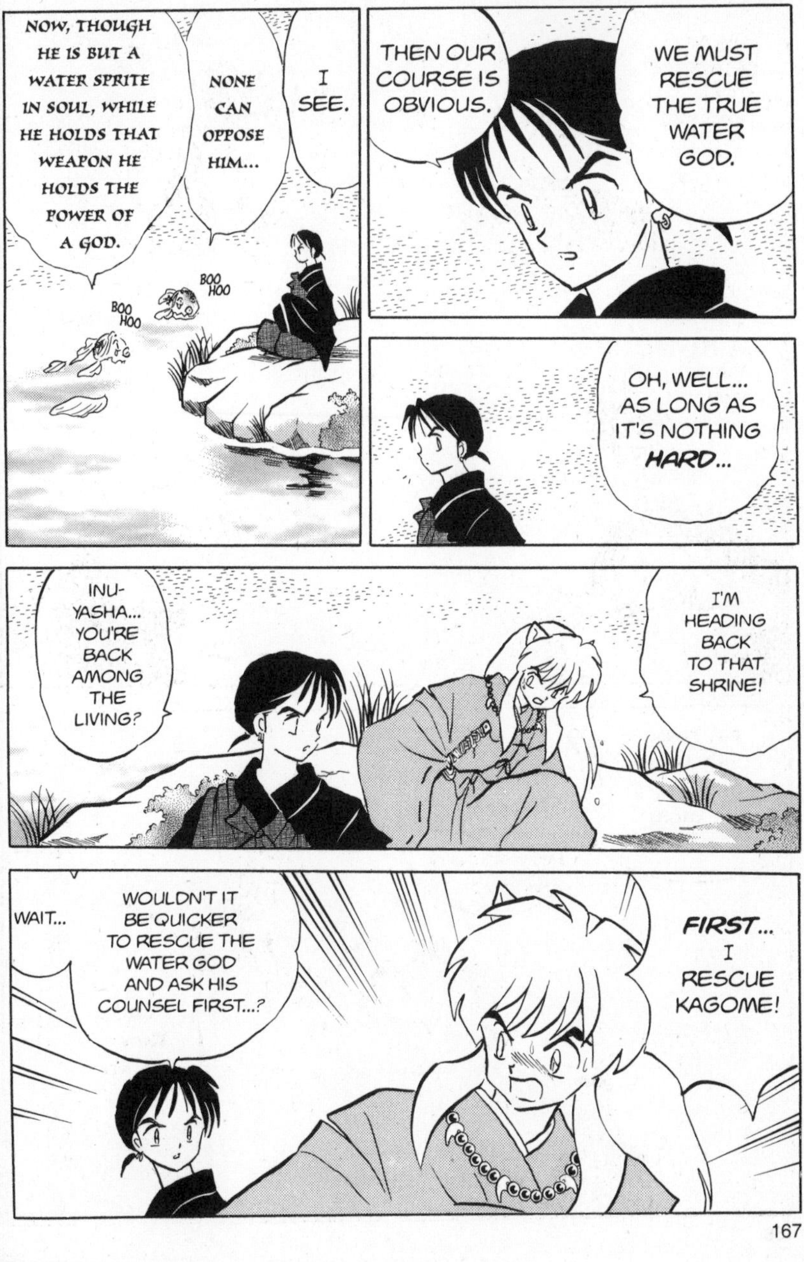
NOW, THOUGH HE IS BUT A WATER SPRITE IN SOUL, WHILE HE HOLDS THAT WEAPON HE HOLDS THE POWER OF A GOD.
NONE CAN OPPOSE HIM...
I SEE.
BOO HOO
BOO HOO
THEN OUR COURSE IS OBVIOUS.
WE MUST RESCUE THE TRUE WATER GOD.
OH, WELL... AS LONG AS IT'S NOTHING **HARD**...
INU-YASHA... YOU'RE BACK AMONG THE LIVING?
I'M HEADING BACK TO THAT SHRINE!
WAIT...
WOULDN'T IT BE QUICKER TO RESCUE THE WATER GOD AND ASK HIS COUNSEL FIRST...?
FIRST... I RESCUE KAGOME!

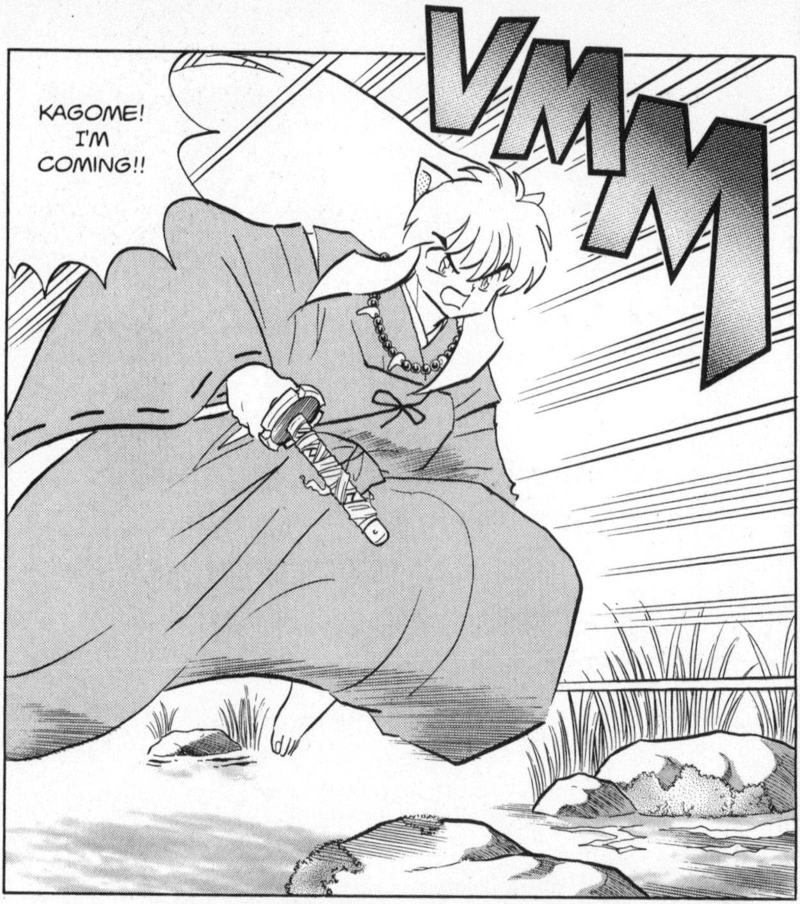
KAGOME! I'M COMING!!
VMM

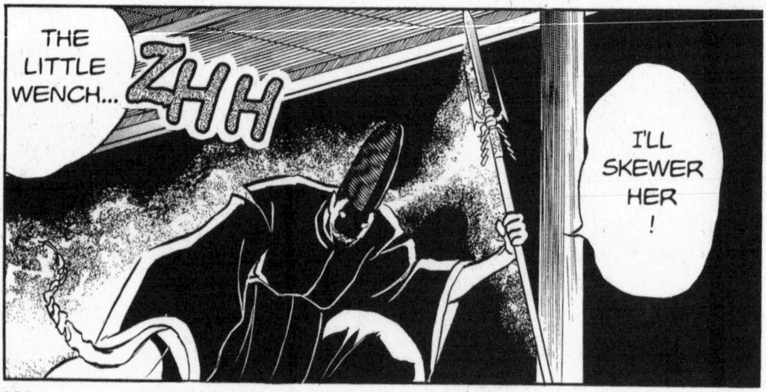
THE LITTLE WENCH...
ZHH
I'LL SKEWER HER!

SCROLL TEN

THE TRUE GOD

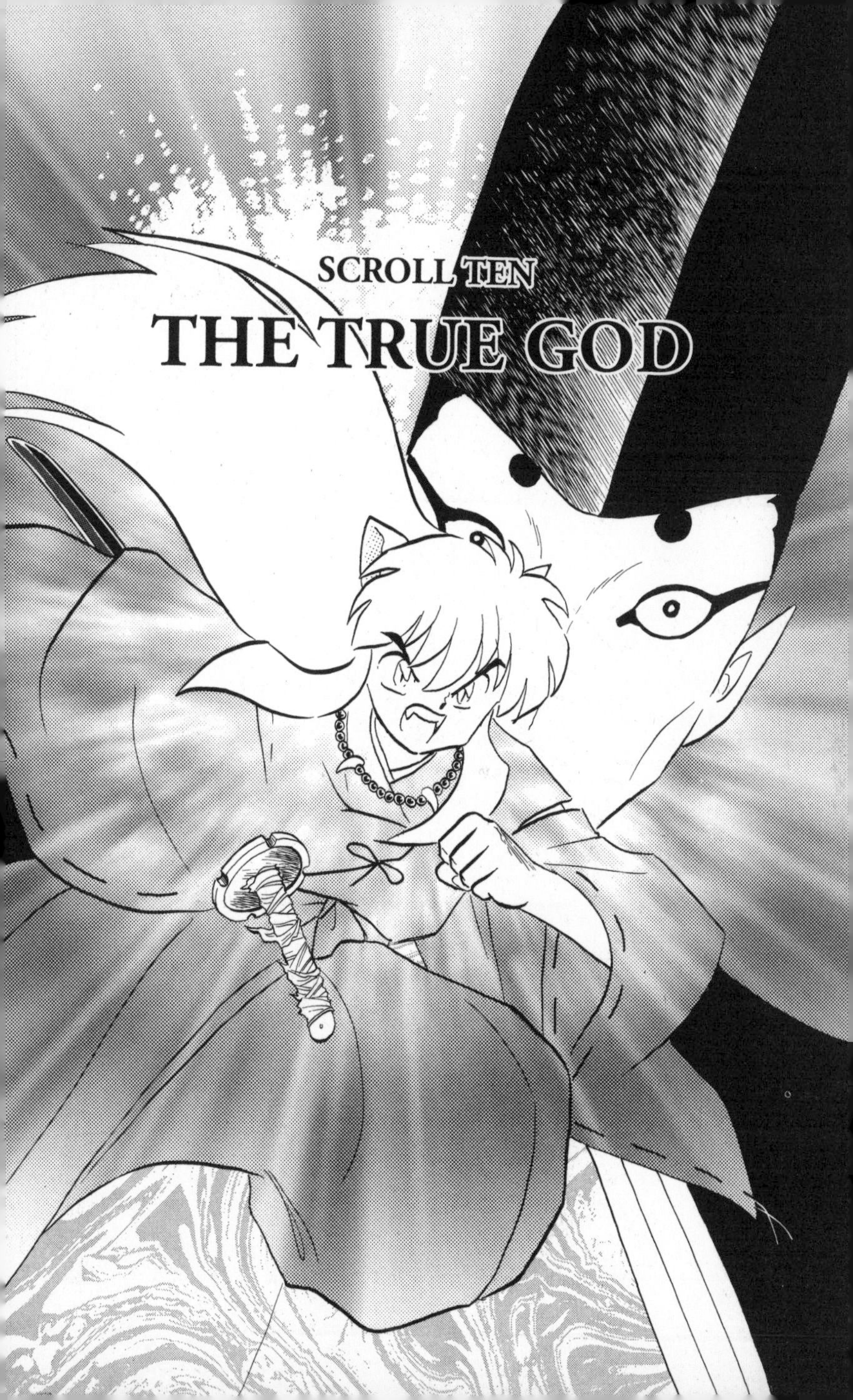

B-DMP
B-DMP
B-DMP

H-HE'S
NOT
COMING...
?

GRSS

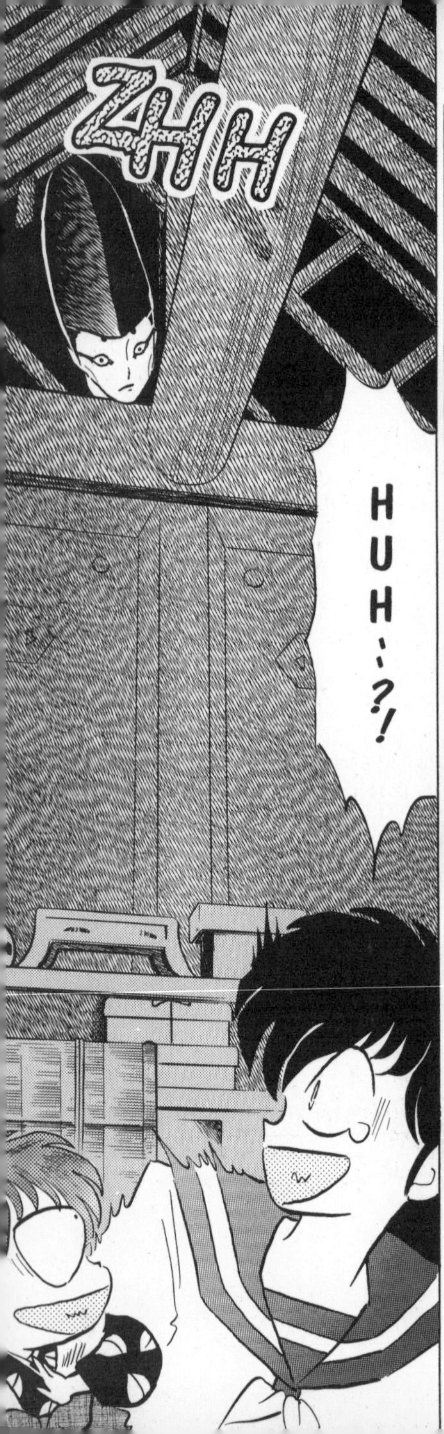
ZHH
HUH...?!

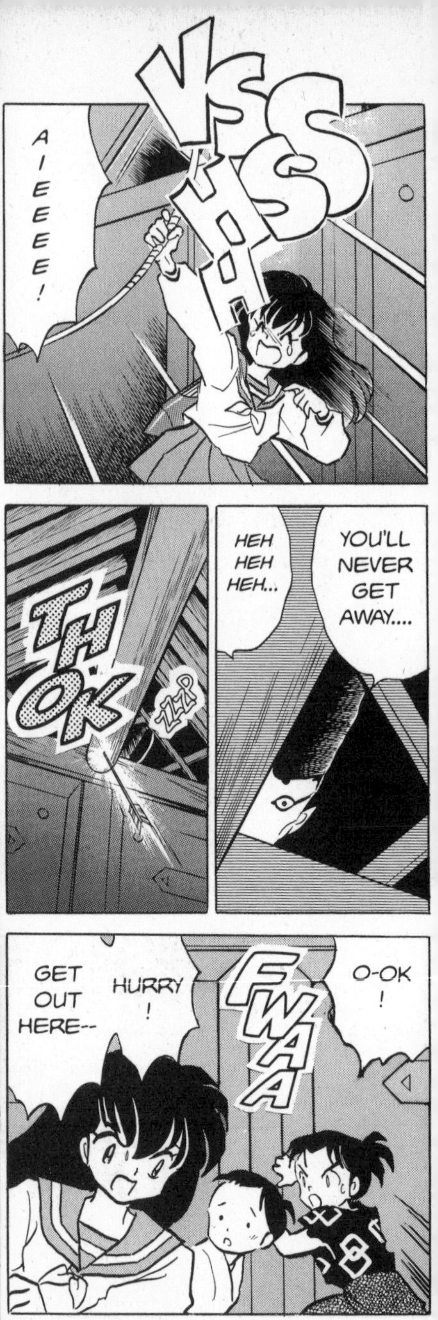
AIEEEEE!
VSSSHH
THOK
ZZZP
HEH HEH HEH...
YOU'LL NEVER GET AWAY....
GET OUT HERE--
HURRY!
FWAA
O-OK!

HUH ?!

I-IT WON'T OPEN ?!

LITTLE WENCH...

I'LL KILL **YOU** FIRST !

NNNH

173

I'M GONNA BE SPEARED--!

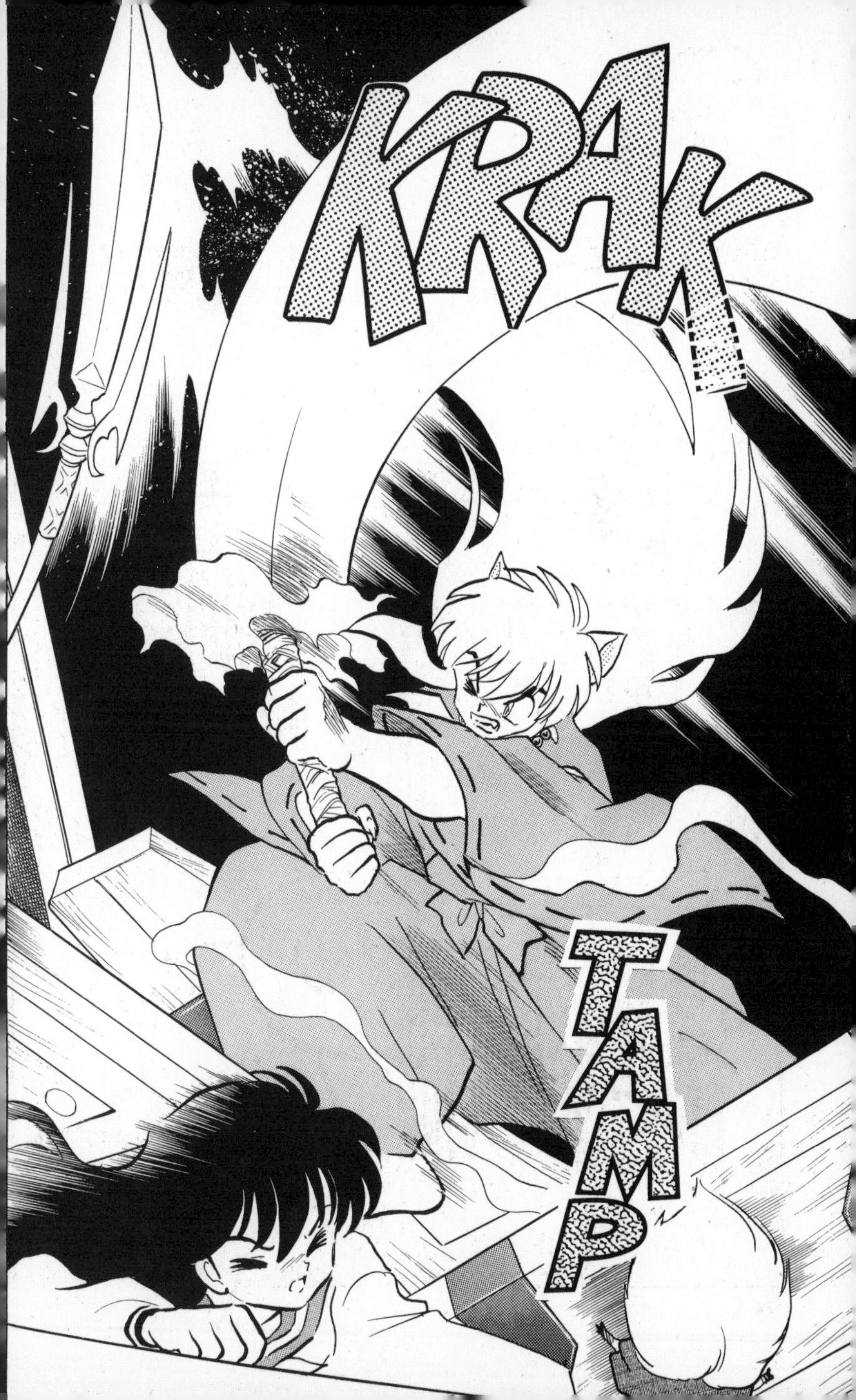
KRAK
TAMP

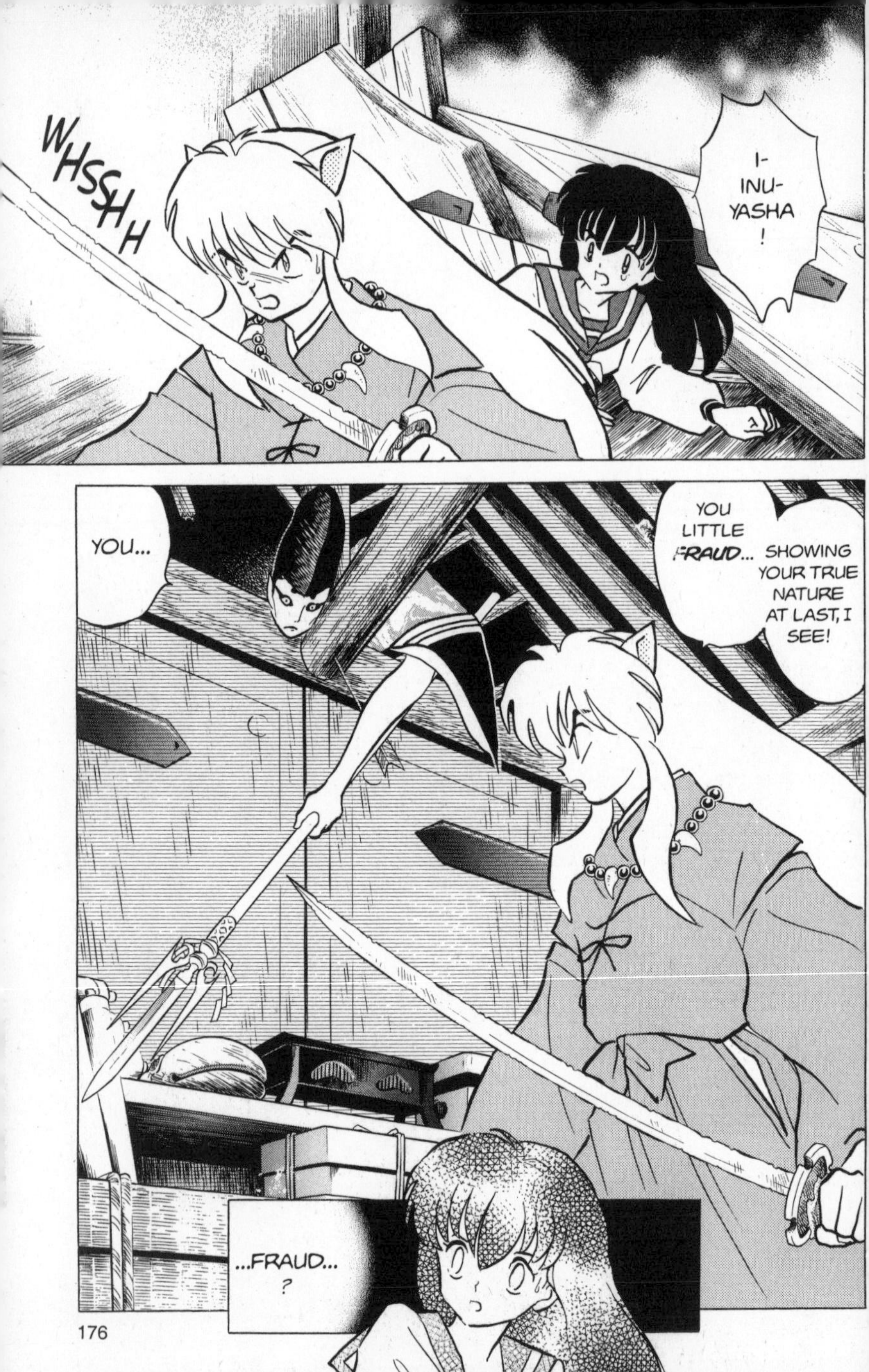

WHSSHH
I-INU-YASHA!
YOU...
YOU LITTLE FRAUD...
SHOWING YOUR TRUE NATURE AT LAST, I SEE!
...FRAUD...?

KAGOME!!

YOU AND THE BRATS ALL RIGHT?!

Y-YEAH.

BUT....

WE **WERE** FINE UNTIL NOW, BUT...

KLATTER

PUFFF

ZZHH...

TRYING TO ESCAPE, ARE YOU?!

!

ZZHHH...!

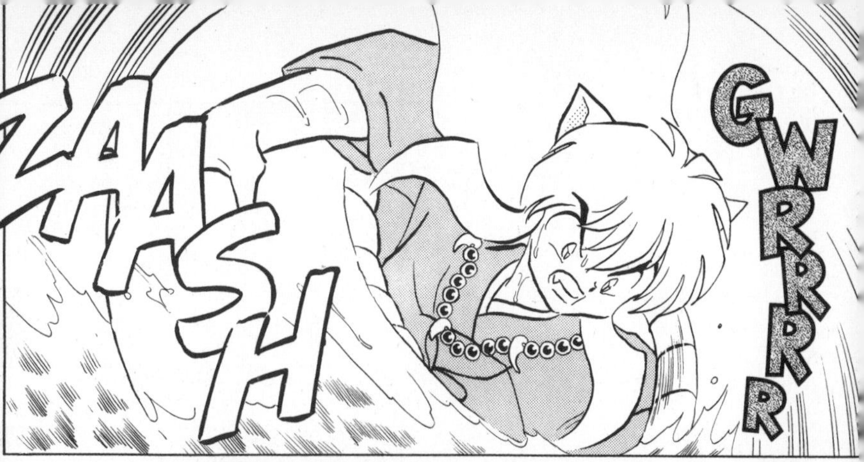
ZAASH
GWRRRRR
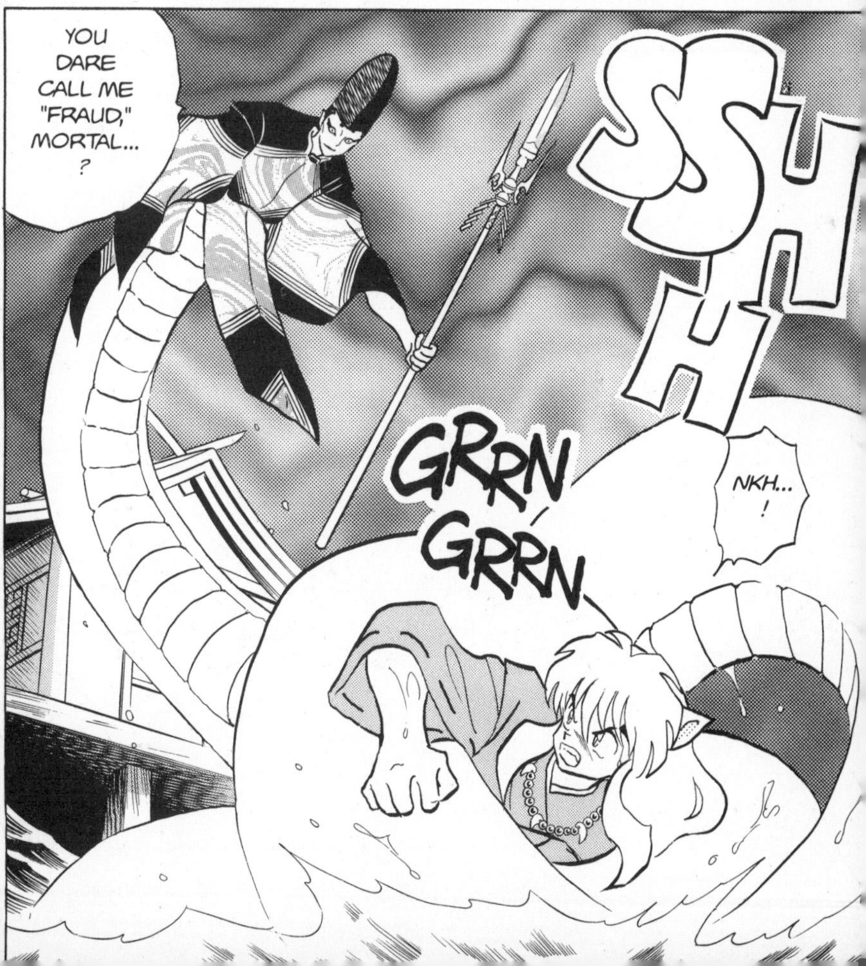
YOU DARE CALL ME "FRAUD," MORTAL...?
SSHH
GRRN GRRN
NKH...!

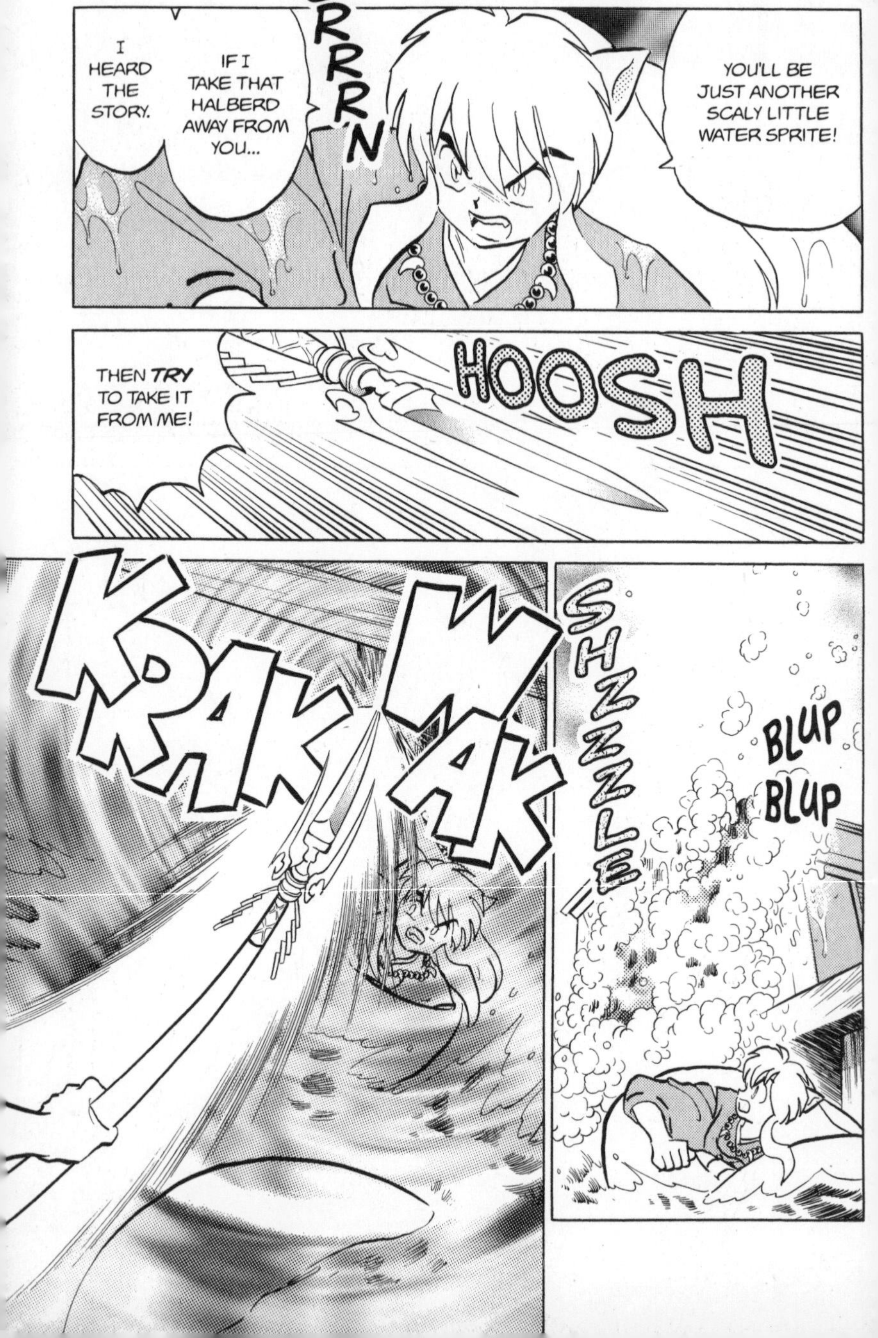
I HEARD THE STORY.
IF I TAKE THAT HALBERD AWAY FROM YOU...
GRRRRN
YOU'LL BE JUST ANOTHER SCALY LITTLE WATER SPRITE!
THEN *TRY* TO TAKE IT FROM ME!
HOOSH
KRAK
WAK
SHZZZZLE
BLUP
BLUP

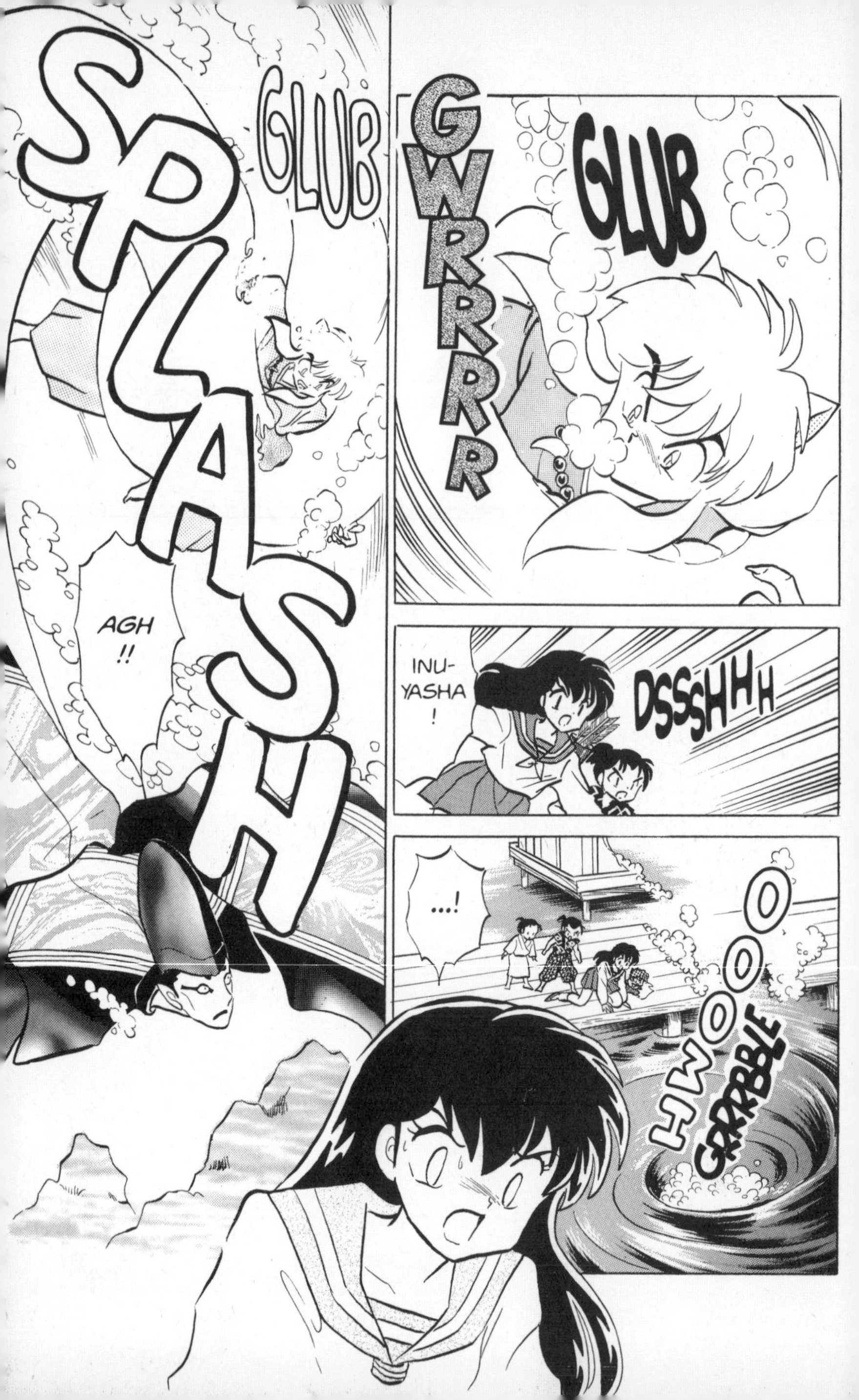
SPLASH
GLUB
AGH !!
GWRRRR
GLUB
INU-YASHA !
DSSSHHH
...!
HWOOOO
GRRRBBLE

OUR BELOVED WATER GOD IS TRAPPED INSIDE THE CAVE AT THE TOP OF THIS BOULDER.

SHAAA

WE UNDERSTAND. WE SHALL FREE HIM.

BOO HOO HOO HOO HOO

LET'S HURRY, MONK!

I'M WORRIED ABOUT KAGOME AND THE OTHERS!

SHFF

THEY SHOULD BE ALL RIGHT.

INU-YASHA'S WITH THEM.

INU-YASHA...

IS HE STRONG ENOUGH?

WELL... IF YOU MEAN PHYSICALLY, THEN I'D SAY...

OH, YES. QUITE STRONG.

AN IDIOT, IN OTHER WORDS....

AH.

A SPELL-SCROLL OF CONFINE-MENT....

THIS MUST BE IT.

DOES SOME-ONE SPEAK ?!

A YOUNG WOMAN'S VOICE...?

THEN, THE WATER GOD...IS A GODDESS!

SHH

HASTEN! REMOVE THE SCROLL OF CONFINE-MENT!

END THIS CAPTIVITY !

RIGHT AWAY, YOUR HOLINESS... !

AHEM

RRRIP

KRAK

CLAT-TAT-TER

!

TH-THIS IS...

THE TRUE WATER GODDESS...

A BIT... SMALL, WOULDN'T YOU SAY?

INDEED I WOULD...

DOINK

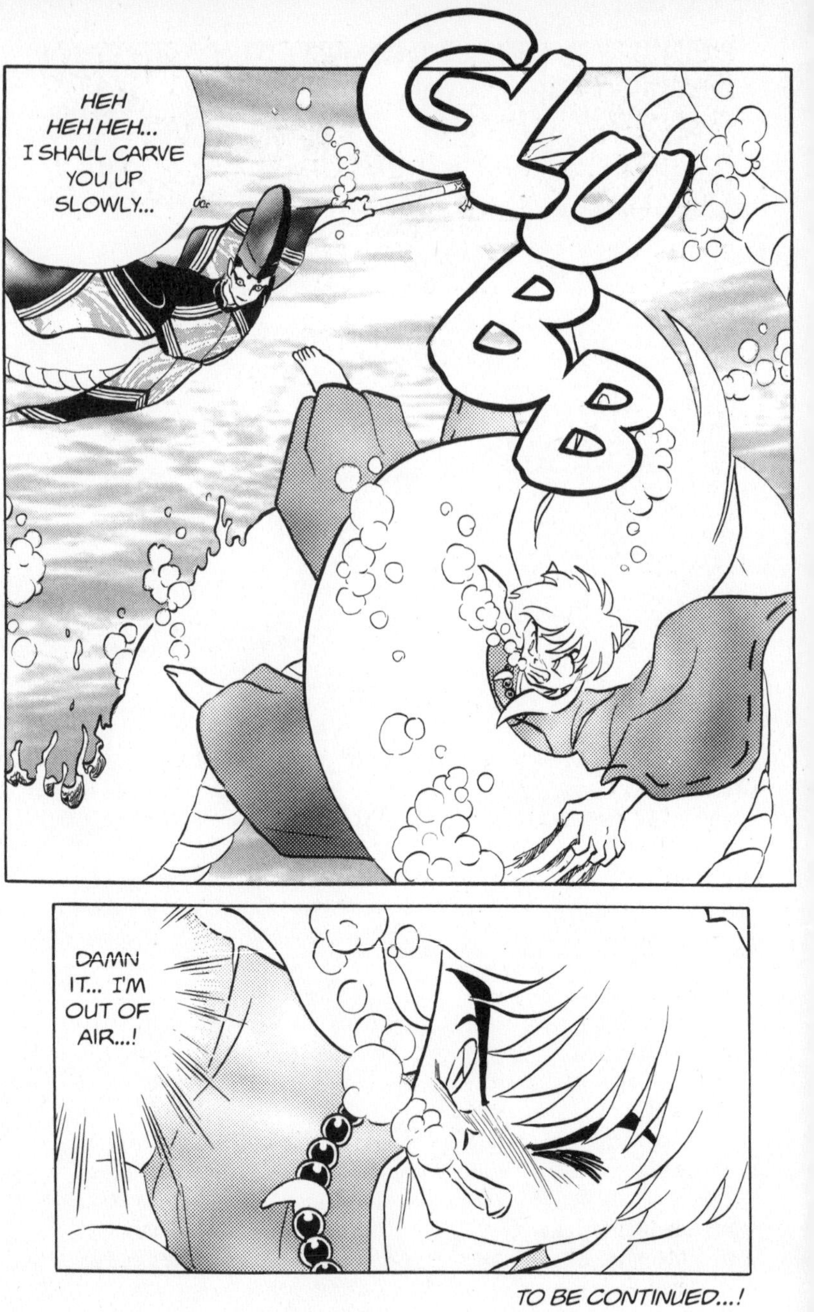
HEH HEH HEH... I SHALL CARVE YOU UP SLOWLY...
GLUBB
DAMN IT... I'M OUT OF AIR...!

TO BE CONTINUED...!

About Rumiko Takahashi

Born in 1957 in Niigata, Japan, Rumiko Takahashi attended women's college in Tokyo, where she began studying comics with Kazuo Koike, author of *CRYING FREEMAN*. She later became an assistant to horror-manga artist Kazuo Umezu (*OROCHI*). In 1978, she won a prize in Shogakukan's annual "New Comic Artist Contest," and in that same year her boy-meets-alien comedy series *URUSEI YATSURA* began appearing in the weekly manga magazine *SHÔNEN SUNDAY*. This phenomenally successful series ran for nine years and sold over 22 million copies. Takahashi's later *RANMA 1/2* series enjoyed even greater popularity.

Takahashi is considered by many to be one of the world's most popular manga artists. With the publication of Volume 34 of her *RANMA 1/2* series in Japan, Takahashi's total sales passed *one hundred million* copies of her compiled works.

Takahashi's serial titles include *URUSEI YATSURA, RANMA 1/2, ONE-POUND GOSPEL, MAISON IKKOKU* and *INUYASHA*. Additionally, Takahashi has drawn many short stories which have been published in America under the title "Rumic Theater," and several installments of a saga known as her "Mermaid" series. Most of Takahashi's major stories have also been animated, and are widely available in translation worldwide. *INUYASHA* is her most recent serial story, first published in *SHÔNEN SUNDAY* in 1996.

EDITOR'S RECOMMENDATIONS

Story & Art by Saki Hiwatari   Vol. 1

story and art by Yû Watase

Did you like INUYASHA? Here's what we recommend you try next:

PLEASE SAVE MY EARTH

A sensitive high school student has recurring dreams that she's part of a team of seven alien scientists from the moon. She doesn't believe this could possibly be true until she meets other people who've been having these dreams as well. Fragments of a past life eventually come to light in an intricate, fascinating story of reincarnation, psychic powers, and eternal, tragic love.

© 1986 Saki Hiwatari/Hakusensha, Inc.

ALICE 19TH

Alice was a typical young girl—hopelessly in love and bored, until she follows a magical rabbit that literally jumps in front of her life. In a *shôjo* twist on *Alice in Wonderland*, this new story by the artist of *Fushigi Yûgi* and *Ceres, Celestial Legend* features two sisters: one who's been pulled into a world of darkness, and another (Alice) who must become a master of the Lotis Words to save her.

© 2001 Yuu Watase/Shogakukan, Inc.

GYO

This horror manga by *Uzumaki* artist Junji Ito dredges up a nightmare from the deep—monstrous, mutant fish and sea creatures that invade an Okinawa town. Ito's artwork is gorgeous and unforgettable—if you're looking for something completely different in manga, this is it.

© 2002 Junji Ito/Shogakukan, Inc.

Ranma Transformed...Again!!

Ranma ½™

Now you can get your favorite martial artist in your favorite form! A must-have to complete your Ranma 1/2 collection.

$69.95 each

COMPLETE OUR SURVEY AND LET US KNOW WHAT YOU THINK!

☐ Please do NOT send me information about VIZ products, news and events, special offers, or other information.

☐ Please do NOT send me information from VIZ's trusted business partners.

Name: _____

Address: _____

City: _____ **State:** _____ **Zip:** _____

E-mail: _____

☐ Male ☐ Female   Date of Birth (mm/dd/yyyy): ___/___/_____   (Under 13? Parental consent required)

What race/ethnicity do you consider yourself? (please check one)

☐ Asian/Pacific Islander   ☐ Black/African American   ☐ Hispanic/Latino

☐ Native American/Alaskan Native   ☐ White/Caucasian   ☐ Other: _____

What VIZ product did you purchase? (check all that apply and indicate title purchased)

☐ DVD/VHS _____

☐ Graphic Novel _____

☐ Magazines _____

☐ Merchandise _____

Reason for purchase: (check all that apply)

☐ Special offer   ☐ Favorite title   ☐ Gift

☐ Recommendation   ☐ Other_____

Where did you make your purchase? (please check one)

☐ Comic store   ☐ Bookstore   ☐ Mass/Grocery Store

☐ Newsstand   ☐ Video/Video Game Store   ☐ Other: _____

☐ Online (site: _____)

What other VIZ properties have you purchased/own? _____

How many anime and/or manga titles have you purchased in the last year? How many were VIZ titles? **(please check one from each column)**

ANIME	MANGA	VIZ
☐ None	☐ None	☐ None
☐ 1-4	☐ 1-4	☐ 1-4
☐ 5-10	☐ 5-10	☐ 5-10
☐ 11+	☐ 11+	☐ 11+

I find the pricing of VIZ products to be: **(please check one)**

☐ Cheap ☐ Reasonable ☐ Expensive

What genre of manga and anime would you like to see from VIZ? **(please check two)**

☐ Adventure ☐ Comic Strip ☐ Science Fiction ☐ Fighting

☐ Horror ☐ Romance ☐ Fantasy ☐ Sports

What do you think of VIZ's new look?

☐ Love It ☐ It's OK ☐ Hate It ☐ Didn't Notice ☐ No Opinion

Which do you prefer? **(please check one)**

☐ Reading right-to-left

☐ Reading left-to-right

Which do you prefer? **(please check one)**

☐ Sound effects in English

☐ Sound effects in Japanese with English captions

☐ Sound effects in Japanese only with a glossary at the back

THANK YOU! Please send the completed form to:

NJW Research
42 Catharine St.
Poughkeepsie, NY 12601

All information provided will be used for internal purposes only. We promise not to sell or otherwise divulge your information.